WHY ISRAEL?

A BIBLICAL LOOK INTO THE NATION'S PAST AND FUTURE

KEAVIN HAYDEN

**WORDS MATTER
PUBLISHING**
OUR WORDS CHANGE THE WORLD

© by Keavin Hayden. All rights reserved.

Words Matter Publishing
P.O. Box 531
Salem, Il 62881
www.wordsmatterpublishing.com

No part of this publication may be reproduced, stored in a retrieval system, or transmitted in any way by any means—electronic, mechanical, photocopy, recording, or otherwise—without the prior permission of the copyright holder, except as provided by USA copyright law.

Scripture quotations are taken from the Holy Bible, New Living Translation, copyright © 1996. Used by permission of Tyndale House Publishing, Inc. Wheaton, Illinois, 60189 All Rights Reserved.

ISBN 13: 978-1-949809-84-8

Library of Congress Catalog Card Number: 2020945772

Though never mentioned specifically in the Bible, the Star of David is recognized universally as the insignia for modern Judaism. Today it is a symbol of great pride among the Hebrew people, but during War World II Adolf Hitler forced Jews to wear it as a "badge of shame" designed to racially profile their identities. The First Zionist Congress in 1897 chose the star as the central emblem for the flag of the future State of Israel. Just 51 years later the new nation of Israel was born on May 14, 1948, thus establishing the first Jewish state in nearly 2,700 years. But where did Israel come from? And what is the significance of their reappearance on the world's political and religious stage? In his book WHY ISRAEL? author Keavin Hayden takes his readers on a spiritual journey through time, uncovering the history of this ancient people, and demonstrating how the existence of Israel will affect the future of everyone living on our planet.

"I have made Israel for myself, and they will someday honor Me before the whole world"
>   --*The Lord's Explanation of Israel's Origin and Prediction for It's Future in Isaiah 43*

"How beautiful on the mountains are the feet of those who bring good news of peace and salvation, the news that the God of Israel reigns! The watchmen shout and sing with joy, for before their very eyes they see the Lord bringing His people home to Jerusalem. Let the ruins of Jerusalem break into joyful song, for the Lord has comforted His people. He has redeemed Jerusalem. The Lord will demonstrate His holy power before the eyes of all the nations. The ends of the earth will see the salvation of our God"
>   --*The Lord's Gospel Declaration in Isaiah 52*

"Judah is my bow, and Israel is my arrow! Jerusalem is my sword, and like a warrior, I will brandish it against the Greeks"
>   --*The Lord's War Cry in Zechariah 9*

"Look at my servant, whom I strengthen. He is my chosen one, and I am pleased with him. I have put my Spirit upon him. He will reveal justice to the nations. He will be gentle – he will not shout or raise his voice in public. He will not crush those who are weak or quench the smallest hope. He will bring full justice to all who have been wronged. He will not stop until truth and righteousness prevail throughout the earth. Even distant lands beyond the sea will wait for his instruction"
   --*The Lord's Introduction of His Chosen Messiah in Isaiah 42*

"'Comfort, comfort my people,' says your God. 'Speak tenderly to Jerusalem. Tell her that her sad days are gone and that her sins are pardoned. Yes, the Lord has punished her in full for all her sins'"
   –*The Lord's Pronouncement of Pardon for Zion in Isaiah 40*

CONTENTS

Dedication ix
Acknowledgments xi
Author's Preface xiii

SECTION I: The Types 1

Chapter 1: The Covenant Call (Abraham And Isaac) 3
Chapter 2: The Birth Of Israel (Jacob) 13
Chapter 3: Law And Order (Moses) 27
Chapter 4: The Chosen King (David) 43
Chapter 5: A Prophet's Warning (Elijah) 55
Chapter 6: Destruction And Captivity (Daniel) 67

Chapter 7: God's Secret Revealed
(The Calling Of Gentiles) 85

SECTION II: The Antitypes 101

Chapter 8: Return Of Jacob (Modern Israel's) 103

Chapter 9: Return Of Jerusalem And It's Temple
(Time Of Gentiles Fulfilled) 123

Chapter 10: Return Of Daniel (Antichrist Revealed) 143

Chapter 11: Return Of Elijah
(Final Calling Of God's Family) 165

Chapter 12: Return Of David
(Second Advent Of Messiah) 179

Chapter 13: Return Of Moses
(Shaking Of The Lawgiver) 199

Chapter 14: Return Of Abraham
(Uniting Of God's Family) 215

Conclusion 235

DEDICATION

This book is dedicated to my wife and co-worker in Christ for her devotion to God, and to our family. Thank you, Lisa, for challenging and encouraging me to study the Bible when I was still a young man seeking after things in this world. You have remained a faithful companion on this incredible spiritual journey we began together nearly 40 years ago. The most exciting part is that our journey is not yet over!

Also, to our four amazing daughters, son in laws, and grandchildren. May your faith always find rest while trusting in the Eternal Rock – the God of Abraham, Isaac, and Jacob – the Promised Seed of Israel.

ACKNOWLEDGMENTS

To Dr. Tom Norvell and the New Beginnings Sunday School Class at Century Christian Church in Owensboro, Kentucky, for inviting me to share my faith with you. Our time together helped to create a new beginning in my own life. The series of 43 lectures you so graciously allowed me to present serves as the foundational material for the writing of this book.

Renowned writer and editor Arthur Plotnik once said, "You write to communicate to the hearts and minds of others what's burning inside you, and we edit to let the fire show through the smoke." This pretty well sums up my relationship with the two men who collaborated with me on this project. To Gerald Wheeler and Steve Wilson, thank you for your tireless efforts in editing this book, enabling me to get through the ruts, and helping me finally say what it was I really wanted to be said.

AUTHOR'S PREFACE

The idea of *Israel* as a nation is an emotionally charged topic. The mere mention of its name can easily set off demonstrations, sometimes resulting in violence and even all-out war. But *Why Israel?* What is it about this tiniest of countries sitting in the midst of massive Middle Eastern nations that constantly seems to keep the world sitting on the edge of its seat? How did it get there, and for what purpose does it exist? These are age-old questions this book seeks to answer. It is not an attempt to solve any current political, religious, or social perplexities, nor a desire to advocate on behalf of Jews, Palestinians, or Christians living in the region. No, what you are about to read is simply an honest attempt to explain from the Bible how, *and why,* Israel appears continually in world affairs and conflicts. To accomplish this task, we must go way back in time to the biblical account of our world's beginning.

Without question, the Bible itself is a controversial document. It is the most interesting, yet mysterious set of writings known to humanity. Not only is it the top-selling book of all time, but it continues to hold a number one sales position year in and year out.[1] Though despised by some, others hold it in highest reverence, believing it holds the key not only to our world's past but also its future. But, why the Bible?

The Bible is primarily a Hebrew book. It largely documents the story of the Hebrew people (Israel) as recorded by Hebrew writers. Yet as we shall see, it was not meant for the benefit of the Hebrews only, but all the earth's peoples.

The question then arises—*Why Israel?* The Bible explains the creation of our world, its collapse into a sinful state, and its final restoration to eternal peace. A singular figure known as the "Messiah" brings about its redemption. Christians believe the Messiah revealed Himself 2,000 years ago as the Jewish Rabbi Jesus Christ. Jews believe that he has yet to come but will appear in the near future. Regardless, the answer to our question, *Why Israel?* is that the Bible teaches humanity's Savior originates from within the Hebrew race.

In Genesis we read that because a man (Adam) sinned, he doomed the entire human race to death.[2] Yet God promised that He would one day bring forth a "seed," or offspring, from the woman (Adam's wife) who would reverse the curse of sin in the earth.[3] It is understandable from the start that God is not partial to any one particular race of people regarding His promise to save them from sin and death, a fact revealed through Adam's choice of a name for his wife. "Then Adam named his wife Eve because *she would be the mother of all people everywhere.*"[4] The Hebrew term for "Eve" means "to give life." So, at the very beginning of the Bible story, the Lord promises to restore life to people everywhere through Eve's offspring.

No doubt at the birth of her first son, Cain, she and her husband were excited to think that maybe he was the fulfillment of God's promise! Then, a second son, Abel, arrived. But their hopes that either child could be the promised Seed completely shattered when the older brother killed the younger.[5] However, their hope renewed when Eve gave birth to another son, whom she named Seth. She said, "God has granted me *another son [seed]* in place of Abel, the one Cain killed."[6]

Though many, many generations have passed since then, the world still waits for that promised Seed to arrive and put an end to the misery caused by sin and death. We find the explanation of how this is to transpire in the future in the past history of the Hebrew people. As stated earlier, the Messiah is to emanate from Israel. To say it another way, Israel is the conduit for the world's salvation through its bringing forth the Messiah. When we read the Bible at face value, we notice the synonymity between Messiah and Israel. Synonymity is defined as "a person or thing so closely associated with a particular quality or idea that the mention of their name calls it to mind."[7] Simply put one cannot discuss the idea of the Messiah without considering Israel. Any attempt to suggest that the Bible teaches otherwise only obscures the Messiah's mission to save the world.

God's plan to redeem the world involved establishing a beta group, of sorts, from Abraham, the father of the Hebrew race. To him, the Lord gave a covenant promise that through his physical offspring He would bring salvation to the world. Abraham's descendants later became known as the *nation of Israel*. Through prophets, God passed on to them the same promise He had first given to Adam and Eve and then Abraham, declaring that He would send them a Savior, known as the *Messiah*. He also staked His reputation that His people would accept this Messiah within a specific time period known as the "*seventy weeks,*" a prophecy recorded in Daniel 9. When this would happen, the world, as we now know it, will come to its end. Obviously, the prophecy's complete fulfillment is still future, yet recent world events strongly suggest it could soon happen. When studied in its entirety, God's divine plan reveals that His initial choosing of physical Israel was simply a prototype demonstrating His intention to offer salvation, not just to the Hebrews, but to all the races scattered throughout the earth. It forcibly speaks to the fact that if God is faithful in keeping the promise He made with Abraham and his physical offspring (Israel), however long delayed, then we can trust Him in making the same guarantee to the rest of humanity also destined to become Abraham's spiritual children.

This book is, therefore, an attempt to make the connection between the salvation of Israel and that of the world as also being synonymous. But to accomplish this task, we must first become better acquainted with the history of Israel—one deep and rich in the knowledge of the Messiah. The giants of Hebrew faith—individuals such as Abraham, Isaac, Jacob, Joseph, Moses, David, Elijah, and Daniel—though not the promised Seed, were personifications of the Messiah. The lessons revealed by their life stories were not just for their day, but continue to teach us regarding some future attribute of the Messiah still destined to be played out in our world.

Why Israel? Because the Bible declares Israel's presence on the world scene is tangible evidence of an intangible God. Although habitual apostasies mark Israel's history, their heritage has remained intact despite attempts by the Assyrians, Babylonians, Romans, and more recently the European Holocaust, to disband or annihilate them. By all accounts, no people on the planet have suffered so much genocide, yet continue with such tenacity to survive. For nearly 2,700 years they were scattered around the world, and then miraculously called back into existence as a nation in May 1948. All the algorithms in the world couldn't have predicted this, but God's prophets did. Isaiah says God alone can predict the future and make it come to pass.[8]

But why does world history chronicle such hatred toward the Jewish people? Well, someone else was present that day in the Garden of Eden when God spoke to Adam and Eve. "So, the Lord God said to the serpent ... *from now on, you and the woman will be enemies, and your offspring and her offspring will be enemies.* He [the Seed of the woman] will crush your head, and you will strike His heel."[9] The book of Revelation clearly defines who that serpent symbolically represents. "This great dragon—*the ancient serpent called the devil, or Satan,* the one deceiving the whole world."[10]

The Bible equates Israel with the woman who will bring forth the promised Messiah Seed. Revelation 12 describes her as "a woman clothed with the sun, with the moon beneath her feet, and a crown of twelve stars on her head. She was pregnant, and she cried out in the pain of labor as she awaited her delivery ... He [the dragon, or Satan] stood before the woman [Israel] as she was about to give birth to her child [Messiah], ready to devour the baby as soon as it was born. *She gave birth to a boy who was to rule all nations with a rod of iron.*"[11] Here we find the outline of a spiritual warfare played out on earth between the forces of darkness and the promised Seed, the offspring of Israel.

Sad to say, but the Bible predicts that at the end of time the earth's nations will unite to reject the coming Messiah.[12] Since He is invisible until His appearing, they will first seek once again to rid the earth of His visible people, Israel. But God will intervene and destroy those nations, thereby saving Israel and convincing the world that He alone is God. The nations will have failed to understand one very important Biblical lesson: "*As you have done to Israel, so it will be done to you.*"[13] Tragically, many will not realize their own eternal destiny is inherent in the salvation of Israel. It's a dire warning all need to heed: "Yes, you nations [who come against Israel] will drink and stagger and disappear from history, as though you had never even existed."[14]

But another group of people will possess spiritual discernment, enabling them to understand God's eternal plan to save the world through the establishment of His eternal kingdom on earth. From every tribe, nation, tongue, and people, He will gather those who choose life. This redeemed group will together worship and celebrate their Messiah. "And they sang a new song with these words, 'You [Messiah] are worthy …. For you were killed, and *your blood has ransomed people for God from every tribe and language and people and nation*. You have caused them to become God's Kingdom and His priests. *And they will reign on the earth.*'"[15] We see once more the same desire that God had in Genesis of not showing partiality. "There will be glory and honor and peace from God *for all who do good— for the Jew first and also for the Gentile*. For *God does not show favoritism*."[16] "He does not want *anyone* to perish."[17]

This book is an appeal to all peoples to find common unity through a comprehension of God's eternal plan to save us all as revealed through the Bible. We can best recognize that plan by studying Israel's past; its future role in this world's destiny; and, the defining of exactly who constitutes the biblical understanding of Israel.

Prayerfully, this volume will aid in removing some of the mystery that the Bible presents for its readers. Unless otherwise noted, I have chosen to use the *New Living Translation* of the Bible so as to make the text more reader-friendly.[18] I have provided biblical references for those who perhaps are not yet acquainted with the Scriptures. Hopefully, they will aid in helping them navigate as we explore the depths of God's sacred Word. Occasionally I have added bracketed material to help clarify the context of a passage and indicated it by an asterisk (*) in the endnotes.

Since beginning our Bible ministry nearly 35 years ago, my wife, Lisa, and I have sought first and foremost to encourage people to study their Bibles, do their own critical thinking, and draw their own conclusions as to what it teaches. We are not so concerned that they agree with what we have presented here. If the ideas offered do nothing more than challenge the reader to go get a Bible and find out for themselves what is right, or wrong, then we have accomplished our mission.

It is to that end this work is now sent forth.

Keavin Hayden
Owensboro, Kentucky
September 29, 2019

SECTION I
THE TYPES

CHAPTER 1
THE COVENANT CALL
(ABRAHAM AND ISAAC)

Ten generations after the Flood violence and injustice filled the world just as it had before God destroyed it. People worshiped multiple gods of their own creation and did whatever they wanted. It was then God revealed to a man named Abram His plan to establish a family of faithful followers on earth. It would not be just any family, as most clans eventually disintegrate and vanish. In contrast, God's household would become a unified dynasty destined to inherit the earth and rule over it throughout eternity. Abram is the foundational patriarch whose covenant with God would serve as a lighthouse of hope to his posterity. Central to this relationship was the identical promise that God had given Eve about a future offspring (Messiah) who would come to earth and reverse the curse of sin.

Abram was born in a place called Ur of the Chaldeans, located in today's Iraq. His father, Terah, was a priest of their local clan. Polytheists, they worshipped multiple gods. When Abram was about 75 years old, he, along with his wife Sarai, father Terah, nephew Lot and his family, and their extended household of servants, moved to Haran whose ruins lie within present-day southern Turkey (some say Northern Syria). There Abram's father died. Then the Lord spoke to Abram saying, "Leave your country, your relatives, and your father's house and *go to the land that I will show you. I will cause you to become the father of a great nation ... I will make you famous ... I will bless those who bless you and curse those who curse you. All the families of the earth will be blessed through you.*"[19]

They thus became the nucleus of the plan God announced to create a "great nation," by which "all peoples of the earth will be blessed." We see that God's strategy of building a family was inclusive, not exclusive. Just as Eve's name meant "mother of all living," Abram's name would later be changed to Abraham, meaning "father of multitudes." Anyone who blessed Abram's family, God in turn would bless, and whoever cursed them would in consequence receive curses. We first see this principle played out when God sent a plague upon the king of Egypt, because he sought Abram's wife, Sarai.[20]

When the Lord unveiled His plan, Abram not only believed it but acted upon it. Imagine banking so earnestly on what God is saying to you that it would cause you to leave your home, family, and livelihood to go somewhere you have never been or had even heard about! That is how Abram's religious experience affected him. No doubt today certain Western societies, such as America in which religion has in many cases become little more than a national past-time, might consider him a religious fanatic. Yet that is what God loved about the man. By faith, Abram realized that the world he knew was only a temporary one, and the Lord gave him a promise of a better, eternal world to come. The book of Hebrews says it best: "It was by faith that Abraham obeyed when God called him to leave home and go to another land that God would give him as his inheritance. *He went without knowing where he was going ... Abraham did this because he was confidently looking forward to a city with eternal foundations, a city designed and built by God.*"[21]

Abram and his family packed up their camels and moved to the land known as Canaan (modern-day Israel). One day God said to him, "Look as far as you can see in every direction. *I am going to give all this land to you and your offspring as a permanent possession. And I am going to give you so many descendants that, like dust, they cannot be counted!* Take a walk in every direction and explore the new possessions I am giving you."[22]

No doubt Abram felt confused. Although he had no children and his wife was old and barren, yet the Lord had promised land for his descendants. Surely, he pondered the puzzle, because when the Lord visited him the next time, he was ready with a question, "'O Sovereign Lord, what good are all your blessings when I don't even have a son ... You have given me no children, so one of my servants will have to be my heir?' Then the Lord said to him, 'No, your servant will not be your heir, for you will have a son of your own to inherit everything I am giving you.' Then the Lord brought Abram outside beneath the night sky and told him, 'Look up into the heavens and count the stars if you can. Your descendants will be like that— too many to count!' And Abram believed the Lord, and *the Lord declared him righteous because of his faith*. Then the Lord told him, 'I am the Lord who brought you out of Ur of the Chaldeans to give you this land.' But Abram replied, 'O Sovereign Lord, how can I be sure that you will give it to me?'"[23]

God Signs the Covenant

The Lord then guaranteed His promises through a legal contract. The Bible is a book of covenants. If we don't understand them, we cannot grasp the Bible. What God made with Abram is the most important agreement in the history of humanity! Today when we make a real estate contract or any other kind of formal agreement, both parties sign the agreement in ink. In those days it was commonplace to sign, or seal, such accords with blood. God instructed Abram to kill three animals and two birds, cut the animals in halves, and then lay them side by side, forming a bloody pathway between them.

Abram did as told, but spent the rest of the daylight chasing away vultures. Fatigued, he sat down at dusk to wait for the Lord's next move, only to fall asleep.[24] In a dream the Lord told him, "'You can be sure that your descendants will be strangers in a foreign land, and they will be oppressed as slaves for four hundred years. But I will punish the nation that enslaves them, and in the end, they will come away with great wealth ... After four generations your descendants will return here to this land ...' As the sun went down and it became dark, Abram saw a smoking firepot and a flaming torch pass between the halves of the carcasses. So, the Lord made a covenant with Abram that day and said, '*I have given this land to your descendants.*'"[25]

Though Abram truly believed that God was honest concerning His promises, he still was in the dark about how He would accomplish them. His wife, Sarai, still unable to have children, came up with her own idea of how God was going to keep His promise. She told Abram to sleep with her servant Hagar, and then he might have the son God promised. As planned, Hagar had a boy, and Abram named him Ishmael.

Thirteen years later, when Abram was 99 years old, God reappeared to him and said, "I am changing your name. It will no longer be Abram; now you will be known as Abraham ... *I will give you millions of descendants who will represent many nations.* Kings will be among them. *I will continue this everlasting covenant ... between Me and your offspring forever. And I will always be your God ... Yes, and I will give all this land of Canaan to you and to your offspring forever. And I will be their God.*"[26]

Then God told him something truly unbelievable. "'Regarding Sarai, your wife—her name will no longer be Sarai; from now on you will call her Sarah. And I will bless her and give you a son from her ... she will become the mother of many nations. Kings will be among her descendants.' Then Abraham ... laughed to himself in disbelief. 'How could I become a father at the age of one hundred?' he wondered. 'Besides, Sarah is ninety; how could she have a baby?' And Abraham said to God, 'Yes, may Ishmael enjoy your special blessing!' But God replied, 'Sarah, your wife, will bear you a son. You will name him Isaac, and *I will confirm my everlasting covenant with him and his descendants.* As for Ishmael, I will bless him also, just as you have asked. I will cause him to multiply and become a great nation ... *But my covenant is with Isaac,* who will be born to you and Sarah about this time next year.' That ended the conversation."[27] "Then the Lord did exactly as He had promised. Sarah became pregnant, and she gave a son to Abraham in his old age ... And *Abraham named his son Isaac.*"[28]

Perhaps now Abraham began to understand that the covenant promise God had made with him would be fulfilled by the Lord's doing and not his own. He and Sarah had believed God's promise to give them a son as his inheritance, but they had tried to make it happen by their own efforts. They had even tried to believe that Ishmael's birth was the divine working in their behalf until He gave them the news the real fulfillment would result from God performing a miracle by making Sarah's barren womb fertile!

Now, as the boys grew, tension filled Abraham's household, because of the growing hostility between the two mothers and their sons. The stress became so intense that one day Sarah came to him and demanded, "'Get rid of that servant and her son. He is not going to share the family inheritance with my son Isaac. I won't have it!' This upset Abraham very much because Ishmael was his son. But God told Abraham, 'Do not be upset over the boy and your servant wife. Do just as Sarah says, for *Isaac is the son through whom your descendants will be counted.* But I will make a nation of the descendants of Hagar's son because he is also your son.' So, Abraham ... sent her away with their son."[29]

The Covenant Extends to Isaac

Abraham would have another opportunity to learn the paramount lesson of faith and teach it to Isaac as well. The experience would lead both to depend on God to keep His promises even though everything in their visible world suggested otherwise. The Lord told Abraham to take Isaac to a mountain that He had chosen in the land of Moriah. There he was to offer him as a burnt offering! When people first learn about this from the Bible, it tends to unnerve them. Sometimes people ask, "What kind of God would ask a parent to sacrifice their child?" Such a concept was not foreign to Abraham, because he had come out of a culture that sometimes called for child offerings. What confused him, however, was that this command had no logical purpose since Isaac was the son through whom would come unnumbered descendants. If he were dead, how would it then be possible?

As they made their journey up the mountain, Isaac asked his father, "'We have the wood and the fire ... but where is the lamb for the sacrifice?' 'God will provide a lamb, my son,' Abraham answered ... When they arrived at the place where God had told Abraham to go, he built an altar and placed the wood on it. Then he tied Isaac up and laid him on the altar over the wood. And Abraham took the knife and lifted it up to kill his son as a sacrifice to the Lord. At that moment the angel of the Lord shouted to him from heaven. 'Abraham! Abraham!' 'Yes,' he answered. 'I am listening.' 'Lay down the knife,' the angel said. 'Do not hurt the boy in any way, for now, I know that you truly fear God. You have not withheld even your beloved son from me.' Then Abraham looked up and saw a ram caught by its horns in a bush. So, he took the ram and sacrificed it as a burnt offering on the altar *in place of his son*. Abraham named the place 'The Lord will provide'."[30]

The lesson of faith was not just for the participants that day. It was for all future generations seeking to know more about the Messiah's purpose. The ram offered that day as a substitute for Isaac represented the Messiah who would in time come as a "lamb to the slaughter" and die as a substitute for sinful humanity (represented that day by Isaac) so that they could live.[31] Taking an oath to Himself, God then reiterated to Abraham the covenant promise: "I will bless you richly. I will multiply your descendants into countless millions, like the stars of the sky and the sand on the seashore. They will conquer their enemies, and through your descendants, *all the nations of the earth will be blessed*—all because you have obeyed Me."[32]

Years later, Sarah died. Abraham purchased the cave of Machpelah located at Hebron as a family burial place, and there he laid her to rest. Nearing the last years of his own life, he decided that Isaac needed a wife. But not just any wife would do. Under no circumstances did he want him to marry any of the local Canaanite women, so he called his most trusted servant

Eliezer and commissioned him to journey back to Abraham's old home of Haran to find Isaac a wife. The story, found in Genesis 24, is quite an amazing account of how God leads in the lives of people who seek to follow His will. Through prayer and divine providence, the Lord led the servant to the home of Bethuel, Abraham's nephew. The man had a son named Laban and a daughter Rebekah whom the Bible describes as "very beautiful, and she was a virgin; no man had ever slept with her."[33]

After telling them why he had come, Eliezer requested that Rebekah return with him to the land of Canaan to become his master Isaac's wife. For her this would mean leaving her home for good, never to see her family or parents again. They left the final decision to Rebekah. Believing what she'd just heard concerning God's promises to her great uncle Abraham and his offspring, she then made the commitment to join his family and become part of this amazing Bible story. As she left, her family gave her a blessing: "'Our sister, may you become the mother of many millions! May your descendants overcome all their enemies.' Then Rebekah and her servants mounted the camels and left with Abraham's servant."[34]

One evening while Isaac walked in the Negev, he saw a caravan approaching. When Rebekah asked Eliezer who the man was, he told her that it was his master, Isaac. Dismounting and covering her face with a veil, she went to him. After hearing the servant's account of how God had miraculously led him, "Isaac brought Rebekah into his mother's tent, and she became his wife. He loved her very much, and she was a special comfort to him after the death of his mother."[35]

Abraham died at the age of 175. Afterward, the Lord appeared twice to Isaac to reaffirm the covenant promise He had before made with his father. Isaac considered migrating to

Egypt, because of a severe famine, but God instructed him, "Do not go to Egypt. Do as I say, and stay here in this land. If you do, I will be with you and bless you ... I will cause your descendants to become as numerous as the stars, and I will give them all these lands. And *through your descendants, all the nations of the earth will be blessed.*"[36] The covenant promise had now passed to Isaac and his generation. According to the covenant terms, from this point forward all future members of the Lord's family would be acknowledged through Isaac in God's final census.[37]

The Bible declares that because Abraham trusted in what God told him would happen, and ordered his life accordingly, the Lord considered him to be "righteous."[38] Abraham believed God's promise that the chosen "Seed" would be born into the world through his lineage. By means of this special child, Abraham's other children would also inherit the Land of Promise. Furthermore, Abraham assumed that though his progeny would die, God was able to bring them back to life again to receive all that He had pledged.[39] His trust in God and in what the Lord vowed was so deep and real that he "was even called '*the friend of God.*'"[40]

Those who share Abraham's faith are his spiritual offspring. They, too, are considered to be God's friends, and not just friends, but His children as well. As children, they will share in the inheritance of the land and the blessings of Abraham's rewards. Those who reject the plan given to Abraham, or attempt to halt or alter it, can, according to the terms of the arrangement, only expect God's curse.

CHAPTER 2
THE BIRTH OF ISRAEL (JACOB)

Sibling rivalry can destroy a family. We saw it brought out in the story of Abraham's two sons. Sarah's determination to protect the interest of her son, Isaac, led her to have Hagar and Ishmael expelled from the family camp. The Bible is mostly silent about the personal relationship between the two boys though it does tell us that they reunited for the burial of their father at the family cave of Machpelah.[41] From there we assume they went their separate ways and that God blessed Ishmael with 12 sons, and through them kept His promise to raise up many nations.

However, the family inheritance went with Isaac. "Abraham left everything he owned to his son Isaac."[42] More importantly, the promise to bless all the nations of the earth with the Messiah would have its fulfillment through his lineage. It is

13

imperative then to continue to study his family line as faithfully chronicled in Genesis 27-33.

Rebekah became pregnant with twin boys. The story of the two brothers, named Jacob and Esau, would become the epitome of the pain and division that sibling rivalry can inflict upon families. Their struggle with each other began while still in their mother's womb. The physical discomfort led Rebekah to inquire of the Lord the reason, and she learned that "the sons in your womb will become two rival nations. *One nation will be stronger than the other; the descendants of your older son [Esau] will serve the descendants of your younger son [Jacob].*"[43] Such a prediction seemed surprising since the custom of that culture always gave the family birthright to the eldest son.

No doubt while growing up Jacob heard his mother recount this strange revelation. Though he hoped it was truly God's will for him someday to obtain the sacred privilege, at the same time he sought to make it happen through his own devious schemes. As the boys grew, they developed opposite interests. Esau loved the outdoors and became a skillful hunter. Jacob was more of a stay at home boy who liked to cook and clean tent. "One day when Jacob was cooking some stew, Esau arrived home exhausted and hungry from a hunt. Esau said to Jacob, 'I'm starved! Give me some of that red stew you've made …' Jacob replied, 'All right, but trade me your birthright for it.' 'Look, I'm dying of starvation!' said Esau. '*What good is my birthright to me now?*' So, Jacob insisted, 'Well then, swear to me right now that it is mine.' So, Esau swore an oath, *thereby selling all his rights as the firstborn* to his younger brother. Then Jacob gave Esau some bread and lentil stew. Esau ate and drank and went on about his business, *indifferent to the fact that he had given up his birthright.*"[44]

Jacob—The Deceiver

As Isaac aged, his eyesight dimmed. Fearing that he would soon die, Rebekah became more concerned to secure the birthright for her younger son. She overheard Isaac tell Esau to get him some wild game as a ceremonial meal and then he would pronounce on him as the oldest son the birthright blessings. When Esau left for the hunt, she quickly directed Jacob to kill two goats. Then she prepared her husband's favorite meal for him and wrapped some of the goat hide around Jacob's hands and neck so as to imitate Esau's naturally hairy skin. Then she sent Jacob in to serve the meal to the nearly blind Isaac in an attempt to pass him off as Esau in order to get the blessing. Jacob lied to his father when asked his identity, and he passed the feel test with his now hair-covered body. Upon closer interrogation, Jacob lied for a second time and then passed his father's smell test.

After eating the meal and convinced that his server was indeed his eldest son, Isaac announced, "May many nations become your servants ... May all your mother's sons bow low before you. *All who curse you are cursed, and all who bless you are blessed.*"[45]

As soon as Jacob left, Esau showed up with the meal he had foraged for his father. "'Sit up and eat it so you can give me your blessing.' But Isaac asked him, 'Who are you?' 'Why, it is me, of course!' he replied. 'It's Esau, your older son.' Isaac began to tremble uncontrollably and said, 'Then who was it that just served me wild game? I have already eaten it, and I blessed him with an irrevocable blessing before you came.' When Esau understood, he let out a loud and bitter cry. 'O my father, bless me, too!' he begged. But Isaac said, 'Your brother was here, and he tricked me. He has carried away your blessing.' Esau said bitterly, 'No wonder his name is Jacob, for he has deceived me twice, first taking my birthright and now stealing my blessing. Oh, haven't you saved even one blessing for me?' Isaac said to Esau, 'I have made Jacob your master ... what is there left to give?' Esau pleaded, 'Not one blessing for me? O my father, bless me, too!' Then Esau broke down and wept."[46]

What a sad commentary on an otherwise godly home! Scripture lays bare the flaws even of God's people. Such stories are revealed to us so that we may become wiser regarding the decisions we make in our own lives. Esau was likely more concerned about receiving his father's material possessions than being a link in the Lord's genealogical chain to bring the Messiah to earth.

And the mother and son conspiracy didn't work out so well for them either. God had told Rebekah before the twins' birth that it was His intent for Jacob to have the birthright, yet like in the case of Abraham and Sarah, she too set about trying to fulfill God's wishes by her own human scheming. One of the hardest spiritual lessons to learn, even for those who truly love God and want His will to be done on the earth, is that we need to "wait patiently and confidently" for the Lord to perform what He says He will do.[47] Had mother and son not been so anxious about God's fulfillment of His promise, the account probably would have had a more peaceful outcome.

Instead, their trickery to swindle Esau out of his inheritance evoked murder in the brother's heart for "he said to himself, 'My father will soon be dead and gone. Then I will kill Jacob.' But someone got wind of what Esau was planning and reported it to Rebekah. She sent for Jacob and told him, 'Esau is threatening to kill you. This is what you should do. Flee to your uncle Laban in Haran. Stay there with him until your brother's fury is spent. When he forgets what you have done, I will send for you. Why should I lose both of you in one day?'"[48]

Jacob Sent Away

Rebekah convinced Isaac they needed to send Jacob back to her homeland to find a wife as she had been for Isaac. Agreeing, he said to Jacob, "May God Almighty bless you and give you many children. And may your descendants become a great assembly of nations. *May God pass on to you and your descendants the blessings he promised to Abraham. May you own this land where we are now foreigners, for God gave it to Abraham.*"[49]

Jacob then fled for his life, leaving behind the very land he had hoped to inherit, and the Bible never indicates that Jacob saw his mother again. The times when we recognize our character flaws, it's often a struggle to rely on the Lord's mercy. Jacob had been convicted of his sin. Though his father had given him the blessing, how did he know it was legitimate? Maybe his trickery had disqualified him in God's eyes? Probably while doubting if God could really trust the family blessing to someone like himself, he fell asleep while still in the dangerous wilderness of Palestine. As he slept, he had his famous dream of a ladder resting on earth but reaching into heaven, with angels going up and down on it. "At the top of the stairway stood the Lord, and He said, *'I am the Lord, the God of your grandfather Abraham and the God of your father, Isaac. The ground you are lying on belongs to you. I will give it to you and your descendants. Your descendants will be as numerous as the dust of the earth ... All the families of the earth will be blessed through you and your descendants.* What's more, I will be with you, and I will protect you wherever you go. *I will someday bring you safely back to this land. I will be with you constantly until I have finished giving you everything I have promised.*'"[50]

Jacob finally made his way to Haran and met his cousin, Rachel, Laban's youngest daughter, whom the Bible describes as being "beautiful in every way, with a lovely face and shapely figure."[51] Instantly falling in love with her, he agreed to give her father seven years of labor in exchange for her becoming his wife. In Laban, though, Jacob had met his match as a hoodwinker. Although Laban agreed to the deal, he broke the contract on the wedding night when he sent his oldest, and less attractive, daughter Leah in place of Rachel into the dark tent of consummation. When Jacob awoke the next morning, he realized he had been duped by the old bait and switch tactic. He demanded that Laban keep his end of the deal and immediately give him Rachel. Detecting that he had the upper hand, Laban managed to negotiate another seven years labor out of Jacob by allowing him to have Rachel at the beginning of the agreed time period. Acquiescing, Jacob began the seven years of additional labor.

During this period Jacob started having children by his two wives and their two maidservants. By the four women, he would eventually sire 12 sons and a daughter. Once he fulfilled his obligation, he told Laban it was time for him to take his family and return home to Canaan. But the two agreed to a livestock deal, so Jacob stayed on so as to build a little wealth for his own family. The Lord overruled yet another attempt by Laban to cheat Jacob by miraculously interfering with the animal's mating patterns.[52] As a result, after six years Jacob acquired a sizable amount of wealth. Then the Lord told him to return to his childhood home.

Jacob Returns as Israel

As Jacob neared his homeland, he learned to his horror that Esau was on his way to meet him with an army of 400 men. Hoping to protect his family, he separated himself and spent the night alone. During the night an unknown man attacked him. The two wrestled until dawn, then the man asked Jacob to release him. But Jacob refused to release him, saying, "'I will not let you go unless you bless me.' 'What is your name?' the man asked. He replied 'Jacob.' *'Your name will no longer be Jacob,'* the man told him. *'It is now Israel because you have struggled with both God and men and have won.'"*[53]

How can a person possibly win a fight with God? And what exactly does it mean to wrestle with Him? We all have at times struggled with believing God's existence. One of the main purposes of the Lord's covenants is to convince us that He is real. When Israel later questioned His presence in their lives, He said, "You will seek Me and find Me when you search for Me with all your heart."[54] Such a search will ultimately lead us to an understanding of His strategy to save the world through the covenant with Abraham. This is what Jacob came to understand--that God had a plan to forgive him personally of all his sins. Believing in it, he held God to His own promise, refusing to let go until He assured him that the Lord would honor His word to him. We can do the same. Holding God accountable for what He has promised, and applying it to us personally, is the secret to our spiritual victory.

Yet, even after we arrive at this realization, we still have a tremendous bent toward wanting to do it our way instead of relying on the Lord to accomplish what He promised. In fact, today the world is still enduring Israel's continual struggle to finally accept their God. Revelation 21:7 has a wonderful promise. "All who are victorious will inherit all these blessings, and I will be their God, and they will be my children." But again, how do we spiritually succeed in a world in which everything resists our desire to please God? We do it the same way Jacob did. We surrender to the Lord our plans to have everything our way and accept His will. "For every child of God defeats this evil world by trusting Christ to give the victory [instead of trying to gain the victory for Christ]. And the ones who win this battle against the world are the ones who believe that Jesus is the Son of God."[55]

Two people may be in agreement with a promise the Lord has given. Yet one prayerfully studies the Word, seeking wisdom as to how God says He will accomplish what He declares He will do, while the other zealously strikes out to enlist forces to make it happen. When Jacob was Jacob (a name meaning "he who supplants") he sought to get the promised birthright through deception. But that night, in the face of death and without any evidence that he would survive the struggle, he finally surrendered all his high expectations and dashed hopes to God. By faith, he simply accepted the provisions of the covenant, thus gaining the victory. It was then the Lord changed his name to Israel, which means "one who struggles with God."

Once Jacob was able to make peace with the Lord, he was then able to make some reconciliation with his brother and return to the land of his youth. But tragedy struck as his family was making their way toward Ephrath (Bethlehem). Though Rachel had been the love of his life, she had for years remained barren. She had watched as her sister Leah provided her husband with six sons and his only daughter, and then both her and her sister's handmaids delivered for Jacob four additional sons. Before the family had left her homeland Rachel finally had a child called Joseph. Now she was pregnant again, and the caravan had stopped near Bethlehem for her to give birth to Jacob's twelfth son. His name would be Benjamin, and the only one of Jacob's sons born in the Promised Land.

The Birth Of Israel (jacob)

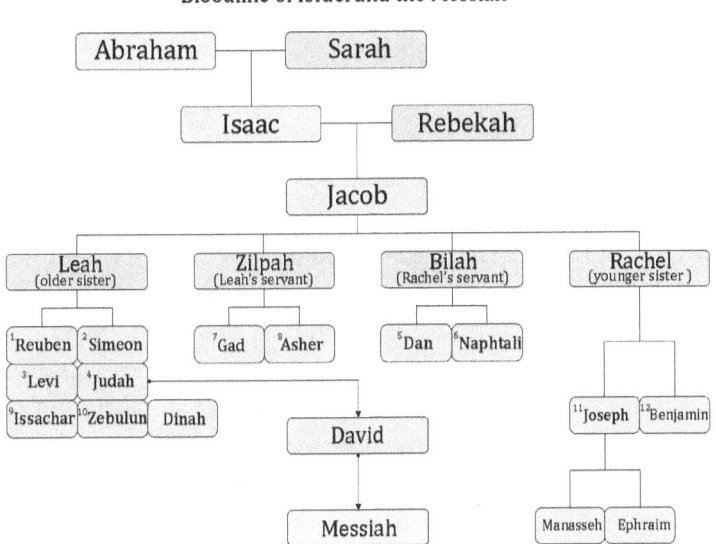

Normally the birth of a child is one of life's great occasions for celebration, but this one resulted in mourning as Rachel died from a complicated delivery. People most often sacrifice their lives in an attempt to prevent another from dying, thus leaving this world. Rachel instead gave her life while bringing a life into it. She experienced the worst of the serpent's sting placed upon women in Eden concerning pain in childbearing.[56] However, her sacrifice would leave a most important and lasting legacy on the entire family of Israel. From Benjamin came king Saul who would first establish his people as a political nation in the earth. Rachel's offspring through Benjamin also reached into New Testament times with the apostle Paul who would inform the Gentile nations that they too were included in the covenants God had made with the Hebrews.

The family buried her by the roadside, and a monument dedicated to this mother of Israel still stands today. Shortly afterwards, Jacob endured more sorrow as he and Esau came together at the family burial cave to honor their father, Isaac, who died at the age of 180.[57]

Though Jacob experienced a spiritual change, he still passed on his fallen nature to his children. His favorite son was Joseph, possibly because he was from his beloved Rachel. A dreamer, the youth shared two of his dreams with his father and brothers, suggesting that someday the family would bow down to his authority.[58] We get the sense that at 17 years old Joseph was just innocently relating these dreams, perhaps in an attempt to find for himself some answers to their meaning. He had heard old family stories about the line of succession of the ones chosen to propagate the promised Seed. Could his dreams be implying that he was the next to be chosen for the divine privilege? His brothers, well aware that Joseph was clearly their father's favorite son, were filled with spite. So, when the opportunity presented itself, they took matters in their own hands and devised a plan to kill Joseph while making it look like an accident. However, for the sake of conscience, they restricted their evil scheme just to selling him to a caravan of Ishmaelite slave traders bound for Egypt. Then they lied to their father, making him assume that a wild animal had killed Joseph.

Joseph in Egypt

Poor Joseph took nothing with him into Egypt except human fear and a faith in the God of his ancestors. The latter proved to be what he needed to endure his lot in life, as it was to get worse for him before it improved. After being bought as a slave, he found himself falsely accused of a sex crime against his master's wife. It landed him in an Egyptian prison where he endured even more suffering. But his faith stood firm. For anyone desiring to know and understand the Bible, the story of

Joseph's plight while in Egypt is a must-read.[59]

And, by the way, exactly what is this faith that Joseph possessed? The same hopefulness available to all of us, it's a belief that no matter what circumstances come our way, God has a better life awaiting us. It is what Abraham and Isaac believed, and Jacob as well. Not much has changed in this wicked world, and will not do so until the Messiah comes and transforms it. While some are content to make their fortunes and live in the luxury and false security it affords, multitudes around the world will never experience anything but dire poverty with no way or means to change it. Some people have lived healthy and happy lives until they learned that they were terminally ill with no chance of survival. Many of today's youth are victims of modern human trafficking, while tens of thousands die daily from lack of nutrition. Still others can only expect to spend the best years of their lives, if not the rest of their lives, in a prison cell. Many endure miserable lives because of their own choices, or, like Joseph, wind up victims of cruel circumstance. The good news is that God has let down to all a chain of hope which if grasped, can lift us above any state of human affairs, however horrible, including death. Speaking of those who found such faith, Scripture declares that they "trusted God and were tortured, preferring to die rather than turn from God and be free. *They placed their hope in the resurrection to a better life.*"[60]

Well, things did get better for Joseph, and his dreams did prove true. Through wisdom provided him by God, he prepared Egypt to endure a great famine by developing a massive system of grain storage facilities. The Pharaoh placed him in charge of the entire country. When the famine did arrive, it was so severe it forced his own family to migrate from Canaan to Egypt in order to get food, reuniting Joseph with his father and brothers.

Afterward, Jacob died in Egypt at the age of 147, and with the king's permission the family briefly returned to Canaan to lay him to rest at Machpelah with his father Isaac and grandfather Abraham. Upon returning to Egypt, his brothers feared that Joseph would now get even with them. When they asked him for forgiveness, he responded, "Don't be afraid of me. Am I God, to judge and punish you? As far as I am concerned, *God turned into good what you meant for evil.*"[61]

But though sin(s) may be forgiven, we usually end up paying a price as a consequence of our actions. The brothers had sought to kill Joseph but instead sold him into slavery. Now, their sins had transplanted the entire family into Egypt where their descendants would end up serving as slaves. "Then a new king came to the throne of Egypt who knew nothing about Joseph or what he had done. He told his people, 'These Israelites are becoming a threat to us because there are so many of them. We must find a way to put an end to this.'"[62] So, he made them slaves to the nation.

Joseph understood that it had all been part of God's original plan to bring His people into Egypt. Remember, God told Abraham that his descendants would spend 4 generations in a foreign land before they settled in the homeland He promised to them.[63] Joseph explained to his family, "'Soon I will die ... but God will surely come for you, to lead you out of this land of Egypt. *He will bring you back to the land He vowed to give to the descendants of Abraham, Isaac, and Jacob.*' Then Joseph made the sons of Israel swear an oath, and he said, 'When God comes to lead us back to Canaan, you must take my body back with you.' So, Joseph died at the age of 110."[64] The New Testament expresses Joseph's faith with the words, "And it was by faith that Joseph, when he was about to die, confidently spoke of God's bringing the people of Israel out of Egypt. *He was so sure of it that he commanded them to carry his bones with them when they left!"* [65]

What was it that gave Joseph such certainty concerning His people's return to their Land of Promise? Simply that He knew God had given them this promise through a covenant, and he believed the Lord was good for His word. They would indeed eventually return to the land just as Jacob did. Repeatedly throughout Scripture, Israel always returns.

From just one man, Jacob, God fashioned a bloodline. They entered Egypt as a family but would exit as a nation called Israel.

CHAPTER 3
LAW AND ORDER (MOSES)

The covenant God made with Abraham and passed on to his offspring Israel is a most powerful motivator. As we saw in the previous chapter, it provides hope for people who aren't doing so well in the present world. It makes their situations more tolerable, because it promises hope for a better life to come. Yet its sway reaches not only those whom many might consider weak, as the irreligious often regard adherents of religion, but as well it can affect the most prominent and powerful on earth. Consider the prophecy given to Israel by the prophet Isaiah: "This is what the Sovereign Lord says: 'See, I will give a signal to the godless nations ... *Kings and queens will serve you. They will care for all your needs. They will bow to the earth before you and lick the dust from your feet. Then you will know that I am the Lord.*'"[66] Imagine someone who possesses all earth's political power and wealth giving it up in expectation of a future promise made by an unseen deity. Well, such is the story of Moses.

By the time of Moses' birth, the Hebrews had lived in Egypt for nearly 400 years, and were now enslaved. The Jewish historian Flavius Josephus claims that Pharaoh's counselors told him that "there would be a child born to the Israelites, who, if he were reared, would bring the Egyptian dominion low, and would raise the Israelites; that he would excel all men in virtue, and obtain a glory that would be remembered through all ages."[67] Whatever the exact motivation, the king ordered all Hebrew male babies drowned in the Nile River.[68] Here we see another attempt by Satan to break the lineage of the promised Seed.

Now Moses was born into the tribe of Levi. In a desperate attempt to protect him, his mother Jochebed placed him in a basket boat and hid him in the reeds along the bank of the Nile. Pharaoh's daughter discovered him and, recognizing that he was a Hebrew child, sought a Hebrew woman to nurse him for her. Moses' sister Mariam, watching nearby, suggested that she knew a woman who was lactating. So, in God's divine providence the infant went back to his biological mother. When he was older the princess called for the child and adopted him as her own son. Though still one of the most powerful nations on earth, Egyptian world dominance was waning. Some Bible scholars believe the royal family hoped to groom Moses to reassert their role among the nations. In his famous New Testament sermon, Stephen told his audience, *"Moses was taught all the wisdom of the Egyptians, and he became mighty in both speech and action."*[69]

Imagine having what many politicians strive for their entire careers—money, position, dominance over the lives of multitudes by imposing rules they exempt themselves from due to elite privilege. Though Moses had been educated in the Egyptian religion, his birth mother had done her best to instill in him the beliefs of his Hebrew ancestors. Herein lay the test for Moses' faith. When the time came for him to get off the fence and make a choice, the Bible tells us, "It was by faith that Moses, when he grew up, refused to be treated as the son of Pharaoh's daughter. *He chose to share the oppression of God's people instead of enjoying the fleeting pleasures of sin* [for the short time he would be on earth]. *He thought it was better to suffer for the sake of the Messiah than to own the treasures of Egypt, for he was looking ahead to the great reward that God would give him* [after his time was over on earth]. It was by faith that Moses left the land of Egypt. He was not afraid of the king. Moses kept right on going *because he kept his eyes on the one who is invisible.*"[70]

Moses Flees Egypt

God was calling Moses to fulfill a major prophecy. He was to help deliver his family from Egyptian bondage and lead them back to the land that God had promised Abraham, Isaac, and Jacob. But first Moses had to flee for his life, because, in his own human effort to do what he felt led by God to do, he killed an Egyptian slave master. It caused his fellow Hebrews to question his zeal and placed him on Egypt's most wanted list. So, he departed to Midian, a desert area around Mount Sinai, where for 40 years he took up the humble occupation of sheep and goat herding. Here he was to learn a most vital lesson—God's people are like sheep in that they must be led, and by nature they will resist being forced. It is a most elementary expression of human nature that people respond more favorably to grace than they do to law.

Now Moses was human as are we all. Surely many times he must have questioned his own calling; wished that he had made a career in Egyptian politics; doubted as to whether or not God could, or would, still use him. But God had not given up on him. "One day Moses was tending the flock ... Suddenly, the angel of the Lord appeared to him as a blazing fire in a bush. Moses was amazed because the bush was engulfed in flames, but it didn't burn up. 'Amazing!' Moses said to himself. 'Why isn't that bush burning up? I must go over to see this.' When the Lord saw that He had caught Moses' attention, God called to him from the bush. 'Moses! Moses!' 'Here I am!' Moses replied. 'Do not come any closer,' God told him. 'Take off your sandals, for you are standing on holy ground ... *I am the God of your ancestors—the God of Abraham, the God of Isaac, and the God of Jacob* ... You can be sure I have seen the misery of my people in Egypt ... So, I have come to rescue them from the Egyptians and *lead them out of Egypt into their own good and spacious land* ... Now go, for I am sending you to Pharaoh. You will lead my people, the Israelites, out of Egypt ...' But Moses protested, 'If I go to the people of Israel and tell them, the God of your ancestors has sent me to you, they won't believe me. They will ask, which god are you talking about? What is his name? Then what shall I tell them?' God replied, 'I AM THE ONE WHO ALWAYS IS. Just tell them, I AM has sent me to you.' God also said, '*Tell them, The Lord, the God of your ancestors—the God of Abraham, the God of Isaac, and the God of Jacob—has sent me to you. This will be my name forever; it has always been my name, and it will be used throughout all generations.*"[71]

Here we get a rare insight into the divine by means of God's own self-identification. He declares that *the God of Abraham, the God of Isaac, and the God of Jacob* has always been His name and always will be. He does not change His identity, unlike heathen deities. For example, the Greek god-king of the sea was Poseidon, but to the Romans he was Neptune. Their worshipers named and identified such gods. The point is that though human beings may call Him by various names (Yahweh; Jehovah; Yeshua; Jesus; etc.), the true Creator of the universe Himself has gone on record as the God who initially made the covenant with Abraham. This is important, because this same God does not change His identity, nor His covenant, from Genesis to Revelation.

The God of the Hebrews obliterates sin and anything associated with it upon contact as was on exhibit at the burning bush. Scripture uses fire metaphorically to instruct us about the holiness of God's nature. Moses later counseled the people, "So be careful not to break the covenant the Lord your God has made with you. *You will break it if you make idols of any shape or form, for the Lord your God has absolutely forbidden this. The Lord your God is a devouring fire*, a jealous God."[72] The New Testament offers the same advice to believers preparing to enter their Promised Land of eternal life. "Since we are receiving a Kingdom that cannot be destroyed, let us be thankful and please God by worshiping Him with holy fear and awe. *For our God is a consuming fire.*"[73]

Plainly stated, sin, unshielded by the protective provisions of the eternal covenant, will be consumed when it comes in contact with the Lord's presence. That's why the antichrist has the freedom to do his thing on the earth, because God's probation of grace allows it. But one day his activities will come to a screeching halt. "For this lawlessness is already at work secretly, and it will remain secret until the One who is holding it back *steps out of the way*. Then the man of lawlessness will be revealed [exposed to the Almighty's presence], whom the Lord Jesus will consume with the breath of His mouth and destroy by the *splendor [brightness as by fire] of His coming*."[74] And what is his final fate along with those who follow him? "Anyone whose name was not found recorded in the Book of Life was thrown into *the lake of fire.*"[75] No wonder God instructed Moses to remove his shoes when he stepped onto the holy ground of the Lord's fiery presence!

But what intrigued Moses most regarding the burning bush was that it wasn't being consumed. That's because just as God's presence is a "consuming fire" to that which is sinful, it preserves that which His righteousness protects. It would be a "pillar of fire" that gave light for nightly travel and kept the Hebrews from freezing to death on the desert floor during the 40 years they spent wandering.[76]

Years later, when the prophet Elisha and his servant found themselves surrounded by a great army sent by the king of Aram to seize him, "the servant of the man of God got up early the next morning and went outside, there were troops, horses, and chariots everywhere. 'Ah, my lord, what will we do now?' he cried out to Elisha. 'Don't be afraid!' Elisha told him. *'For there are more on our side than on theirs!'* Then Elisha prayed, 'Oh Lord, open his eyes and let him see!' The Lord opened his servant's eyes, and when he looked up, he saw that the hillside around Elisha was filled with horses *and chariots of fire.*"[77]

And, while the flames of a Babylonian furnace, "heated seven times hotter than usual," didn't even singe the hair or clothing of God's three faithful witnesses, "the *flames leaped out and killed the soldiers* as they threw the three men in!" Astonished that the young men *"didn't even smell of smoke,"* the king sought to learn *the means of their safeguarding*. He inquired of his aids, "'Didn't we tie up three men and throw them into the furnace?' 'Yes,' they said, 'we did indeed, Your Majesty.' 'Look!' Nebuchadnezzar shouted. 'I see four men, unbound, walking around in the fire. *They aren't even hurt by the flames! And the fourth looks like a divine being!'*"[78]

Most of the things we think are so grand in the world will not be around forever. All of humanity's works designed to attract and tether us to our earthly sinful existence will someday perish. Peter reminds us, "The heavens will pass away with a terrible noise, and *everything in them will disappear in fire, and the earth and everything on it will be exposed to judgment.*"[79] Fire will then test everything! If inspired by trust in the Messianic covenants it will stand. If not, it won't. "For no one can lay any other foundation than the one we already have—Jesus Christ [the Messiah Seed]. Now anyone who builds on that foundation may use gold, silver, jewels, wood, hay, or straw. But there is going to come a time of testing at the judgment day to see what kind of work each builder has done. Everyone's work will be put through the fire to see whether or not it keeps its value. *If the work survives the fire*, that builder will receive a reward. But *if the work is burned up*, the builder will suffer great loss. The builders themselves will be saved, *but like someone escaping through a wall of flames.*"[80]

Like Elisha's servant, we need to have our eyes opened to see what is transpiring around us in the spiritual realm instead of being entertained and mesmerized by the latest circus arriving in town. The things that we have been tricked into believing are important in this life are not real. That is why the Bible advises us to "fix our eyes not on what is seen, but on what is unseen, since what is seen is temporary, but what is unseen is eternal."[81] The concepts we have been discussing here are not negotiable. They are not crazy ideas of some fanatic who said God talked to him from a burning bush. Moses was dead serious when he told his people "These instructions are not mere words—*they are your life!*"[82]

Moses Returns to Egypt

The book of Exodus testifies to how closely Moses followed God's instructions. After 40 years of absence, the Lord sent him back to Egypt to confront Pharaoh. "Then you will tell him [Pharaoh], this is what the Lord says: *'Israel is my firstborn son*. I commanded you to let him go, so he could worship Me. But since you had refused, be warned! *I will kill your firstborn son!*'"[83] Instead of heeding the divine warning, Pharaoh did everything he could to make the lives of the Hebrews more difficult and keep them as slaves. His resistance precipitated a showdown between the supreme god/ruler of Egypt and the Supreme God/Ruler of the universe! Ten plagues designed to expose the fraudulent powers of the Egyptian deities now pummeled the land. Moses foretold the most devastating one. "This is what the Lord says: 'About midnight I will pass through Egypt. *All the firstborn sons will die in every family in Egypt, from the oldest son of Pharaoh, who sits on the throne, to the oldest son of his lowliest slave.* Even the firstborn of the animals will die. Then, a loud wail will be heard throughout the land of Egypt ... But among the Israelites it will be so peaceful that not even a dog will bark. *Then you will know that the Lord makes a distinction between the Egyptians and the Israelites.* All the officials of Egypt will come running to me, bowing low. 'Please leave!' they will beg. 'Hurry! And take all your followers with you.'"[84] To the Israelites, the Lord announced: "I am the Lord. *I appeared to Abraham, to Isaac, and to Jacob as God Almighty ... And I entered into a solemn covenant with them. Under its terms, I swore to give them the land of Canaan, where they were living.* You can be sure that I have heard the groans of the people of Israel, who are now slaves to the Egyptians. *I have remembered my covenant with them* ... I will free you from your slavery in

Egypt ... *I will bring you into the land I swore to give to Abraham, Isaac, and Jacob. It will be your very own property.*"[85]

The night the angel of death swept through the land of Egypt, carrying out the fatal sentence, brought the Hebrews their first real test of faith. God had directed them to sacrifice a lamb and smear its blood upon the doorposts of their dwellings. When the angel of death saw the blood, that household would be "passed over," saving all who dwelt in it. Exodus 12 recounts the story of this first Passover which the people of Israel continue to celebrate annually. Of course, it was a lesson designed to teach future believers that by trusting in the shed blood of the Messiah they, too, will be "passed over" in the day of God's final judgment. As Paul later told the newly formed church at Corinth, *"For indeed Christ, our Passover, has been sacrificed in our place.* Therefore, let's keep the feast."[86] Or, as it reads in the *Orthodox Jewish Bible*, "our Korban Pesach has been sacrificed, Mashiach. [SHEMOT 12:3-6, 21]."

It happened just as God said. The firstborn throughout Egypt, including Pharaoh's son, died, while the Hebrews remained safe under the blood. Finally, Pharaoh ordered their exit from the land. "And the people of Israel did as Moses had instructed and asked the Egyptians for clothing and articles of silver and gold ... *and they gave the Israelites whatever they asked for. So, like a victorious army, they plundered the Egyptians.*"[87]

The Exodus of Israel

We begin to see a pattern here. Ecclesiastes 3:15 brings out a major prophetic principle: *"Whatever exists today and whatever will exist in the future has already existed in the past. For God calls each event back in its turn."* The Bible is a book of types and anti-types, or models presented only to be replicated in the future. If we don't grasp this, it will be difficult to gain any real understanding of the lessons the scriptures are trying to teach. Editors call them literary patterns. For example, just as Jacob had left Canaan in exile to work for his uncle Laban in Haran, he later returned as "Israel" with wealth. His family was exiled to work for the Egyptians only now to return to Canaan as a nation [Israel] with wealth. So, too, in the last days Israel, having been serving in the bondage of the world's nations, will return to the Promised Land and obtain wealth. The prophet Isaiah wrote, "Arise, Jerusalem! Let your light shine for all nations to see ... All nations will come to your light ... Look and see, for *everyone is coming home!* Your sons are coming from distant lands; your little daughters will be carried home ... merchants from around the world will come to you. *They will bring you the wealth of many lands ... For though I have destroyed you in my anger, I will have mercy on you through my grace. Your gates will stay open around the clock to receive the wealth of many lands ...* For the nations that refuse to be your allies will be destroyed *... You will know at last that I, the Lord, am your Savior and Redeemer, the Mighty One of Israel ... I, the Lord, will bring it all to pass at the right time.*"[88]

Just as those nations opposing Israel at the end of time will face destruction, so Pharaoh's mighty army was wiped out when he sent them to chase the Hebrews through the Red Sea. "The waters covered ... the entire army of Pharaoh. Of all the Egyptians who had chased the Israelites into the sea, *not a single one survived.* The people of Israel had walked through the middle of the sea on dry land, as the water stood up like a wall on both sides. This was how the Lord rescued Israel from the Egyptians that day."[89] "There were about 600,000 men, plus all the women and children ... *Many people who were not Israelites went with them.*"[90]

Here Comes the Law

Two months after their deliverance, the Hebrews arrived in the mountainous desert area of Sinai. There God revealed Himself to them. "All Mount Sinai was covered with smoke because the Lord had *descended on it in the form of fire.*"[91] The people were terrified as God gave them the law of Ten Commandments. He told them, "I am the Lord your God, who rescued you from slavery in Egypt. *Do not worship any other gods besides Me. Do not make idols of any kind*, whether in the shape of birds or animals or fish. You must never worship or bow down to them, for *I, the Lord your God, am a jealous God who will not share your affection with any other god!*"[92] This first commandment was of utmost importance. Israel would struggle with it throughout their entire history, resulting in almost continuous chastisement from the Lord. But why?

In a precarious world in which crop failures were frequent and human mortality high, maintaining fertility was an obsession. The ancient Near East believed that its deities were responsible for preserving life. They brought the rains to water the crops and made them grow and mature. Human conception and childbirth were under the control of various gods. But they had to be encouraged to maintain that vital fertility. The gods, people believed, easily forgot what humanity needed. The best thing to do was to keep reminding and even showing them how fertility should happen. Naturally, that appealed to fallen human nature. They projected their own sinful desires into their gods. But the Bible declares that such false gods are nothing more than a figment of humanity's sinful imagination. Obviously, if the gods are just like us, it makes us feel less guilty about what we are like.

The apostle Paul hit this nail on the head when he wrote, "they began to think up foolish ideas of what God was like. The result was that their minds became dark and confused. Claiming to be wise, they became utter fools instead. And instead of worshiping the glorious, ever-living God, they worshiped idols made to look like mere people, or birds and animals and snakes … Instead of believing what they knew was the truth about God, *they deliberately chose to believe lies*. So, they worshiped the things God made but not the Creator himself."[93] That is why God continually reminded the Hebrews not to make such images, and certainly not to settle into any false security such self-deception can offer. He was the true and only source of life and fertility.

"The Israelites at the foot of the mountain saw an awesome sight. *The awesome glory of the Lord on the mountaintop looked like a devouring fire.* Then Moses disappeared into the cloud … He stayed on the mountain forty days and forty nights."[94] There he received special instructions from God about how the people were to worship Him through the construction of a tabernacle and the appointment of a priesthood selected from among the tribe of Levi (later to be called the Levites). Moses returned with a pair of stone tablets containing the Ten Commandments written by the finger of God Himself. But the people had become impatient, and being concerned about their fate, had fashioned a golden calf, placing their trust in it to lead them. The people declared, "O Israel, these are the gods who brought you out of Egypt!"[95] When God vowed to destroy the Hebrews, Moses interceded, reminding the Lord, "*Remember your covenant with Your servants—Abraham, Isaac and Jacob. You swore by your own self, 'I will make your descendants as numerous as the stars of heaven. Yes, I will give them all this land that I have promised to your descendants, and they will possess it forever.'* So, the Lord withdrew His threat."[96]

Here again, as when Jacob had wrestled with God, Moses held God to His word of honor regarding the covenant promise He had made with Abraham. Here is the one pledge God will never discredit simply for the reason that He promised it. Shortly thereafter the Lord told the people to provide their jewelry for the construction of His tabernacle, and they complied. A later Jewish teacher commented about their behavior. "Rabbi Abba bar Aha said: 'One cannot determine the nature of this people. When asked to contribute for making the golden calf, they give; and when asked to contribute for constructing the tabernacle, they give.'"[97]

The Lord then instructed them how they could successfully settle their new homeland. "*It is not at all because you are such righteous, upright people that you are about to occupy their land.* The Lord your God will drive these nations out ahead of you because of their wickedness, and to *fulfill the oath He swore to your ancestors Abraham, Isaac, and Jacob.* I will say it again, The Lord your God is not giving you this good land because you are righteous, *for you are not—you are a stubborn people.*"[98] He sternly warned, "When the Lord your God destroys the nations and you drive them out and occupy their land, *do not be trapped into following their example in worshiping their gods.* Do not say, 'How do these nations worship their gods? I want to follow their example.'"[99] And, "D*o not make treaties of any kind with the people living in the land.* They are spiritual prostitutes, committing adultery against Me by sacrificing to their gods. *If you make peace with them, they will invite you to go with them to worship their gods*, and you are likely to do it."[100]

In addition to religious guidelines, holy days, and numerous social rules, He gave them health principles designed to combat disease, even against microscopic enemies unknown at the time. He forbade them to consume the blood of animals, or eat scavenger or bottom feeders from the sea and waterways due to their proneness to contain parasites. If they found a dead rodent or reptile in any household vessel, they were to destroy that vessel even though it might incur a monetary loss. Wooden cooking utensils were not to be used because of potential bacterial contamination. He even instructed them, "Mark off an area outside the camp for a latrine. Each of you must have a spade as part of your equipment. Whenever you relieve yourself, you must dig a hole with the spade and cover the excrement."[101] The Lord provided many details about maintaining the cleanliness of their environment, individual hygiene, or personal and communal conduct. To the ancient Hebrews cleanliness was next to godliness.

In all, they received 613 ordinances, or *Mitzvot*, recorded in the first five books of the Hebrew Scriptures [the Torah]. Another significant reason for such specific commands was that they would serve as a common bond for Hebrews during the coming centuries when they would find themselves exiled in other lands. Such rules would help insulate them from surrounding cultures, and provide them spiritual bonds though they would at times be physically separated. Thus, their Hebrew heritage would be preserved all the way to the world's end.

Israel's Disbelief

It should come as no surprise that the devil could easily convince the Gentile world to dismiss the certainty of the covenants that the Lord had made with the Hebrews. After all, they "*had no part in the promises* God had made to them."[102] The shocking proof of the great deceiver's power to mislead appears in the history of the Hebrews themselves as they began to doubt their own divine calling. It has been a reoccurring pattern that plagues them to this day. The good news is, the Bible predicts that one day they will throw off their spirit of doubt concerning God's commitment to them, and enter into the glory of their promised inheritance.

That last generation of Israelites will come to an understanding of their divine calling. Speaking in a broader context of both the preserving and destructive nature of eternal fire, Isaiah's words of encouragement to their ancestors will someday resonate with them. "But now, O Israel, the Lord who created you says: 'Do not be afraid, for I have ransomed you. I have called you by name; you are mine ... *When you walk through the fire of oppression, you will not be burned up; the flames will not consume you.* For I am the Lord, your God, the Holy One of Israel.'"[103]

Upon leaving Sinai, Moses announced, "I am giving all this land to you! Go in and occupy it, *for it is the land the Lord swore to give to your ancestors Abraham, Isaac, and Jacob, and to all their descendants.*"[104] Although God promised to clear out the land of Canaan for their occupation, they decided to send 12 spies to determine their chances of defeating its inhabitants. Upon their return, they said, "'We can't go up against them [the occupants of Canaan]! They are stronger than we are!' So, they spread discouraging reports about the land among the Israelites: 'The land we explored will swallow up any who go to live there. All the people we saw were huge. We even saw giants there, the descendants of Anak. We felt like grasshoppers next to them, and that's what we looked like to them!'"[105] Only two of the 12 spies, Caleb and Joshua, fully accepted God's promise of victory. Though they tried to persuade the people to believe in the Lord's covenant promise that He would give them the land, the people sided with the 10 doubters, and so the Lord informed them they would spend the next 40 years wandering in the wilderness—a year for each day that they had spent spying out the land. After hearing it, the people then decided to seize the land even though told that God would now not be with them. Badly defeated in battle, as predicted, they spent the next 40 years dying off while wandering in the desert.

Hebrews 3:19 documents that the people did not enter their land of rest because of disbelief in the covenant promise God made to their fathers. Yet, His presence continued to be with them those 40 years they roamed as vagabonds. "The Lord guided them by a pillar of cloud during the day and a pillar of fire at night. That way they could travel whether it was day or night. And the Lord did not remove the pillar of cloud or the pillar of fire from their sight."[106] Here we find a huge lesson to be learned and never forgotten. *Scripture constantly emphasizes that though God punishes Israel, He never eternally forsakes them.* It is a principle that goes all the way back to the original assurance God gave Abraham concerning his descendants: "I will be with you, and I will protect you wherever you go. I will someday bring you safely back to this land. I will be with you constantly *until I have finished giving you everything I have promised.*"[107]

CHAPTER 4
THE CHOSEN KING (DAVID)

While it took God only one night to get Israel out of Egypt, it would take 40 years to remove Egypt from Israel. In actuality, they spent 40 years on what normally would have been an 11- day trip.[108] Finally, the chastisement brought about by their earlier refusal to enter the Promised Land came to an end. It happened just as God said it would. Everyone, excepting Caleb and Joshua from the generation who had exited Egypt, had died, including Moses at the age of 120. He viewed the Promised Land from a mountaintop but never set foot on its soil. The divine appointment to guide Israel across the Jordan River then fell to Joshua, a leader from the tribe of Ephraim.[109]

Joshua was well seasoned in his faith, having survived the Exodus and wilderness trials. He understood the answer to our question, *Why Israel?* He knew the Lord had called his nation into being and was using them to:

1. Document God's existence and character to the world nations (Ezekiel 36:22, 23)
2. Be a blessing to the nations (Genesis 22:18)
3. Be a witness to the nations (Isaiah 43:10-13)
4. Deliver to the nations the written revelation of God's word (Romans 3:2)
5. Deliver to the nations the promised Messiah (Romans 11:26-28)
6. Be a sign to the nations of the world's end (Luke 21:24)
7. Establish and offer the nations an eternal kingdom of peace (Isaiah 9:7)

God told Joshua to "be strong and courageous, for you will lead my people to *possess all the land I swore to give their ancestors.*"[110] Israel did occupy the land, and at the end of his life, Joshua reminded them of the eternal covenant God had made with them as a people. He assured them that no outside forces could put an end to God's promise of using them to bless the world. Joshua recounted the story of Balaam, who for a fee sought to change God's promise to Israel, but ended up prophesying, "*Blessed is everyone who blesses you, O Israel, and cursed is everyone who curses you.*"[111] Just as God pronounced blessings and curses to the Hebrews based on their loyalty, He *also pronounced blessings and curses on all Gentiles on the basis of how they relate to them.*

The only thing that could frustrate the divine plan was not external adversaries, but Israel's own choices. Their leader told them, "*Deep in your hearts you know that every promise of the Lord your God has come true. Not a single one has failed;* But as surely as the Lord your God has given you the good things he has promised, *he will also bring disaster on you if you disobey him....* If you break the covenant of the Lord your God by worshiping and serving other gods, his anger will burn against you, and *you will quickly be wiped out from the good land he has given you.*"[112] He then presented them with his famous challenge, "Serve the Lord alone. But if you are unwilling to serve the Lord, *then choose today whom you will serve.* Would you prefer the gods your ancestors served beyond the Euphrates [referring to Abraham's polytheistic background]? Or will it be the gods of the Amorites in whose land you now live? But as for me and my family, *we will serve the Lord.*"[113]

Establishment in the Land

During the next 14 centuries, Israel lived uncertainly in their Promised Land. As we shall see, the original promise that God had selected their family for a special purpose sustained the faith of those who remained faithful to Him. It was this promise, pregnant with God's vow to deliver Abraham's *"Seed"* to save the world, that Satan most feared and sought to abort. He knew the Lord chose the Hebrew people, whom the Bible metaphorically depicts as a "woman," to serve as the bloodline for the Messiah.[114] No wonder that race has been the most persecuted people in the history of our planet!

Then came the time of the Judges. With Israel now established in the land, the Lord sent encouragement to them through Bokim, saying, "I brought you out of Egypt into this land that I swore to give your ancestors, and I said *I would never break my covenant with you.*"[115] However, the following generations had a proclivity to do "what was evil in the Lord's sight and worshiped the images of Baal. They abandoned the Lord, the God of their ancestors, who had brought them out of Egypt. They *chased after other gods,* worshiping the gods of the people around them. And they angered the Lord."[116] Not only did it weaken their faith, it resulted in judgments, usually in the form of invasions by enemies. The Israelites would then plead to the Lord for help, and He would send judges (deliverers)—Gideon, Jephthah, and Samson, to name a few—to defeat their enemies and direct them back to the historical promise made to them by the one, true God. The tragic cycle continued for nearly 300 years.

Battle of the Kings

The thirteenth and last of the judges, Samuel, served at the tabernacle and was also Israel's first major prophet. God anointed him for his position as a leader in Israel when he was still a youth. He had been born at a time when the spiritual condition of Israel was at an all-time low. "In those days Israel had no king, so the people did whatever seemed right in their own eyes."[117] Samuel faithfully served the Lord and Israel his entire life, and nearing his end, appointed his two sons to carry on his work. But the leaders of Israel didn't like them, and met with Samuel. "'Look,' they told him, 'you are now old, and your sons are not like you. Give us a king *like all the other nations have.*' Samuel was very upset with their request and went to the Lord for advice. 'Do as they say,' the Lord replied, '*for it is me they are rejecting, not you.* They don't want me to be their king any longer. Ever since I brought them from Egypt they have continually forsaken me and followed other gods. And now they are giving you the same treatment. Do as they ask, but solemnly warn them about how a king will treat them.'"[118]

In spite of Samuel's warnings and pleadings, they declared, "'Even so, we still want a king.' They said, 'We want to be like the nations around us. Our king will govern us and lead us into battle.'"[119] So, the Lord led Samuel to anoint Saul and present him as their ruler. Later, the prophet asked God to send rain out of season as a testimony to the people's rebellion in asking for a king. When the thunder and rain came "the people were terrified of the Lord and of Samuel. 'Pray to the Lord your God for us, or we will die,' they cried out to Samuel. 'For now, we have added to our sins by asking for a king.'"[120] Just as their fathers had done, they had rejected the Lord, because of their desire to be like the world around them, and now they greatly feared His judgment. But Samuel said, "Don't be afraid.... *The Lord will not abandon his chosen people, for that would dishonor his great name.* He made you a special nation for himself."[121]

Once again, Israel would harvest the bitter fruit of their sowing during the reign of Saul, but the Lord did not spurn His chosen people. On the contrary, He was preparing to make another major commitment to them. Perhaps none of the characters recorded in the Old Testament were as legendary as David. His anointing by Samuel as Saul's replacement remained secret for a time, yet as history unfolded, so did David's destiny. But his road to kingship would prove a difficult one. Called from his father's farm at an early age, he went out to face and defeat Israel's greatest nemesis—the giant Goliath. "But something happened when the victorious Israelite army was returning home after David had killed Goliath. Women came out from all the towns along the way to celebrate and to cheer for King Saul, and they sang and danced for joy with tambourines and cymbals. This was their song: 'Saul has killed his thousands, and *David his ten-thousands*!' This made Saul very angry. 'What's this?' he said. 'They credit David with ten thousands and me with only thousands. Next, they'll be making him their king!' So from that time on *Saul kept a jealous eye on David.*"[122]

Saul, who was supposed to be leading Israel, now sought to break a major link in God's genealogical chain destined to bring forth the promised Seed. Time and again he tried to kill David, who fled the palace to live in caves with a band of about 400 supporters. Society regarded them as rebels and misfits, people "who were in trouble or in debt or who were just discontented."[123] Saul's soldiers continuously hunted them like animals, yet David told them, "Stay here with me, and I will protect you with my own life, for the same person wants to kill us both."[124] No doubt those rejects from Israelite society felt safe with David, because *they believed he was God's chosen one who in time would ascend to Israel's throne.*

Even Saul, deep down in his heart, knew it to be God's will. David didn't presumptuously try to make it happen but instead patiently waited on the Lord's timing. After one of the occasions when he had the opportunity to kill Saul, yet instead spared his life, the king confessed to David, "And now I realize that you are surely going to be king, and *Israel will flourish under your rule.*"[125] Amazingly, he still afterward chose to allow Satan to work through him to oppose God's selection of David. Here is a classic example of a lack of spiritual discernment. Instead of using his position of power and influence to help execute God's plan for Israel, Saul instead spent his time and resources to counteract it. What a contrast to Nabal's wife, Abigail, who had David's best interest in mind when she said to him, "The Lord *will surely reward you with a lasting dynasty*, for you are fighting the Lord's battles."[126] Though her husband was anti-Davidic, she was in tune with God's plan. In fact, she was so wise that after her husband died, David married her![127]

God Makes Another Covenant

Israel's craving for a worldly king was a slap in God's face. So, as He often does with us, He allowed them to have and experience what they thought they wanted in order to realize

God's way is always better. Yet He does not abandon them. Just so that we understand the level of God's commitment to choosing the Hebrew race for His eternal purpose, it is vital that we grasp what He was preparing to do next. Instead of discontinuing His promises to Israel, *He doubled down on His commitment to them by giving another eternal covenant through King David.* "I have made a solemn agreement with David, *my chosen kings forever; they will sit on your throne from now until eternity.*"[128] Like Abraham, David believed the Lord said what He meant, and meant what He said to him. No wonder that he praised God so much! The king's final words were, "*It is my family God has chosen*! Yes, he has made an everlasting covenant with me. *His agreement is eternal, final, sealed.*"[129] Out of all the clans of Israel God selected one particular family as a royal dynasty to rule eternally over all the families of the earth.

Here is where it gets a bit complicated, yet every bit as fascinating. We need to go back to Jacob's foretelling of his son Judah's role in God's eternal plan. "The *scepter will not depart from Judah, nor the ruler's staff from his descendants, until the coming of the one to whom it belongs, the one whom all the nations will obey.*"[130] It is a biblical demonstration of God's sovereignty. He first chose Abraham over all other Gentiles; then Isaac over Ishmael; Jacob over Esau before the twins were ever born or committed any acts of right or wrong; Judah over his brothers; David over Saul; and now the tiny kingdom of Judah over the rest of Israel. The Lord selected His chosen ones not because their human performances were more stellar than others, for that would have based God's eternal government on human accomplishment rather than divine leading. Those God chose had one thing in common. They had heard and understood God's eternal plan, and believed it would come to pass even though everything around them suggested otherwise.

The intersection of God's sovereignty and man's free will has stumped both students and skeptics of the Bible for ages. God's foreknowledge doesn't determine the decisions of our free will, even though He already knows the outcome of our race before we run it. Though we cannot fully understand or explain it because of divine participation, we do receive some insight into its inner workings.

Perhaps an example from the Bible would better serve our attempt at understanding this theological difficulty. God told Saul that if he had obeyed, his progeny would have ruled forever.[131] Yet David didn't have a perfect track record either--no, far from it. His misdeeds included not only adultery but the premeditated murder of his lover's husband who was a devoted soldier in David's own army, risking his life daily to protect the king and his country. Then to make matters worse, David engaged in a cover-up to hide his crimes from the nation, and even tried to fool God. Yet, when the prophet Nathan pointed out his sins to him, David repented.[132] Though the Lord forgave David, the king still reaped the consequences, both good and bad, of his choices. In spite of all David's shortcomings, God still predicted his offspring would rule from His throne for eternity.

So, why David and not Saul? Because *David's heritage came through Judah upon whom Jacob had years earlier bestowed the royal promise*, and Saul came from the tribe of Benjamin, one not chosen to produce the Messiah. Here is the key that unlocks the rest of Scripture and human history. The book of Revelation declares Christ to be "the Lion of *the tribe of Judah*, the *heir to David's throne*." "He is the one who has the *key of David*."[133]

Again, we encounter the gospel God preached to Abraham concerning his "Seed," saying, "in thee shall all the nations of the earth be blessed."[134] Christ's obedience *fulfilled all the required covenants* that God had made with His people, thus paving the way for them to receive grace despite their failure. David was but a forerunner to the real King of Israel—the Messiah. Even David's disobedience could not thwart God's purposes nor cancel the promise to establish His throne through him. That throne was to be eternally instituted, not as a result of David's obedience, but the Messiah's. Though it is a mystery, *all obedience or disobedience brought about by human choice contributes to the eternal purpose of God.* It is simply for us to believe this, or not believe it, and thus play out our parts accordingly.

"David was thirty years old when he began to reign, and he reigned forty years in all."[135] His small army which began with only a few hundred followers swelled to more than 340,000 Israelite men of war![136] Concerning them, Scripture records: "They were all eager to see David become king instead of Saul, just as the Lord had promised."[137] Saul's failed leadership had severely divided the tribes. But now after the death of Saul at the hands of the Philistines "all Israel went to David at Hebron and told him, 'We are all members of your family. For a long time, even while Saul was our king, *you were the one who really led Israel.* And the Lord your God has told you, *You will be the shepherd of my people Israel.* You will be their leader.'"[138] So the divided members of Jacob's offspring found unity under the banner of King David. Someday it will be the same when all of Israel reunites under the authority of his ultimate successor—Messiah David.

A Kingdom Divided

But Saul's spirit of rejecting the chosen of God didn't die with the king. David's son Solomon succeeded him, and his reign led to a period of peace and prosperity in Jerusalem.

Yet it would not last. God "had warned Solomon specifically about worshiping other gods, but Solomon did not listen to the Lord's command. So now the Lord said to him, 'Since you have not kept my covenant and have disobeyed my laws, I will surely tear the kingdom away from you and give it to one of your servants ... *I will take the kingdom away from your son [Rehoboam]. And even so, I will let him be king of one tribe [Judah], for the sake of my servant David and for the sake of Jerusalem, my chosen city.*'"[139]

Upon Solomon's death, the people of Israel made their choice to go against the Davidic covenant. Just as predicted, Solomon's servant Jeroboam, along with the 10 northern tribes, rebelled against Rehoboam. They shouted, "'*Down with David and his dynasty!* We have no share in Jesse's son! Let's go home, Israel! Look out for your own house, O David ...' So *only the tribe of Judah* [which by this time included the tribes of Simeon and part of Benjamin] *remained loyal to the family of David.*"[140] Rehoboam then mobilized 180,000 troops to restore the kingdom to himself, but the Lord instructed him, "Do not fight against your relatives, the Israelites. Go back home, for what has happened is my doing."[141] To this day the divided kingdom has never reunited—for that day is still to arrive as the Bible predicts they once again will come together.

In time the Assyrians conquered the rebellious northern kingdom and dispersed it throughout Mesopotamia. Judah would slip further into idolatry and see its beloved Temple and holy city of Jerusalem destroyed by the Babylonians six centuries before the birth of Christ. Yet, in compliance with God's desire, many of those sent into exile returned 70 years later, aided by decrees made by Persian kings who funded the rebuilding of both the city and Temple during the days of Ezra and Nehemiah.

And, for what purpose did they come back? Promises relating to the first coming of the successor to David's eternal throne in Jerusalem required descendants of Judah to be there at the time of His appearance. Their return from captivity wasn't coincidental, but providential! To a tiny village in Galilee God sent his angel to tell Mary, "You will become pregnant and have a son, and you are to name him Jesus ... And *the Lord will give Him the throne of His ancestor David. And he will reign over Israel forever; his kingdom will never end!*"[142] As news of the pregnancy spread to Zechariah, the father of John the Baptist, he prophesied, "Praise the Lord, the God of Israel ... He has sent us a mighty Savior *from the royal line of His servant David, just as he promised through His prophets long ago* ... He has been merciful to our ancestors *by remembering his sacred covenant with them, the covenant he gave to our ancestor, Abraham.*"[143] In this Promised Land, the King of kings received His anointing from a questionable woman while in the home of a leper; had His coronation as He rode into His chosen city on the back of a donkey; and was crowned with a diadem of thorns. Surely Pilate got it right when he had a sign placed on His cross that read, "This is Jesus, the King of the Jews."[144]

The apostle Paul in a sermon to both Jews and Gentiles made it unequivocally clear. "And *it is one of King David's descendants, Jesus, who is God's promised Savior of Israel... Brothers—you sons of Abraham, and also all of you devout Gentiles who fear the God of Israel—this salvation is for us!* The people in Jerusalem and their leaders fulfilled prophecy by condemning Jesus to death ... When they had fulfilled all the prophecies concerning his death, they took him down from the cross and placed him in a tomb. But God raised him from the dead. ... God's promise to our ancestors [concerning the promised Seed] has come true in our own time, in that God raised Jesus

... For God had promised to raise him from the dead, never again to die. This is stated in the Scripture that says, *'I will give you the sacred blessings I promised to David.'* [Isaiah 55:3] ... *Now this is not a reference to David,* for after David had served his generation according to the will of God, he died and was buried, and his body decayed. *No, it was a reference to someone else—someone whom God raised and whose body did not decay* [Psalms 16:10] ... Brothers, listen! In this man Jesus there is forgiveness for your sins. *Everyone who believes in him is freed from all guilt and declared right with God*—something the Jewish law [from Mount Sinai] could never do. Be careful! Don't let the prophet's words apply to you. For they said, 'Look, you mockers, be amazed and die! For I am doing something in your own day, *something you wouldn't believe even if someone told you about it.*'" [Habakkuk 1:5][145]

The world has not seen the last of King David's dynasty, nor yet the reuniting of Israel and Judah under His authority.

CHAPTER 5
A PROPHET'S WARNING (ELIJAH)

When you look at a map of Israel you will notice a point of land in the northwest stretching out into the Mediterranean Sea. Here lies a mountain called Carmel. Today it is home to Israel's third-largest city–Haifa. One of the most visited tourist spots in the city is a statue of Elijah with a drawn sword. It sits on the supposed site where nearly 3,000 years ago Mount Carmel hosted one of the most dramatic spiritual battles recorded in the entire Bible.

The glory days of Israel's united monarchy vanished as it split into two kingdoms.[146] The 10 tribes to the north, afterward known as Israel, would be governed by a series of family dynasties after establishing Samaria as its capital city. Judah, to the south, continued under the rulership of one of David's descendants from their capital at Jerusalem. The two nations would wage war against each other, often forming alliances with other nations for support. Both kingdoms would slip into idol worship, leading to God's judgments, but the Lord remained faithful to each of them. Prophets continually reproved them for their departure from God. In some instances, they even killed God's representatives.

"It must be borne in mind that the Old Testament is a theological history rather than a political one. *The biblical editors were less concerned with the survival of the state than with the survival of the faith.* Occupants of the throne were rated good or bad according to the extent that they cherished or neglected the overriding covenant with God, or that they resisted or yielded to the encroaching forces of paganism. The triumphs or disasters of the nation were rewards or punishments for its behaviour. It is in that broad framework of reference that the Bible tells the fascinating human stories of the Hebrew kings."[147] It is also in that same framework that we gain better insight into the call and purpose of the prophets. The Lord's faithful seers warned the people of things going on in the spiritual world which they were not privy to see. They also brought encouragement at the nations' darkest moments, reminding them that they were all part of the larger chosen family of God—called into being for the special purpose of making His name known to the world. For that reason, the covenant promise given them remained valid.

While the prophets delivered notices of divine punishment, in doing so they always had the whole of Israel's best interest in mind. They knew that God's own reputation was at stake. Again and again we see prophet after prophet—Isaiah, Jeremiah, Nehemiah, and others—declaring the same truth. *Though God would always be faithful in punishing them for their rebellion, He would never utterly cut them off from His mercy.*

To do so would be to break His own covenant and dishonor His name before the world. The prophets understood it could never happen because the Lord had taken an oath to Himself that He would be true to the promises He made to His friend Abraham, and His decision was final the moment He made it. They recounted the words of the psalmist, "O children of Abraham, God's servant, O descendants of Jacob, God's chosen one. He is the Lord our God. His rule is seen throughout the land. *He always stands by his covenant*—the commitment he made to a thousand generations. *This is the covenant he made with Abraham and the oath he swore to Isaac. He confirmed it to Jacob as a decree, to the people of Israel as a never-ending treaty*: I will give you the land of Canaan as your special possession."[148] Nehemiah 9 gives a detailed account of just how disobedient and rebellious Israel had been up to Nehemiah's day, and yet he concludes, "But in your great mercy, *you did not destroy them completely or abandon them forever*. What a gracious and merciful God you are!"[149]

One of the most prominent of the prophets was Elijah. The Lord sent him to prophesy against the northern kingdom of Israel once it reached its pinnacle of idolatry. The record of his ministry appears in 1 Kings 16-19. He emerged on the scene shortly after the reign of the sixth king of the northern kingdom, Omri, the founder of Samaria. Seeking to bring long-term security and economic prosperity to Israel, he forged a marriage between his son Ahab and a Phoenician princess named Jezebel of Sidon. Ahab replaced his father as king and began building altars to Baal and erecting Asherah cultic poles. Such worship sought to secure blessings from Baal, the Canaanite god in charge of rain and dew, vital for Israel's agrarian economy. Asherah was the Sidonian fertility goddess thought to have the power to aid in the conception of the large families needed for human survival and the workforce, and was worshiped through fertility monuments placed throughout the country.

The Bible sets the scene this way: "But Ahab did what was evil in the Lord's sight, even more than any of the kings before him. And as though it were not enough to live like Jeroboam, he married Jezebel, the daughter of King Ethbaal of the Sidonians, and *he began to worship Baal*. First, he built a temple and an altar for Baal in Samaria. Then, he set up an Asherah pole. *He did more to arouse the anger of the Lord, the God of Israel, than any of the other kings of Israel before him.*"[150]

Ahab and Jezebel's union resulted in a powerful political and religious institution that would last for two decades. Their self-serving means of governing led to injustice and cruelty toward their subjects as we see displayed in the story of Naboth's Vineyard.[151] How pitiful it would be to have the Bible conclude one's life as it did Ahab's: "No one else so *completely sold himself to what was evil* in the Lord's sight *as did Ahab, for his wife, Jezebel, influenced him.*"[152]

Jezebel imported 450 prophets of Baal and 400 prophets of Ashtoreth from her homeland to teach the Israelites how to worship both false gods. Placed on the royal payroll and eating from the queen's own table, they taught the people how to, among other things, slash their bodies to invoke the blessings of their gods. Then Jezebel launched a campaign of killing the prophets of God so as to extinguish any knowledge of the nation's Israelite heritage.

God Sends the Prophet

Enter Elijah. After all, he is the central figure in this story as visitors still observe his statute while on tours in modern-day Haifa. Scripture does not reveal much about his background except that he was from a town in Gilead called Tishbe, but the resume he left among Bible characters is quite impressive. Through him, the Lord performed many miracles, including the first recorded resurrection, that of the widow's son at Zarephath; calling down fire from God out of heaven; and mounting a fiery chariot becoming one of only two people ever recorded to enter heaven without experiencing death. Elijah also later accompanied Moses with Christ at His transfiguration.[153]

At the height of Ahab and Jezebel's political power, God told Elijah to pay a visit to the king and tell him, "'As surely as the Lord, *the God of Israel,* lives, the God whom I worship and serve—*there will be no dew or rain during the next few years* unless I give the word.' Then the Lord said to Elijah, 'Go to the east and hide by Kerith Brook at a place east of where it enters the Jordan River. Drink from the brook and eat what the ravens bring you, for I commanded them to bring you food.'"[154] The servant of God dwelt outdoors while relying on birds to airlift him his meals. Not only that, but as the drought worsened, his water supply from the brook dried up, and the Lord told him to go see a widow in the village of Zarephath for food. When Elijah asked her for something to eat, she responded, "'I swear by the Lord your God that I don't have a single piece of bread in the house. And I only have a handful of flour left in the jar and a little cooking oil in the bottom of the jug. I was just gathering a few sticks to cook this last meal, *and then my son and I will die.*' But Elijah said to her, '*Don't be afraid!* Go ahead and cook that last meal, but bake me a little loaf of bread first. Afterward, there will still be enough food for you and your son. For this is what the Lord, the God of Israel, says: There will always be plenty of flour and oil left in your containers until the time when the Lord sends rain and the crops grow again.' So she did as Elijah said, and she and Elijah and her son continued to eat from her supply of flour and oil for many days. For no matter how much they used, there was always enough left in the containers, just as the Lord had promised through Elijah."[155]

What a contrast! While Jezebel's 850 prophets sat wining and dining in luxury at the primitive palace, God sent His prophet from a bad situation to a worse one. Elijah asks a poor Gentile woman preparing her last earthly meal for food for himself! Talk about degrading. The proud would never stoop so low. But to Elijah, it wasn't about human pride, but rather the honor and integrity of God's claim over Israel. It was about Him strengthening Elijah's faith for the big showdown. Before the Lord uses His chosen ones to represent Him in public, He first demonstrates to them in their personal lives His great power and majesty. Elijah's survival experiences during the three years of severe drought made him fearless of what any human enemy threatened to do to him. Not to mention that the Lord used him to raise the woman's son from the dead, proving to him that the God of Israel even holds power over death itself.[156]

Elijah believed in the God who made covenants with Abraham and David. Believers know from studying the past that the Lord consistently keeps His promises about the future. Sometimes those promises may get delayed, other times they appear as if impossible to happen at all, but eventually they do, because He said they would. In fact, speaking of those who have gone before us who trusted in the covenant promises, the Bible says, "All these people were still living by faith when they died. They did not receive the things promised; they only saw them and welcomed them from a distance, admitting that they were foreigners and strangers on earth. People who say such things show that they are looking for a country of their own. If they had been thinking of the country they had left, they would have had opportunity to return. Instead, they were longing for a better country—a heavenly one. Therefore, God is not ashamed to be called their God, for he has prepared a city for them."[157]

Experiencing this type of trust in God perfects our love toward Him. "And as we live in God [trusting in His promises], our love grows more perfect. So, *we will not be afraid on the day of judgment, but we can face him with confidence because we are like Christ here in this world.* Such love *has no fear* because *perfect love expels all fear.*"[158]

The Power of the Covenants

We thus become like Elijah, and others before us, who also trusted in those same covenant promises. We become like Moses who marched back into the country from which he had earlier fled for fear of his life and now demanded that Pharaoh let his people go. And we become like David, a mere youth, who when Israel's entire army of grown men trembled at the sight of the giant warrior, Goliath, asked, "Who is this pagan Philistine anyway, that he is allowed to defy the armies of the living God?"[159] He then told his opponent, "Today the Lord will conquer you, and I will kill you and cut off your head ... and *the whole world will know that there is a God in Israel ... It is His battle, not ours.*"[160]

Or perhaps we could become like Gideon whose one encounter with God transformed him from a yellow-belly into Israel's powerful deliverer from the Midianites. As he attempted to harvest some food in secret, God approached and addressed him as a "mighty hero!"[161] Can we not picture a surprised look on his face as if to say, "Who, me?" "How can I rescue Israel? *My clan is the weakest* in the whole tribe of Manasseh, and *I am the least* in my entire family!" Gideon's lack of faith continued when he questioned, "If the Lord is with us, *why has all this happened to us?* And *where are all the miracles our ancestors told us about?* Didn't they say, 'The Lord brought us up out of Egypt? But now *the Lord has abandoned us* and handed us over to the Midianites.'" After revealing His identity, the Lord said to Gideon, "It is alright. *Do not be afraid.* You will not die." Later, though, after Gideon watched the Lord whittle his troop numbers from 32,000 down to 300, he would courageously tell his freedom fighters even before the battle began, "Get up! *For the Lord has given you victory* over the Midianites!"[162]

Or, do we dare say, we might even become like Jesus when, facing His moment of doubt and pain, He cried out to His Father, saying, "Everything is possible for you. Please take this cup of suffering away from me. Yet *I want your will, not mine.*"[163] Yes, this is how we become like Christ in this world. We become so trusting of the same promises the Bible heroes believed in that nothing can shake our certitude. Things may not happen the way we want them to or expect them to, but that is okay. We still do what we in our spirit feel summoned to do, and trust that the Lord will use it to His glory. Peter told us, "Now, who will want to harm you if you are eager to do good? But *even if you suffer for doing what is right, God will reward you for it.* So *don't be afraid and don't worry.*"[164]

After all, the most anyone can do is get us fired from our job while attempting to take away our livelihood; destroy our most precious relationships with the ones we love dearest; topple our positions of power, influence, and authority, thus tarnishing our reputation among our earthly peers; or, if God allows it, take us down to death. It's all okay, because "even when I walk through the dark valley of death, *I will not be afraid*, for you are close beside me. Your rod [covenant of law] and your staff [covenant of grace] protect and comfort me."[165] It is vital that we reach the place where we "do not fear anything except the Lord Almighty. He alone is the Holy One. If you fear him, you need fear nothing else."[166] Such is indeed the "beginning of wisdom."[167]

Students of the covenants have studied the biblical storyline and see how it keeps repeating itself. Knowing the plot well, they celebrate its outcome—the eventual return of the Messiah! They realize whatever lot they have received in our present life—good, or not so good—is nothing in comparison to the glorious things that will come to them after their resurrection to eternal life! Paul encouraged his Gentile converts, "So, *you should not be like cowering, fearful slaves.* You should behave instead like God's very own children, adopted into his family—calling him 'Father, dear Father.' For his Holy Spirit speaks to us deep in our hearts and *tells us that we are God's children.* And since we are his children, we will share his treasures—*for everything God gives his Son, Christ, is ours, too.* But if we are to share in his glory, we must also share his suffering."[168]

May the Best God Win

Now it was Elijah's time to fearlessly face the forces of darkness gathering around him. In the third year of the drought, and after the king hunted him like Saul had David, as a fugitive accused of trying to subvert the government, God said to Elijah, "Go and present yourself to King Ahab. Tell him I will soon send rain!"[169]

"'So, it's you is it—Israel's troublemaker?' Ahab asked when he saw him. 'I have made no trouble for Israel,' Elijah replied, 'You and your family are the troublemakers, for you have refused to obey the commands of the Lord and have worshiped the images of Baal instead. Now bring all the people of Israel to Mount Carmel, with all 450 prophets of Baal and the 400 prophets of Asherah, who are supported by Jezebel.' So, Ahab summoned all the people and the prophets to Mount Carmel.

Then Elijah stood in front of them and said, 'How long are you going to waver between two opinions? If the Lord is God, follow Him! But if Baal is God, then follow him ...' Then Elijah said ... 'Now bring two bulls. The prophets of Baal may choose whichever one they wish and cut it into pieces and lay it on the wood of their altar, but without setting fire to it. I will prepare the other bull and lay it on the wood on the altar, but not set fire to it. Then call on the name of your god, and I will call on the name of the Lord. The god who answers by setting fire to the wood is the true God ...' Then they [the prophets of Baal] called on the name of Baal all morning shouting, 'O Baal, answer us!' But there was no reply of any kind. Then they danced wildly ... About noontime, Elijah began mocking them. 'You'll have to shout louder,' he scoffed, 'for surely he is a god! Perhaps he is in deep thought, or he is relieving himself. Or maybe he is away on a trip, or he is asleep and needs to be wakened!' So, they shouted louder, and following their normal custom, they cut themselves with knives and swords until the blood gushed out. They raved all afternoon until the time of the evening sacrifice, but still, there was no reply, no voice, no answer. Then Elijah called to the people, 'Come over here!' They all crowded around him ... He took twelve stones, *one to represent each of the twelve tribes of Israel*, and he used the stones to rebuild the Lord's altar. Then he dug a trench around the altar large enough to hold about three gallons. He piled wood on the altar, cut the bull into pieces, and laid the pieces on the wood. Then he said, 'Fill four large jars of water, and pour the water over the offering and the wood.' After they had done this, he said, 'Do the same thing again.' And when they were finished, he said, 'Now do it a third time!' So, they did as he said, and the water ran around the altar and even overflowed the trench. At the customary time for offering the evening sacrifice, Elijah the prophet walked up to the altar and prayed, '*O Lord, God of Abraham, Isaac, and Jacob, prove today that you are God in Israel* and that I am your servant. Prove that I have done all this at your command. O Lord, answer me! *Answer me so these people will know that you, O Lord, are God and that you have brought them back to yourself.*' Immediately the fire of the Lord flashed down from heaven and burned up the young bull, the wood, the stones, and the dust. It even licked up all the water in the ditch! And when the people saw it, they fell on their faces and cried out, 'The Lord is God! The Lord is God!' Then Elijah commanded, 'Seize all the prophets of Baal. Don't let a single one escape!' So, the people seized them all, and Elijah took them down to the Kishon Valley and killed them there."[170]

Then Elijah prayed three times for rain, and his servant saw "a little cloud about the size of a hand rising up out of the sea … And sure enough, the sky was soon black with clouds. A heavy wind brought a terrific rainstorm."[171]

Here again, as with similar testimony and purpose like the prophets before him, Elijah summoned Israel back to its covenantal God—the God of Abraham, Isaac, and Jacob. But one person missed the worship service that day—Jezebel. When Ahab told her that Elijah had executed her prophets of Baal, she took an oath to have him killed. Amazingly, the Bible records the brave prophet's response: "Elijah *was afraid* and fled for his life."[172] Here is the human side of life. We may at times speak fearlessly for truth, but when the spiritual surge within us fades, we succumb to our fear of earthly retribution even though our heavenly reward is sure to follow. The cross always looms before the crown. The type of bravery the prophet had earlier demonstrated is called the *spirit of Elijah*. It is a God-infused exhibition of courage that we can only experience by believing in the covenant story. Ahab was willing to give the hope of Israel away through his connection with Jezebel. Elijah fought for his Hebrew family's inheritance by calling out false worship for what it is—a laughable fraud. A similar scenario will reoccur at the end of time, and *the corresponding spirit of Elijah will return to meet it.*

Elijah had one more lesson to learn. He thought he was the only one with such a spirit, but the Lord informed him, "Yet *I will preserve seven thousand others in Israel who have never bowed to Baal* or kissed him."[173] Yes, God's covenant plan always triumphs through a chosen few, but the few sometimes turn out to be more than we think. Ahab and Jezebel had met their match. The Lord later appointed Jehu as king over Israel to deliver justice to the house of Ahab. Ahab's entire family perished, and none of his descendants ever again ruled in Israel. Jezebel's foretold death occurred when servants pushed her out of the palace window and a pack of dogs literally ate her body.[174] And Elijah? Well, the Lord sent a chariot of fire and transported him to heaven. As for the northern 10 tribes making up the kingdom of Israel, it lasted only a little more than 200 years from the time of their split with the House of David under Jeroboam. Eventually the Assyrians conquered and dispersed them throughout their territories.

CHAPTER 6

DESTRUCTION AND CAPTIVITY (DANIEL)

"Judaism, the religion of the Bible, is the classical paradigm of a God-made religion. It is the assertion—not the philosophical proof—that God exists and that He has spoken and speaks to man, *giving him clues to the road that he must follow.*"[175]

Because Satan knows that Judaism is a reminder to the world of God's existence by calling attention to the history of Abraham's family, it infuriates him. He also knows it is a religious system that God called forth to produce the sacred "Seed" destined to "crush his head."[176] Here is a consistent theme throughout Scripture—God revealing Himself through His dealings with the Hebrew people. That is why He takes such interest in their disciplining. *"From among all the families on the earth, I chose you alone. That is why I must punish you for all your sins."*[177] Such punishment usually came in the form of persecution when God allowed Satan to try his best to replace or eradicate Judaism.

The northern kingdom of Israel had practiced idolatry and ceased to exist as a nation. Judah was guilty of the same sins as demonstrated under their King Jehoram who, "followed the example of the kings of Israel and *was as wicked as King Ahab*, for he had married one of Ahab's daughters ... But the Lord was not willing to destroy Judah, *for He had made a covenant with David and promised that his descendants would continue to rule forever.*"[178]

About 130 years after the demise of the northern kingdom, the mighty Babylonian ruler Nebuchadnezzar overthrew the southern kingdom of Judah. After destroying Jerusalem's walls and the sacred Temple built under Solomon, he took captive some of the princes of Judah, including one young man named Daniel. Daniel's story depicts oppression and deliverance under the severest circumstances, but ultimately it teaches that God is always with His people. Whether it be three faithful boys mercilessly thrown into a fiery furnace (Daniel 3) or Daniel himself being left as lunch for lions (Daniel 6), God was there to protect them. Such accounts teach believers that they have nothing to fear from the threats of world leaders who think they are all-powerful. The latter deceive themselves by thinking they can do what they want regarding God's people. Every politician and/or religious leader who wields any authority should read, and re-read, the book of Daniel until they understand its most major lesson: *"the Most-High rules over the kingdoms of the world and gives them to anyone He chooses."*[179]

That's what the Median king, Darius learned as he personally witnessed God save Daniel from the lions. He afterward sent the following message throughout his emerging world empire: "I decree that everyone throughout my kingdom should tremble with fear before the God of Daniel. For *he is the living God*, and he will endure forever. *His kingdom will never be destroyed, and his rule will never end. He rescues and saves his people.*"[180]

Daniel, a young Jew who had witnessed the destruction of his beloved city of Jerusalem along with its sacred Temple, found himself taken captive to a foreign land to serve an idolatrous king. Why had this happened to him and his people? The prophets of old had foretold that the Messiah was to come to Jerusalem to save His people. Jacob had told his son, Judah, that royal authority would not leave his family until Messiah appeared through his lineage. The Lord Himself even confirmed it by making a covenant with David that his family would rule forever from Jerusalem! How could all this be possible with Jerusalem destroyed? Daniel turned to reading the Hebrew prophets to make sense of it all. They explained why his people had suffered their horrendous fate—mainly their disobedience in worshiping false gods. It also established in Daniel's mind a framework for further revelations concerning the future of the Jews and their city of Jerusalem.

The Lord revealed to him that in spite of his people's rebellion, His promises to them were good all the way to the end of the world. Daniel found the most comfort and hope when he read predictions made by the prophet Jeremiah prior to their captivity. "I, Daniel, was studying the writings of the prophets. I learned from the word of the Lord, as recorded by Jeremiah the prophet, *that Jerusalem must lie desolate for seventy years.*"[181] "The truth is that *you [Judah] will be in Babylon for seventy years*. But then I will come and do for you all the good things I have promised, and *I will bring you home again...to your own land.*"[182]

Visited by an Angel

Thus, Daniel received assurance that the captivity of his people in that foreign land was temporary. Finding comfort in knowing that God's plan for his people was still intact, he began praying and confessing the sins of his nation. He acknowledged that God had pre-warned them and was justified in allowing such a fate to fall on them, because of their disregard for the instruction given to them through Moses concerning idol worship.[183] Furthermore, he also began to plead with God to restore Jerusalem along with its desolated Temple and return the Hebrew people to it, not from a selfish motive, but because the honor of God's name was at stake. "O my God, do not delay, *for your people and your city bear your name.*"[184]

What happened next is absolutely amazing! While Daniel was praying, the angel named Gabriel gave him a most wonderful prophetic vision. It presented a timetable that not only pinpointed *when* the Jews would return to Jerusalem, but also *when* their Messiah should arrive there, and *what* He would accomplish! Today, Bible scholars refer to this as the "Seventy Weeks" time prophecy. As in the case of algebraic equations, we need to break down the prophecy into segments to understand it fully. After learning the value of each segment, then we can plug them back into the overall equation to get a fuller grasp of its meaning. The prophecy appears in its entirety in Daniel 9:24-27, but here we will examine it point by point.

Point 1 – "Seventy weeks are determined for your people and your holy city" (Daniel 9:24).

The seventy weeks mentioned here is the ultimate amount of time that God assigned for Judah to finally be purified from its idolatrous ways. A week has seven days, so seventy weeks equals 490 days (7 x 70 = 490). However, it is crucial to understand that one day in Bible prophecy equates to one literal year, a concept firmly established in other scriptural accounts in which the Lord assigned punishment for Israel's sins. For example, in Numbers 14:34 the Lord presented the consequences for Israel's refusal to enter the Promised Land at the time of the Exodus. He said, "Because the men who explored the land were there for *forty days*, you must wander in the wilderness for *forty years—a year for each day suffering the consequences of your sins.*" In another place God instructed Ezekiel, "You will bear Israel's sins for 390 days—*one day for each year of their sin.* After that, turn over and lie on your right side for 40 days—*one day for each year* of Judah's sin."[185]

So, here the Lord established a period of 490 literal years for Daniel's people (Jews) and His holy city (Jerusalem). We can think of it as a scheduled period of time during which they would be purified through future events of chastisement that would befall them. So, what was to happen during the 490 years?

Point 2 – Daniel 9:24 instructs that six things were to be accomplished during this time period.

They were:

- "to put down rebellion"
- "to bring an end to sin"
- "to atone for guilt"
- "to bring in everlasting righteousness"
- "to confirm the prophetic vision"
- "to anoint the Most Holy Place."

Israel was in a real predicament. If that was what needed to happen for their purification, then they were helpless. Such things are obviously beyond human achievement. In fact, the fulfillment of the prophetic to-do list is still future to our day. For example, sin and rebellion continue to exist in our world, and "everlasting righteousness" is a concept still only hoped for. But the prophecy promises that within the seventy-week period Messiah will completely put down all things rebellious toward God and thus bring an end to sin. Daniel understood this can only occur when He takes His rightful place upon David's throne in His holy city of Jerusalem, and from there usher in a new era of global government guided by everlasting principles of righteousness.

Point 3 – The vision tells us what God intends to achieve through His Messiah during this time frame of 490 years. Now we need to know when the prophetic period of time would begin. The angel provides Daniel the starting point when he declares, "Know and understand this: *From the issuing of the decree to restore and build Jerusalem, until the Messiah, the Prince, there will be seven weeks and sixty-two weeks.*"[186]

Jeremiah proved right concerning his prediction that the Jews would serve their time of retribution for only 70 years. A new ruler arrived on the world stage—the Persian King Cyrus the Great. More than 100 years before his birth, the Lord called Cyrus by name as His chosen instrument to free the Jewish exiles that his government would inherit from the Babylonians. "I will raise up Cyrus to fulfill my righteous purpose, and I will guide all his actions. *He will restore my city and free my captive people.*"[187] The Persians would not only allow the Jewish people to return to their homeland but would provide the financial aid needed to repair Jerusalem and erect a new Temple there.

This all took place during the time of Ezra and Nehemiah. The Persian kings actually proclaimed four decrees relating to the restoration of Jewish society and culture. They include:

- ✔ King Cyrus granting Ezra authority to rebuild the Temple in 539 B.C. (Ezra 1:1-4; 5:13-17).
- ✔ King Darius the Mede giving Ezra authority to rebuild

the Temple in 519 B.C. (Ezra 6:6-12).
- ✓ King Artaxerxes reaffirming Ezra's permission, along with providing protection and supplies, to rebuild the Temple in 457 B.C. (Ezra 7:11-26).
- ✓ King Artaxerxes granting Nehemiah permission, along with protection and supplies, to rebuild the city of Jerusalem and its wall in 444 B.C. (Nehemiah 2:1-8).

So how do we know which decree to use as our starting point? Remember, the angel instructed Daniel it would be the *"command to restore and build Jerusalem."* That is the last decree made by Artaxerxes to Nehemiah in 444 B.C. The previous three proclamations involved the rebuilding of the Temple but said nothing about restoring the city.

Yet, here is where we have to be careful or we will fail the math exam. Gabriel took the original 490 years and divided out of it "seven weeks and sixty-two weeks" (49 days and 434 days; see again Daniel 9:25). Added together that calculates to be 483 days (49 + 434 = 483), or prophetically speaking 483 literal years. Now, Daniel was familiar with the Jewish calendar which had 360 days per year, not our solar calendar containing 365.25 days. Therefore, we must take the 483 years and multiply it by 360, giving us a total of 173,880 days. Because we are attempting to pinpoint a date using our solar calendar, we divide the 173,880 days by 365.25 days leaving 476 solar years (173,880 / 365.25 = 476). If this is confusing, think of it in terms of converting the U.S. system of measurement to the metric system. The amount of time is the same, but we simply shifted it from Hebrew reckoning to determine a date on our solar calendar.

So, hang on now. Gabriel was telling Daniel that from the time Artaxerxes would make the decree to Nehemiah in 444 B.C. the Jewish Messiah would appear on the scene 476 years later. If the reader understands this, then they have just discovered one of the most astounding Messianic prophecies in the entire Bible. The apostle Paul would later write: "*When the time came to completion, God sent His Son, born of a woman, born under the law, to redeem those under the law, so that we might receive adoption as sons.*"[188]

So, let's do the math. Taking 444 B.C. (the issue date of the command) and advancing 476 years into the future places us around the spring of 33 A.D.[189] This was the time when Jesus fulfilled Zechariah's messianic prophecy by riding a donkey into Jerusalem, thereby openly announcing His claim as the rightful heir to David's throne.[190]

69 weeks; 483 Jewish years or 476 solar years

444 B.C.	A.D. 33
Artaxerxes grants Nehemiah permission to "restore and build Jerusalem" Nehemiah 2:1-8	Until Messiah the Prince Zechariah 9:9 John 12:12-16 Galatians 4:4

Point 4 – Next the angel provided Daniel with a chronological list of things to take place once the Messiah appeared at the end of the 69-week period. They were:

- ✓ The Anointed One will be killed, appearing to have accomplished nothing (Daniel 9:26).
- ✓ A ruler will arise whose armies will destroy the city [Jerusalem] and the Temple (Daniel 9:26).
- ✓ War and its miseries would continue from that time to the very end (Daniel 9:26).

We know that after Jesus rode into Jerusalem and laid claim

to Israel's kingship, events of great importance took place. He went to the Temple and turned over the tables of the money changers and vendors of sacrificial animals, thus laying bare their false profession. As time advances, these same messianic prophecies will reveal God's true agenda, thereby exposing the falsity of today's earthly religions. In order to protect their power base, the religious leaders killed the very One they professed to be looking for. Some 37 years later a series of attacks began against Jerusalem that resulted in the complete destruction of the city and its Temple. And, since that time the world has not become more peaceful, but with every passing generation more dangerous and miserable. Not only have the number of wars increased over the past 2,000 years, but also the scope of their devastating effects on human life as evidenced by two world wars in the past century.

The Messiah's Mission

The question as to whether or not Jesus Christ was the promised Seed is of utmost importance. Everything discussed in this book, including all the prophecies and events, past, present, and future, hinge upon the appearance of the Messiah. Today, Christians proclaim Jesus as the Messiah, the Jews say he was an imposter, and Muslims make no claim of his Messiahship, but declare that he was just a prophet and a righteous man.

Once, Jesus spoke to some Jewish religious leaders about a future resurrection after which His followers would never die. They then protested "'Are you greater than our father Abraham, who died? Are you greater than the prophets, who died? *Who do you think you are?'* Jesus answered ... 'Your ancestor Abraham rejoiced as he looked forward to my coming. He saw it *and was glad.*' The people said, 'You aren't even fifty years old. How can you say you have seen Abraham?' Jesus answered, '*The truth is, I existed before Abraham was even born!*'"[191]

Another time Jesus asked His disciples, "'Who do people say I am?' 'Well,' they replied, 'some say John the Baptist, some say Elijah, and others say you are one of the other prophets.' Then Jesus asked, 'Who do you say I am?' Peter replied, 'You are the Messiah ...' Then Jesus began to tell them that he, the Son of Man, would suffer many terrible things *and be rejected* by the leaders, the leading priests, and the teachers of religious law. He would be killed, and three days later he would rise again."[192]

It should come as no surprise that even His own people rejected Him at His first appearance. Just as the angel told Daniel, even to those who first believed in Him it appeared that He had accomplished nothing at the time of His crucifixion. Such was the sentiment His followers from Emmaus expressed when recounting the events leading to His death. They said, "*He was a prophet* who did wonderful miracles. *He was a mighty teacher*, highly regarded by both God and all the people. But our leading priests and other religious leaders arrested him and handed him over to be condemned to death, and they crucified him. *We had thought he was the Messiah who had come to rescue Israel.*"[193]

The Old Testament prophets said this would happen. Writing about his people's unbelief regarding the appearance of their Messiah, the prophet Isaiah stated, "Who has believed our message? ... He was despised *and rejected*—a man of sorrows and acquainted with bitterest grief. We turned our backs on him and looked the other way when he went by. He was despised, and we did not care."[194] As we just studied in Daniel's seventy-week Messianic prophecy, the "Anointed One [Messiah] will be killed, *appearing to have accomplished nothing.*[195] But the Psalmist had already declared, "The stone *rejected* by the builders has now become the cornerstone. *This is the Lord's doing*, and it is marvelous to see."[196]

This but follows a pattern of rejection the chosen of God have endured throughout the ages. Jacob had to flee his home only to return later to fulfill his role in laying the foundation for a clan called Israel. Joseph's brothers sold him into slavery, but though being counted as dead, he later reappeared to save his people from famine. Moses sought to protect his people when he killed the Egyptian, but his fellow Hebrews spurned his intentions, forcing him into 40 years of obscurity in the Midian desert. Afterward, he showed back up in Egypt and led his people out of their terrible bondage. Saul turned against David simply for successfully fighting Israel's enemies, compelling him to live in wilderness conditions all the while fearing for his life. Subsequently, he ascended Israel's throne. Elijah likewise fled to the wilderness after Ahab opposed his attempt to help restore Israel back to God's favor. When the great drought ended, he weighed in on Mount Carmel to finish the mission he had started.

Such events were but forerunners designed to demonstrate what was to be the Messiah's experience. It should come as no surprise that He too would first be rejected and killed, disappear at His ascension, only to return again at a later date to save His people, Israel, from their sins. So, once again we ask, *Why Israel?* Is it any wonder that they, too, would vanish from the history books only to resurface on the world stage at the end of time to fulfill their God-given role? As believers in the Messiah understand this pattern, it reinvigorates their own faith as they experience rejection by employers, family, friends, fellow believers, or sometimes even be tempted to think that God has given up on them. It is all part of a baptismal purging of their earthly consciousness, resulting in a more acute spiritual awareness of their calling.

Israel's long history demonstrates a tendency to reject the One who summoned them into existence. In this whole sad, story it is He who is really the victim of rejection, something best illustrated by what happened at His first coming. Yet, miraculously, the Bible states that at His second coming a remnant of Israel will break the pattern of rejecting their God and thus embrace Him. Then, at last, Israel's eternal relationship with God will be consummated.

After Jesus came in fulfillment of the prophetic predictions, the apostle John wrote, "But although the world was made through him, the world didn't recognize him when he came. Even in his own land and among his own people [the Jews], *he was not accepted*. But to all who believed him and accepted him, he gave the *right to become children of God. They are reborn!* This is not a physical right *resulting from human passion or plan [natural birth]*—this rebirth comes from God."[197]

Speaking to those returning to Emmaus, Jesus said, "'Wasn't it clearly predicted by the prophets that the Messiah would have to suffer all these things before entering his time of glory?' *Then Jesus quoted passages from the writings of Moses and all the prophets, explaining what all the Scriptures said about himself.*"[198] Will not anyone claiming in the future to be Israel's Messiah need to show credentials of prior suffering, and rejection, in order to meet the expectations of the prophets?

Here is the gospel that Paul sought to teach the Gentile believers in Rome: "This Good News was promised long ago by God through His prophets in the Holy Scriptures. It is the Good News about His Son, Jesus, who came as a man, *born into King David's royal family line*. And Jesus Christ our Lord was shown to be the Son of God when *God powerfully raised him from the dead* [after being rejected] by means of the Holy Spirit."[199] To Paul, it was the essence of the Messiah's mission. If He died and was resurrected to life, then all who believe in Him, though they may die, will be resurrected and spiritually speaking "never die," just as He told the religious leaders that day.[200] If He wasn't the Messiah and wasn't resurrected, then His follower's "faith is useless," and they "are the most miserable people in the world."[201] But those who believe know they will disappear in death only to re-appear in a future resurrection.

Modern Day Confusion

Peter assures us, "For *we were not making up clever stories* when we told you about the power of our Lord Jesus Christ and his coming again."[202]

It is a sad commentary on the three great religions of the world who claim Abraham as their father that they cannot agree as to the identity of the "Seed" promised him. What chance, then, do others have of intelligently finding their way into Abraham's spiritual family? All three make the Messiah's identity subjective to their own theologies, or their own earthly political agendas, rather than seriously searching what the Scriptures teach about Him.

Let's apply a little critical thinking here. If Jesus was the Messiah, Islam has it wrong and should give Him proper homage. If Jesus wasn't the Messiah, then Islam still has it wrong, because He apparently lied about who He was, thus making Him a false prophet, a liar, and not a good man as the Quran teaches. They might want to re-think basing any spiritual reliance on the teachings of someone who lied about being the Messiah.

If Jesus wasn't the Messiah, the Jews had it right in saying he was an imposter. But if He was the Messiah, then that chosen nation will need to re-examine itself spiritually and give Him the worship He deserves, something that their prophets predict they will someday end up doing. The Jews by their own admission accept Old Testament forecasts about the Messiah they believe is still to come. Well, again, won't this future Messiah first need to experience the rejection and shame those prophets wrote about before He receives His final acceptance and glory?

And gentile Christians who think they have it all figured out that Jesus was the Messiah will face the future challenge of making sure the one who appears a second time is the same Person who came the first time. That is because there will be a personality who will arise from their own ranks and falsely claim that he is Christ.[203] Conceptually speaking the Messiah is part and parcel of Israel, thus those Christians who have exchanged their role for that of Israel's will more easily adopt a false Christ for the true one.

When you boil it all down, it really is pretty cut and dry. Either Jesus is who He says He is and whom His disciples claimed Him to be—Israel's Messiah—or He isn't. It is not an issue to be determined at the ballot box of human opinion. Rather, it is a divine decision of the sovereign God made from eternity past, "before the world was made."[204]

Now let's be clear on one point. What any person, or group of people, believe about this matter does not in any way alter the authenticity of Jesus' claim to be the Messiah. He is who He is regardless of what we think. He is either the Master Designer of the universe, or He is another false god offering another false wish. Yet an inherent power results when a person believes that He not only was the Messiah when He appeared 2,000 years ago but that He is the resurrected, living Christ who is preparing to return to earth a second time to save His people.

Sometimes people ask, "What's the big deal about whether or not Jesus was the Messiah?" Can't salvation come through some other means? Well, let's ask Abraham. God promised to give him a specific offspring who would be the Savior of the world. Remember, the Lord made His unilateral commitment as demonstrated when He walked alone through the bloody pathway while Abram slept. When the Messiah should show up, He would ratify this same covenant with His own blood, thus becoming its sole grantor. Much like a last will and testament, no one can change or alter the terms of the decision after it has been established through the death of the testator. The book of Hebrews explains how this legal instrument relates to the death of the Messiah: "Now when someone dies and leaves a will, no one gets anything until it is proved that the person who wrote the will is dead. The will goes into effect only after the death of the person who wrote it. While the person is still alive, no one can use the will to get any of the things promised to them ... He [the Messiah] came once for all time, at the end of the age [His first coming], to remove the power of sin forever by his sacrificial death for us [on Calvary's cross] ... He will come again [His second coming] but not to deal with our sins again. This time he will bring salvation to all those who are eagerly waiting for him."[205]

The inheritance He is leaving to us as beneficiaries is eternal life and possession of the entire earth. No wonder the apostle exclaimed, "What can we say about such wonderful things as these? If God is for us, who can ever be against us? Since God did not spare even his own Son but gave him up for us all, won't God, who gave us Christ, also give us everything else?"[206] And what do we have to do to receive His wonderful gift? Merely accept it. Gifts are to be received, not earned. God won't allow humanity to take any credit for its own redemption. Not because He is arbitrary, but because it is impossible. As hard as we try, humans can't even prevent our own physical deaths. How in the world, then, do we expect to forestall our spiritual deaths? Contrary to human logic, we must do as Abraham did and look beyond what is possible in our earthly realm and accept the spiritual solution God is offering. That is why Jesus said, "I am the resurrection and the life. Those who believe in me even though they die like everyone else, will live again. They are given eternal life for believing in me and will never perish [by dying a spiritual and eternal death]."[207]

Study all other world religions and you will find none guaranteeing such a promise. The true religion of Abraham is the only one that teaches that we are saved entirely by God's doing, and not any of our own. Many belief systems promise some kind of existence after death, yet they are at best sketchy regarding exactly how it is to happen or what it will be like. The thing they all have in common is some degree of creature merit resulting in their followers doing something to aid in effecting their own redemption. To accept Jesus Christ as the Messiah means to give up on ourselves so that we can inherit the hope of eternal life through a future resurrection from the dead. And it is all in accordance with the terms of God's eternal contract, meticulously explained in His book of covenants–the Bible.[208] Such a promise brings us hope, and makes all of this life's rejections and disappointments bearable as we wait for His reappearing.

Daniel's prophecies were not meant to be fulfilled in his day, but a time far into the future. The angel told him, "Now I am here to explain what will happen to your people [the Jews] in the future, for this vision concerns a time yet to come."[209]

Again, at the close of his account, Daniel repeats what the angel had told him: "But he said, 'Go now, Daniel, for what I have said is for the time of the end. *Many will be purified, cleansed, and refined by these trials.* But the wicked will continue in their wickedness, and none of them will understand. Only those who are wise will know what it means.'"[210] Then the angel assured Daniel of his own personal, future resurrection, "As for you [Daniel], *go your way until the end.* You will rest, and *then at the end of the days* [at the Second Coming], you will rise again to receive the inheritance set aside for you."[211]

There is still one week, or seven factual years, left in Daniel's seventy-week prophecy. We will explore it in more detail later.

CHAPTER 7
GOD'S SECRET REVEALED (THE CALLING OF GENTILES)

It has always been a popular misconception that we cannot understand the Bible. But nothing could be further from the truth. Anyone who gets an appropriate translation of the Bible and reads it completely through will know what it is saying. The problem arises when we only read bits and pieces, or when we try to apply our own interpretation so as to make it say something that we have already predetermined. As we have noted thus far, the Bible is primarily a book about the Hebrew people and their covenantal relationship with the God who summoned them into being as a nation—the God of Abraham, Isaac, and Jacob.

This same God tells us, "I am the Lord ... and there is no other. I publicly proclaim bold promises. *I do not whisper obscurities in some dark corner so no one can understand what I* mean. *And I did not tell the people of Israel to ask me for something I did not plan to give ... Gather together and come, you fugitives* [Gentiles] *from surrounding nations. What fools they are who carry around their wooden idols and pray to gods that cannot save! Consult together, argue your case, and state your proofs that idol worship pays. Who made these things known long ago? What idol ever told you they would happen? Was it not I, the Lord? For there is no other God but me—a just God and a Savior—no, not one! Let all the world look to me for salvation.... I have sworn by my own name, and I will never go back on my word: Every knee will bow to me, and every tongue will confess allegiance to my name.*"[212]

There is simply no credibility to the claim that God's Word—the Bible—is beyond human comprehension. Nor is there any excusable argument that we cannot know what God expects of us. In addition to the testimony of His Word, we have the witness of His divine creation, the natural world that instinctively speaks to us concerning His existence. According to Paul, because of this even Gentiles "have no excuse whatsoever for not knowing God."[213]

As one follows the biblical narrative they will see that after the Messiah's first visit to His chosen people Israel, Old Testament prophecies would then begin to be fulfilled concerning the spreading of God's covenant message among the Gentile world. Israel was getting ready to go dormant as the baton temporarily passed to those who had previously been alienated from the Lord's plan. Another convincing argument of the Bible's authenticity is not just that this actually happened, but that it was accurately predicted centuries before it transpired.

God plainly said to Israel, "From among all the families of the earth, I chose you alone. That is why I must punish you for all your sins .... But always, *first of all, I will warn you through my servants the prophets.*"[214] He cautioned through the prophet

Moses, "If you disobey me, *you will quickly disappear from the land* you are crossing the Jordan to occupy. You will live there only a short time; then you will be utterly destroyed. *For the Lord will scatter you among the nations*, where only a few of you will survive."[215] Thus far in our study, we have documented the history of this happening. But the Lord made another amazing prediction. He said of the Hebrews, "They have roused my jealousy by worshiping non-gods; they have provoked my fury with useless idols. *Now I will rouse their jealousy by blessing other nations; I will provoke their fury by blessing the foolish Gentiles.*"[216]

Paul's Mission and Message

This prophecy lies behind the apostle Paul's calling, mission, and message. In fact, in his letter to the Gentile believers in Rome Paul quoted this very verse from Deuteronomy.[217] God gave him the daunting task of explaining to Gentiles how their eternal salvation derived from a homeless Jew whom the leadership of His own people had rejected. Yet Paul was not deterred, because He understood the historical certainty of the consummated promises God had made to his people—the Jews—particularly those relating to the Messiah. He started by giving the Gentiles a history lesson of the Hebrew people. "They are *the people of Israel, chosen to be God's special children.* God *revealed his glory to them.* He *made covenants with them and gave his law to them. They have the privilege of worshiping him and receiving his wonderful promises.*"[218]

To the church at Ephesus, Paul differentiated between Israel's calling and that of his Gentile audience. He reminded them, "Don't forget that you Gentiles used to be *outsiders by birth* .... In those days you were living apart from Christ. *You were excluded from God's people, Israel, and you did not know the promises God had made to them.* You lived in this world without God and without hope. But now you belong to Jesus Christ. Though you once were far away from God, now you have been brought near to him because of the blood [covenant] of Christ."[219]

The apostle explained that the Lord was including them into His spiritual family *without abandoning the covenant promises He made to Israel.* "Remember that Christ *came as a servant to the Jews to show that God is true to the promises he made to their ancestors.* And He came *so the Gentiles might also give glory to God* for his mercies to them. ... Rejoice, *O you Gentiles, along with His people, the Jews.*"[220]

Ethnic Israel is the lure God uses to catch and net Gentiles. Jesus told His first followers, who were all Jews, "Come, be my disciples, and I will show you how to fish for people."[221] In Paul's day, the Jews in Judea had a type of national pride that caused them to despise the Gentiles. So, along with telling Gentiles a door of adoption into God's spiritual family had opened for those who believed, he also had to inform the Jews that though God continued to work through their corporate disobedience, it did not guarantee them individual salvation. They were to receive it like anyone else, the same way their father Abraham did—through faith!

To the natural eye, God may appear unfair in singling out a certain ethnic group to call His chosen people. However, spiritual vision reveals God's fairness. "Nowhere is it suggested that Israel's advantageous position *guaranteed* salvation to all members of the nation, neither did it *exclude* that Ishmael and those who did not descend from Isaac and Jacob, could experience salvation. On the contrary, according to the terms of the covenant, the blessing of salvation was to become *available to all families of the earth through the elect nation of Israel* (Genesis 12:3; Isaiah 49:5,6; Galatians 3:8-14)."[222]

After asking "Has God failed to fulfill his promise to the Jews?" Paul explained the puzzling concept: "No, for *not everyone born into a Jewish family is truly a Jew! Just the fact that they are* descendants of Abraham doesn't make them truly Abraham's children. For the Scriptures say, *'Isaac is the son through whom your descendants will be counted,'* though *Abraham had other children,* too. This means that Abraham's physical descendants are *not necessarily* children of God. *It is the children of the promise who are considered to be Abraham's children.*"[223] And, just who are the children of the promise? "The *only way* to receive God's promise *is to believe in Jesus Christ*. ... There is no longer Jew or Gentile, slave or free, male and female. ... you are one in Christ Jesus. And now that you belong to Christ, you are the *true children of Abraham*. You are His heirs, and *now all the promises God gave to him belong to you.*"[224] Many have used this passage of Scripture as an argument to prove that no longer any distinction exists between Jew and Gentile, thereby suggesting God's promises to the Jewish nation are no longer pertinent. However, upon closer examination, and in the same context, there are still free people and those in bondage, and there obviously remains a physical distinction between males and females. The verse is not talking about blurring the lines between identifiable traits of race, status, or gender, but simply that God accepts anyone from any background who comes to Him by faith.

Let's try saying it this way. While a Jew's biological DNA may have come from Isaac, that does not mean all of them will be a part of Isaac's spiritual family if they reject the Messiah. In like manner, though a Gentile's biological DNA didn't result from Isaac, some of them will be counted as part of Isaac's spiritual family, because of their faith in Christ.

Paul knew that giving this empowerment of gospel privilege to the Gentiles would be a slippery slope. Just as the Jews became proud and jealous about their calling from God, would Gentiles react any different to their invitation to join God's family? Human nature is human nature. That is why Paul gave stern warnings to the Gentile believers in Rome. He knew that in their infantile faith they would have a tendency to think that since the Lord had now chosen them, it must mean He had abandoned His devotion to the Jews. He told them, "No, God has not rejected his own people [Jews], whom he chose from the very beginning. ... *God has put them into a deep sleep.*"[225] He explained that "the Jews' rejection meant that God offered salvation to the rest of the [Gentile] world," and "this will last only until the complete number of Gentiles come to Christ." After this, there will be an awakening of Israel, and God says then, "I will keep my covenant with them [by sending the Messiah] and take away their sins."[226] Then the apostle spoke with blunt language, "Many of the Jews are now enemies of the Good News. ... Yet the Jews are *still his chosen people because of his promises to Abraham, Isaac, and Jacob. For God's gifts and his call can never be withdrawn.*"[227]

Did you catch the full impact of what Paul just said? The very people whom God designated as His "chosen," the natural offspring of Abraham, He declares to be the enemies of the gospel of Christ! But he states more. Though enemies they are "still His chosen people," because of the covenant promises He made with their ancestors. Not only that, but God can never withdraw His initial choice of the Hebrew people. Honestly, all prejudices aside, if we don't grasp this fact about God, then we can't understand who He really is, or what He plans to do. All the prophets, both major and minor, indicate that God will restore His people Israel to Himself. If this is untrue, then it is up to the Gentiles to strategize their own way to the eternal kingdom.

God's Secret Plan

In his letter to the Ephesians, the apostle makes a startling revelation. "I was chosen for this special joy of *telling the Gentiles* about the endless treasures available to them in Christ. I was chosen to *explain to everyone this plan that God*, the Creator of all things, *had kept secret from the beginning.*"[228] Just what is this eternal mystery Paul was so eager to reveal? "And this is the secret plan: The *Gentiles have an equal share with the Jews in all the riches inherited by God's children ... God's purpose was to show his wisdom in all its rich variety to all the rulers and authorities in the heavenly realms.* They will see this *when Jews and Gentiles are joined together* in His church. *This was his plan from all eternity*, and it has now been carried out through Jesus Christ our Lord."[229]

Such is in keeping with what the prophet Isaiah had centuries before revealed was God's stated mission for the Messiah. Notice that it is twofold: "You will do more than *restore the people of Israel* to me. I will make you *a light to the Gentiles, and you will bring my salvation to the ends of the earth.*"[230] It was the covenant law given at Mount Sinai that had excluded Gentiles from being a part of Israel. So, what did God do? When time for calling the rest of the human family came, did He abandon His namesake Israel to start a new separate family from among the Gentiles—a church? No! Paul said He "made peace between us Jews and you Gentiles by *making us all one people. He has broken down the wall of hostility that used to separate us.* By his death, he *ended the whole system of Jewish law that excluded the Gentiles.* His purpose was to *make peace between Jews and Gentiles* by creating in himself *one new person from the two groups.*"[231]

Thus, God provided a way for the Gentiles to become: "*adopted* into His own family [Israel];" "*fellow citizens* along with all God's holy people [Israel];" "*heirs* according to the promise [that God made with Israel]."²³² Here we see that the Lord did not disenfranchise the Jews to start a new family of Gentile believers. No, just the reverse. He adopted the Gentiles so they could become members of the family He had already established with the Hebrews. Adoption is a unique phenomenon resulting in a deep spiritual experience to all parties involved. Ask any loving parent who has adopted children and they will emphatically tell you those children are no less special than biological offspring. So, it is with the Lord. He said, "And *my blessings are for Gentiles, too,* when they commit themselves to the Lord. *Do not let them think that I consider them second-class citizens.*"²³³

Because Christ was crucified, *"now all of us, both Jews and Gentiles,* may come to the Father through the same Holy Spirit *because of what Christ has done for us.*"²³⁴ Paul then gives his epic appeal for unity to both groups. "Be humble and gentle. Be patient with each other, *making allowance for each other's faults* because of your love. Always keep yourselves united in the Holy Spirit, and bind yourselves together in peace. *We are all one body*, we have the same Spirit, *and we have all been called to the same glorious future.*"²³⁵ He said that if we follow this plan, "we will no longer be like children, *forever changing our minds about what we believe because someone has told us something different or because someone has cleverly lied to us* and made the lie sound like the truth."²³⁶ No longer will we always be looking for the right church with the right message. No longer will we be fooled by preachers and various religious sects whose real intent is to get rich by attracting followers. And no longer will we "take pride in following a particular leader [or religious affiliation]."²³⁷ Those who find the New Covenant Christ find the *hidden treasure of Scripture* and are eager to give everything for it.²³⁸ When Israel awakes at the end of time, they "will not need to teach their neighbors, nor will they need to teach their family, saying 'You should know the Lord.' For everyone, from the least to the greatest, will already know me."[239] That's because the gospel will have by then already gone to the Gentile world, and their full number will have been made up as mentioned in Romans 11:25.

Herein is revealed Christ's true spiritual body of believers—"*the assembly of God's firstborn children, whose names are written in heaven,*" as contrasted to names entered on earthly church roles.[240] The concept of a spiritual body of believers stands in stark contrast to the world's pseudo-religions. It aids in identifying the threefold division of humanity—"Jews, or Gentiles, or *the Church of God.*"[241] Just as Paul taught that there is a physical body, which at the resurrection gives way to a spiritual one, there are also visible, physical religions, which give way to the Lord's invisible, spiritual body of believers. Such are the Lord's true chosen ones – His covenantal children! They have passed through that transformation from the physical realm into a spiritual understanding that, "Since Christ lives within you, even though your body will die because of sin, *your spirit is alive* because you have been made right with God."[242] Each will have personally met the God of Abraham, Isaac, and Jacob, and by believing in the covenant that He made with them, they are forever changed. Now as children of that covenant, they can say, "So we are always confident, even though we know that as long as we live in these bodies we are not at home with the Lord. This is why *we live by believing and not by seeing.*"[243]

Paul also knew that some on both sides would resist God's eternal plan for unity among His people. "I know very well how foolish the message of the cross sounds to those who are on the road to destruction. But we who are being saved recognize this message as the very power of God. As the Scriptures say, 'I will destroy human wisdom and discard their most brilliant ideas,' [Isaiah 29:14]. So where does this leave the philosophers, the scholars, and the world's brilliant debaters? God has made them all look foolish and has shown their wisdom to be useless nonsense. Since God in his wisdom saw to it that *the world would never find him through human wisdom*, he has used our foolish preaching to save all who believe. *God's way seems foolish to the Jews* because they want a sign from heaven to prove it is true [that Jesus was the Messiah]. *And it is foolish to the Greeks* because they believe only what agrees with their own wisdom [that lacks an understanding of how Jesus fulfilled Hebrew prophecies concerning the Messiah]. So when we preach that Christ was crucified, *the Jews are offended,* and *the Gentiles say it's all nonsense.* But to those who are called by God to salvation, *both Jews and Gentiles,* Christ is the mighty power of God and the wonderful wisdom of God. *This foolish plan of God is far wiser than the wisest of human plans,* and God's weakness is far stronger than the greatest of human strength."[244]

We see this natural animus played out when Jesus interacted with His fellow Jews in His home village of Nazareth. After reading from the scroll of Isaiah, *He emphasized Gentile inclusion* by stating that often the prophets' own people did not accept them. He said, "Certainly there were many widows in Israel who needed help in Elijah's time when there was no rain for three and a half years and hunger stalked the land. Yet Elijah was not sent to any of them. He was sent instead to a *widow of Zarephath—a foreigner [Gentile]* in the land of Sidon. Or think of the prophet Elisha, who healed *Naaman, a Syrian [Gentile],* rather than the many lepers in Israel who needed help."[245] By showing from their own Hebrew history that God never intended to overlook the Gentile world, He unmasked their prejudiced view of thinking they were the only ones worthy of divine care. They became so upset by their jealousy they tried to kill Jesus right then and there.[246]

It is no coincidence the Gospel of Luke begins with the devout Simeon, who when He saw the Christ Child presented in the Temple, prophesied concerning Him, "I have seen the Savior you *have given to all people*. He *is a light to reveal God to the nations*, and He *is the glory of your people Israel.*"[247] Luke's story then ends with the words of the Messiah Himself as He commissions His Jewish followers: "Yes, it was written long ago that the Messiah must suffer and die and rise again from the dead on the third day. With My authority, take this message of repentance *to all the [Gentile] nations*, beginning in Jerusalem: There is forgiveness of sins *for all* who turn to me."[248]

God's New Israel

Concerning God's exercise of divine sovereignty, Ronald Diprose points out, "God's decision to set His affection on Israel *was in no way determined by their performance* or national greatness *but rather by His free will and sovereign purposes* [Deuteronomy 7:7, 8; 9:4-5] ... the election of Jacob and his descendants gave expression to *God's sovereign will* [Romans 9:11]. The fact that it was already determined before the twins were born or had done anything good or bad demonstrates that the election of Jacob rather than Esau did not depend *in any way* on the merits or demerits of the persons concerned. The corollary of this truth, often repeated by the Hebrew prophets, is that *the full outworking of God's purpose through Israel will not depend on their faithfulness* [Isaiah 54:10-17; 65:1-8; Jeremiah 5:10, 11,18; 31:35-37; Ezekiel 16:59-63; Hosea 1-14; Romans 11:28, 29]."[249] God is working out His covenant promise through *ethnic Israel*, the biological offspring of Isaac and Jacob. He is also calling the world's attention to Himself through a related Gentile-driven religion called Christianity.

Like Israel, it also has a long shameful history of corruption, yet it, too, has been God's chosen messenger. Out of the Christian world, and all other pagan walks of life, God will one day call His faithful to join the pure extract of faith that He still finds in Israel. He will then unite *spiritual Israel*, a collection of *believing Jews and Gentiles*, through whom ultimately the promises given to Abraham, Isaac, and Jacob will be realized.

Paul describes the experience of this group, who trusts solely in the merits of Christ, by declaring, "Because of that cross, my interest in this world died long ago, and the world's interest in me is also long dead. ... What counts is whether we really have been changed into new and different people. May God's mercy be upon all those who live by this principle. *They are the new people [Israel] of God.*"[250] While Christ's transforming grace is rebirthing these *new creatures* into the *new Israel* on earth, God is busy preparing a *New Jerusalem* to be their home when someday He recreates for them a *new earth!*[251]

A Replacement for Israel?

By A.D. 135 Jerusalem had been completely destroyed, and the southern kingdom of Judah dispersed throughout the nations of the earth. Rome became the center of Christianity. Early church fathers such as Augustine, in his book *City of God*, taught that the Christian Church centered at Rome was God's present-day kingdom on earth, and that it would eventually conquer the world. "The development of the strong anti-Semitic spirit and the teaching that the organized church is the future Messianic Kingdom foretold by God through the Old Testament prophets were part of a *concept of replacement*. According to that concept, since Israel, as a nation, rejected Jesus Christ as its Messiah during His first coming, *God rejected that nation forever as His people*. This theology claims that *God has no future program for Israel* and that He *replaced Israel with the church as His people*. Thus, the church became the 'Israel of God' and inherits the blessings promised to national Israel."[252]

With all due respect to Augustine, however, nowhere does the New Testament teach that because the Jewish leadership crucified Christ, God forever rejected the Jewish people. In fact, it teaches the opposite. The rejection of Messiah by His own people came as no surprise to Him, but was actually forecasted through the Old Testament prophets. "For Herod Antipas, Pontius Pilate the governor, the Gentiles, and the people of Israel were all united against Jesus. ... In fact, *everything they did occurred according to your [God's] eternal will and plan.*"[253] In spite of this, the early apostles still continued to look forward with faith to God's future fulfillment of the covenants He had made with their past Hebrew fathers. Even after the crucifixion, Peter stated, "'People of Israel ... what you did to Jesus was done in ignorance' ... and '*you are included in the covenant God promised to your ancestors.*' For God said to Abraham, 'Through your descendants all the families on earth will be blessed.'"[254] Even after the Jewish leadership said "no" to Yeshua ben Joseph, the apostle James, quoting Old Testament prophets, still proclaimed God as saying, "I *will [in the future] restore the fallen kingdom of David ... so that the rest of humanity might find the Lord, including the Gentiles.*"[255] Paul went on record as saying, "Now I am on trial because I am *looking forward to the [future] fulfillment of God's promise made to our ancestors. In fact, that is why the twelve tribes of Israel* worship God night and day, and they *share the same hope* I have."[256] And finally Jesus Himself, after His crucifixion and resurrection, when asked by His disciples, "Lord, *are you going to free Israel now and restore our kingdom?*" did not discount His Jewish brethren but replied in the affirmative, "*The Father sets those [future] dates ... and they are not for you to know.*"[257]

How appropriate to our discussion is the message that God gave to Jeremiah: "*Have you heard what people are saying? — 'The Lord chose Judah and Israel and then abandoned them.' They are sneering and saying that Israel is not worthy to be counted as a nation. But this is the Lord's reply: 'I would no more reject my people than I would change my laws of night and day, of earth and sky. I will never abandon the descendants of Jacob or David, my servant, or change the plan that David's descendants will rule the descendants of Abraham, Isaac, and Jacob. Instead, I will restore them to their land and have mercy on them.'*"[258]

The Lord clarified the Gentile position when He spoke to Paul near the Damascus gate. The apostle himself later testified regarding the commission that God gave him. "Yes, I am going to send you to the Gentiles, to open their eyes so they may turn from darkness to light, and from the power of Satan to God. Then they will receive forgiveness for their sins and *be given a place among God's people*, who are set apart by faith in me."[259] Notice that he said Gentiles would receive "*a place among*" God's people and were not chosen "*in place of*" them. Israel is the people whom God "set apart by faith."[260] In fact, they are called, or identified, by God's own name. Amos told us, "Now the Lord has sworn this oath *by his own name, The Pride of Israel.*"[261]

A favorite Bible promise among Christians is that God will never leave or forsake His people. Yet, the Lord originally made that promise to Israel through Moses. "When those bitter days have come upon you *far in the future, you will finally return to the Lord your God and listen to what he tells you. For the Lord your God is merciful—he will not abandon you or destroy you or forget the solemn covenant he made with your ancestors.*"[262] Their prophets repeated this identical promise to Israel numerous times throughout their history. The only time it appears in the New Testament is in the book of Hebrews—*a letter written to those of Jewish descent who had accepted Christ as the Messiah.*[263] So, with this in mind, here is the vital question Gentiles who desire to see themselves as a replacement for Israel must ask: If God does not remain faithful in His promise to never forsake Israel, then how can Gentiles trust Him not to abandon them? Surely the answer is obvious? God is not a covenant breaker, so it is impossible for Him to renege on His original commitment to Israel. The Scriptures declare, "God is not a man, that he should lie. *He is not a human, that he should change his mind.*"[264]

After all, didn't Jesus ask God to forgive the Jewish leaders at the very moment they were crucifying Him?[265] If so, then why are some so insistent that God somehow exercised an escape clause to the contract He made with them as a nation? Is it really wise for Gentiles to use such arguments thus following the example of Balaam by trying to "curse" what the Lord has "blessed," just so that they can support their own earthly institutions of religion? "How terrible it will be for them … Like Balaam, they will do anything for money."[266] The truth is that God's plan always *included Gentiles in the promises* He made to Israel. *But never did He intend them as a replacement for Israel.* Such is a gross perversion of God's eternal design, a usurpation that carries eternal consequences, a covetous stealing of a birthright rather than the gracious acceptance of a free gift.

The Lord has stated His warnings for Gentile believers just as He forewarned Israel of their religious pride. "But some of these branches from Abraham's tree, some of the Jews, have been broken off. And you Gentiles, who were branches from a wild olive tree, were grafted in. So now you also receive the blessing God promised to Abraham and his children, sharing in God's rich nourishment of His special olive tree. *But you must be careful not to brag about being grafted in to replace the branches that were broken off. Remember, you are a branch, not the root.* 'Well,' you may say, 'those branches were broken off to make room for me.' Yes, but remember—those branches, the Jews, were broken off because they didn't believe God, and you are there because you do believe. *Don't think highly of yourself, but fear what could happen. For if God did not spare the branches he put there in the first place, he won't spare you either* ... But if you stop trusting [in God's covenant with Israel], you also will be cut off. And *if the Jews turn from their unbelief [regarding that same covenant], God will graft them back into the tree again.* He has the power to do it. For if God was willing to take you who were, by nature, branches from a wild olive tree and graft you into his own good tree—a very unusual thing to do—he will be far more eager to graft the Jews back into the tree where they belong."[267]

SECTION II
THE ANTI-TYPES

CHAPTER 8

RETURN OF JACOB (MODERN ISRAEL)

I n our quest to understand Israel's purpose, it is vital that we have a clear grasp of the reason for the nation's calling. Perhaps the following analogy will be helpful. A college professor, assigned the challenge of teaching an unusually large class, develops a strategy to give each student the individual attention required to adequately learn the curriculum. His novel plan is similar to the old children's game *Follow the Leader*. He will select from the vast group a specific student. The person is not chosen based upon any prior success, or by any other distinguishable qualities. In fact, the only reason why the student would become noticed is that the professor *chose* and placed the young person on display. Then he instructs the remaining classmates to *pay careful attention* throughout the semester to the interaction between him and the student. The unique relationship between them *is but a representation* of how the professor would deal with every other student in the class if given the opportunity. If the class is doing poorly and needs correction, he will single out the model student. And if the overall class is to be commended, again the special student will receive accolades in front of everyone.

It is not surprising that the model student would become the object of both ridicule and envy. While many may have hoped that the professor had picked them for the position, others may also have been glad that it had been someone else. Students thus behaved according to their understanding of why the professor had appointed the model student in the first place. While some empathized, many blamed the individual for their own failures, even treating the person shamefully. Yet they failed to understand one very crucial point. Through the student the professor was communicating to them as individuals. The student was but a representative to the professor on their behalf. If he or she were failing, it was but a reflection on the performance of the overall class, a forewarning that they were going to fail as well! Any negative treatment of the student representative was nothing more than the whipping of a scapegoat in an attempt to escape one's own responsibilities. What's more, how they regarded the student would be how the professor at the end of the semester would respond to their own personal accountability.

In a similar way, the model student is Israel. However, our focus should not be on the Hebrew people themselves, however good or bad we may perceive them to be, but instead on God's purpose in choosing them. Their story is our story whether we know it or not. Yet the world is so blinded to this biblical principle that it has always sought to erase the Lord's chosen. Such a spirit is destined to bring the world to its end.

The prophet Daniel described the most fearful time of earth's history: "Then there will be a time of anguish *greater than any since nations first came into existence.*"[268] Speaking of the same time and event, Jeremiah got a bit more specific. *"In all history there has never been such a time of terror. It will be a time of trouble for my people Israel.* Yet in the end they will be saved ... Foreigners [Gentiles] will no longer be their masters. For my people will serve the Lord their God and *David their king, whom I will raise up for them.* So, do not be afraid, Jacob, my servant; do not be dismayed, Israel, says the Lord. *For I will bring you home again from distant lands, and your children will return from their exile. Israel will return and will have peace and quiet in their own land,* and no one will make them afraid ... I will completely destroy the nations where I have scattered you, but I will not destroy you. *But I must discipline you; I cannot let you go unpunished."*[269]

In His Olivet Discourse Jesus gave an even more chilling version of this horrific prediction. *"For that will be a time of greater horror than anything the world has ever seen or will ever see again.* In fact, unless that time of calamity is shortened, *the entire human race will be destroyed.* But it will be shortened *for the sake of God's chosen ones."*[270] Many think it will be a time of trouble for the world. Obviously, if the entire human race faces extinction it will certainly concern everyone on the planet. However, on closer examination, Jeremiah specifically stated: *"It will be a time of trouble for my people Israel."*[271] It will be the unbelieving nations of the world (the student majority) that will bring this trouble upon Israel (the model student) and throw the planet (the class) into irretrievable chaos.

For such a scriptural forecast to prove true, it first *logistically requires the Jewish people to be back in the land of Palestine.* Again, looking into the future, Moses foretold that because of

Israel's idolatry, "In great anger and fury the Lord *uprooted His people from their land and exiled them* to another land."[272] But he also assured them, "*He will have mercy on you and gather you back from all the nations where he has scattered you. Though you are at the ends of the earth, the Lord your God will go and find you and bring you back again. He will return you to the land that belonged to your ancestors, and you will possess that land again.*"[273]

As we have already established, by A.D. 135 foreign powers had dispersed the vast number of Jews throughout the world. But according to Moses, the Hebrew people would be scattered only to be regathered! It was a consistent theme for all the prophets who would come after him. Following are just a few examples:

"Though I have *scattered them like seeds among the nations*, still they will remember me in distant lands. With *their children, they will survive and come home again to Israel.*"[274]

"I will gather you and your children from east and west and from north and south. *I will bring my sons and daughters back to Israel from the distant corners of the earth.*"[275]

"Although I have scattered you in the countries of the world ... *I, the Sovereign Lord, will gather you back from the nations where you were scattered, and I will give you the land of Israel once again.*"[276]

Those prophets also gave us the Red Sea analogy. Ever since the rescue of the Lord's chosen people from Egypt, that event has served as one of the most striking stories in world history. In 1956 Hollywood made a movie about it, *The Ten Commandments*, even though it happened thousands of years ago. However, the prophet Jeremiah stated the Lord will do something comparatively miraculous for Israel in our more modern times. "'But the time is coming,' says the Lord, 'when people who are taking an oath will no longer say, as surely as the Lord lives, *who rescued the people of Israel from the land of Egypt*. Instead, they will say, as surely as the Lord lives, *who brought the people of Israel back to their own land from the land of the north and from all the countries to which he had exiled them. For I will bring them back to this land that I gave their ancestors.*'"[277]

Ezekiel's Visions of Sticks and Bones

The prophet Ezekiel received two astonishing visions in regard to the end time regathering of Jacob's offspring. The first is known as the "Dry Bones" prophecy. God showed Ezekiel a valley filled with bones scattered across the land. The Lord then asked, "Son of man, can these bones become living people again?"[278] The Lord then caused the bones to assemble themselves and breathed life into them. "They all came to life and stood up on their feet—a great army of them. Then he said to me, 'Son of man, *these bones represent the people of Israel.* They are saying, 'We have become old, dry bones—all hope is gone.' Now give them this message from the Sovereign Lord: O my people, *I will open your graves of exile and cause you to rise again. Then I will bring you back to the land of Israel. When this happens, O my people, you will know that I am the Lord* ... You will see that I have done everything just as I promised.'"[279] Here is the anti-typical realization of Jacob's journey home, and also a foretelling of the future resurrection of all God's faithful followers.

Family feuds are commonplace among humanity. They usually arise as a power struggle between certain members, forcing the rest of the clan to choose sides. It can result from a myriad of issues such as control of family political, legal, or financial matters. Resulting divisions often run deep and can last for generations. Sometimes such severed relations get healed, sometimes not. It has been no different within the family of Jacob. The division of the nation came when the northern tribes rebelled against the covenant God made with the House of David. They afterward became identified as "Israel" while the tribes remaining loyal to David were known as "Judah." In time other nations removed both from their homeland and scattered them into various countries throughout the earth. But the Old Testament prophets foretold a future time when descendants of both houses of this broken family would return to the land of Palestine and be reunited.

Which brings us to the second and more precise of Ezekiel's visions. It describes the reunification of Jacob's family this way: "Again a message came to me from the Lord. 'Son of man, take a stick and carve on it these words: *This stick represents Judah and its allied tribes.* Then take another stick and carve these words on it: *This stick represents the northern tribes of Israel.* Now hold them together in your hand as one stick. When your people ask you what your actions mean, say to them, this is what the Sovereign Lord says: *I will take the northern tribes and join them to Judah. I will make them one stick in my hand.* Then hold out the sticks you have inscribed, so the people can see them. And give them this message from the Sovereign Lord: *I will gather the people of Israel from among the nations. I will bring them home to their own land from the places where they have been scattered. I will unify them into one nation in the land. One king will rule them all: no longer will they be divided into two nations.* They will stop polluting themselves with their detestable idols and other sins, for I will save them from their sinful backsliding. I will cleanse them. Then *they will truly be my people,* and I will be their God. *My servant David will be their king,* and they will have only one shepherd. They will obey my regulations and keep my laws. *They will live in the land of Israel where their ancestors lived, the land I gave my servant Jacob.* They and their children and their grandchildren after them will live there forever, generation after generation.

And *I will make a covenant of peace with them, an everlasting covenant.* I will give them their land and multiply them, and I will put my Temple among them forever ... I will be their God, and they will be my people. And ... *the nations will know that I, the Lord, have set Israel apart for myself to be holy.*"[280]

***

Could this be what Paul was talking about in Romans 11:26 when he stated: "all Israel will be saved"? Many consider this preposterous by thinking there is no way that all Jews will be saved in the end. But, is he referring to individual Hebrews, or instead alluding to the restoration of the offspring of all 12 of Israel's tribes as evidenced in Revelation 7:5-8? After identifying the 144,000 (12,000 from each of Israel's 12 tribes), John then said, "After this I saw a vast crowd, too great to count, *from every nation and tribe and people and language*, standing in front of the throne and before the Lamb."[281] Here we again see blood descendants of Israel and believing Gentiles from around the world co-existing as one, big happy family of God, yet distinctly numbered. Paul's prediction is a powerful affirmation of Ezekiel's two visions depicting the return of the Israelites back to their homeland.

A number of declarations inherent in both of Ezekiel's visions contextually places their ultimate fulfillment as yet future to our day. *First*, the return of Jacob's descendants to the land of Israel, something already occurring. We will explore that in more detail shortly. *Second*, we cannot find the reuniting of the two houses of the nation in any historical accounts after the time they divided under Rehoboam some 900 years before the birth of Christ. *Third*, the people of Israel will stop polluting themselves with sins, be cleansed by means of an everlasting covenant, and become obedient to God. *Fourth*, David will be their king even though Ezekiel's vision occurred some 350 years after the human ruler passed off the scene. *Lastly*, the Lord will establish His Temple in Jerusalem and live among them forever, inferring that when God comes to live with His people there will be a Temple situated in Jerusalem.

Notice that Scripture uses all these events to enlighten the entire world on just who the true God is. First, by the resurrection of Israel's "dry bones," the Hebrew people *"will know that I am the Lord."*[282] Then, when God makes His dwelling place with them, *"the nations will know that I, the Lord, have set Israel apart for myself to be holy."*[283] As we can see, there will be little, if any, wiggle room for skeptics who try to deny that Israel's return is God's doing. Their last option will be a hardness of heart leading to the denial of God's true identity in spite of overwhelming evidence. Their disbelief in the God of Israel will mirror that of Pharaoh. When informed it was time for God to make good on the promise that He made to Abraham by restoring his offspring to the land, he responded, "And *who is the Lord* that I should listen to him and let Israel go? *I don't know the Lord*, and I will not let Israel go."[284]

It's All Hard to Believe

How can anyone claim to believe in Abraham's God and not joyfully anticipate the accomplishment of those things the Lord promised to him? Yet, when commenting on God answering the prayers for His chosen people's restoration, Jesus asked, "But when I, the Son of Man, return, how many will I find who have faith? [in God's original plan revealed to Abraham]"[285] Unfortunately, it is part of our human makeup to doubt and disbelieve, and to disagree with what we do not yet understand. Though world news now mentions Israel daily, some who profess to believe in the Bible still dismiss the Jews' recent return to their land as a legitimate fulfillment of the prophecies we have been discussing.

Modern skeptics use at least three arguments in an attempt to support the incredulousness of such prospects. The first is the old reasoning that all these prophecies *were fulfilled in antiquity* and therefore cannot refer to any future events. They cite the Exodus from Egypt, or the regathering of the Jews from Babylon. Twentieth-century author Clarence Larkin addresses the biblical emptiness of such arguments. He begins by quoting, "though I make a full end of all nations whither I scattered thee, yet will I not make a full end of thee," and, "I will plant them upon their land, and they shall no more be pulled up out of their land."[286] Larkin next makes the following observation: "*But you say this prophecy was fulfilled in the restoration from the Babylonian Captivity? Not so*, for they were driven out of the land after that, and this promise is, that they shall no more be pulled up out of their land, and *must refer to some future restoration*. The return from Babylonian Captivity was the First restoration, *and the Scriptures speak of a Second....* The Jews have never been restored but ONCE, and that was from Babylon. The march from Egypt to Canaan was not a restoration. *You cannot have anything restored to you unless it has been in your possession before, and Palestine was never in the possession of the Children of Israel until after its conquest by Joshua.*"[287] An even more amazing fact is that Mr. Larkin wrote his opinion in 1918, 30 years before the creation of the modern Israeli State.

The second argument is that we need to be careful not to interpret the prophecies too literally, but instead look for their spiritual explanation. A group known in the first century A. D. as the Gnostics employed a similar approach to explain the mysteries of God. One of their central teachings was that while Jesus was the Messiah, His appearance on earth was in the form of a spirit rather than actual human flesh. The apostle John addressed this heresy: "For there are many false prophets in the world. This is the way to find out if they have the Spirit of God: If a prophet acknowledges that *Jesus Christ became a human being*, that person has the Spirit of God. If a prophet does not acknowledge Jesus [as coming in human flesh], that person is not from God. Such a person has the spirit of the Antichrist."[288] In other words, if you didn't interpret the first-century advent of the promised Seed as having taken place literally, then you were teaching heresy.

John Walvoord observed, "The great prophecies of Isaiah, Jeremiah, and Ezekiel treat the predictions concerning the nations in the context of Israel's coming day of restoration and glory. Unquestionably the main theme in the prophet's mind, whether it is stated or not, is that *Israel in contrast to the nations which surround them is destined for glory and honor in God's ultimate kingdom on earth. This tremendous truth has been blurred by the unfortunate tendency to spiritualize these prophecies in the attempt to make them describe the glory of the church. If they are taken literally, however, they provide a pattern of fulfilled prophecy in the past and a program of unfulfilled prophecy in the future* which is tremendously significant in unfolding the great purposes of God for the nations of the world."[289]

Certainly, if someone doesn't believe in the first literal coming of the Messiah, in no way can we expect them to concede to a similar teaching about His second arrival. However, those who embrace the reality of His literal advent 2,000 years ago should have no problem accepting prophecies related to His second coming as transpiring in the same manner. Just as the Jews needed to return to Palestine and Jerusalem for the first arrival of the Messiah, so they must come back there for the fulfillment of prophecies relating to His second appearance. Attempting to give a "spiritual" definition of Israel in an effort to avoid acknowledging the "literal" successors of Jacob grossly distorts the factual meaning of the Bible's prophecies.

Once a truth gets spiritualized away, then the theological ship has left the port and God only knows what seas it will travel. A new hermeneutical captain is in command and can steer the rudders in any direction, all the while using the scriptures as an excuse for passport. The truth of any scriptural passage can only be found in its historical or prophetic context. Failure to do so has led numerous Gentile-derived denominations to identify themselves as "spiritual Israel," seeking to apply the prophecies intended for literal Israel to themselves. Though the Bible does teach that Gentiles will comprise a significant clan within God's spiritual family, when it speaks of "Israel" it most often is referring to a tangible people group descending from the patriarch Jacob, and who stand today as a visible world nation reminding us all of a living, yet invisible God. Let all the world be honest and admit that if Israel wasn't on the table of discussion, we wouldn't even be considering Abraham's God.

The third, and perhaps the most fallacious testimony employed against Israel, is one that also grossly misrepresents God's character. It assumes that God's promises to the Jews are null and void, because of their disobedience, particularly their leaders' rejection of Jesus Christ as the Messiah. While the people most often partake of the consequences of their leader's wrong decisions, God still maintains a personal relationship with each individual. Did the average Jew at that time reject the Messiah? Of course not. The Bible mentions many who did accept Him. Sadly, they had to share the repercussions of the leaders' actions much as we still do today in our political societies. The debunking of this falsified claim that God rejected the Jewish people requires just one single Bible verse: *"But the Lord will have mercy on the descendants of Jacob. Israel will be his special people once again. He will bring them back to settle once again in their own land."*[290]

Remember, God chose Israel to demonstrate to the world who He is, and what He is like. As the world's inhabitants have throughout history observed His great displeasure toward their embracement of false gods by allowing destruction to come upon them, they must also acknowledge them as the recipients of His amazing grace, demonstrating that He is a God of great mercy! To spare a guilty one of their deserved punishment is foreign to humanity's degraded nature. But mercy is the hallmark of a human heart touched by the divine, which in turn demonstrates this sacred characteristic toward others. According to Webster, "mercy is a distinguishing attribute of the Supreme Being."[291] In God's throne room it is the "mercy seat" that overlays the law, allowing sinful worshipers to meet with Him.[292] Eternal life is the fruit of this glorious aspect of God's character. When He grants it to someone, He then expects it to be passed on. In writing to the "Jewish Christians scattered among the nations," James instructed, "For there will be no mercy for you if you have not been merciful to others. But *if you have been merciful, then God's mercy toward you will win out over His judgment against you.*"[293]

For Gentiles to say that the Lord will not exercise mercy and compassion to the Jews because of their disobedience is a false witness to His nature. It robs Him of His greatest attribute and places a stain upon His holy character. Not only that, it denies their own chance of returning to the Lord. Remember our text from Isaiah which says that because of God's mercy to the Jews they will return to their homeland? Well, the same verse further states, "And *people from many different nations [Gentiles] will come and join them there and become part of the people of Israel. The nations of the world will help the Lord's people return.*"[294] The mercy calling Israel home is the same mercy that allows Gentiles to be part of the restoration.

God's plan to unite Jewish and Gentile believers actually

works! We ask, *Why Israel?* Here we have it. It is God's illustration to the world of how He can change a human heart and unite all people groups into His one, true Israel, just as He promised Abraham, Isaac, and Jacob that He would do! As we are about to see, and as Isaiah imagined, the Hebrew people are now returning to Israel, because of the Lord's mercy being shown toward them through the Gentiles. More and more Gentiles (students) in the world (class) are finally understanding and cooperating with God's (the professor's) calling of Israel (the model student). The mercy they are showing to Israel is but a reciprocation of the mercy that God has shown to them.[295]

Modern Day Realities

Olehs is the name given to people of Jewish identity who migrate to Israel. In 1991 a covert Israeli military plan called *Operation Solomon* succeeded in transporting 14,325 Ethiopian Jews into Israel. In 1950 the newly-organized Israeli Parliament passed legislation known as *The Law of Return*. It declared that *"every Jew has the right to come to this country* as an *oleh* [immigrant]."[296] The increasing number of Jews living in Israel in the past 100 years is astonishing. They accounted for only 8 percent (60,000) of the total population in 1918. As of 2019, that number had risen to 6,697,000 (74.2 percent).[297]

What is impressive is not the existence of large numbers of Jewish people in the world, but how few there are considering their ancient history. They are one of the oldest surviving people groups. At the time of their exodus from Egypt nearly 3,500 years ago the Bible tallied their numbers at between one to one and a half million (only males 20 years or older were counted).[298] Today worldwide the estimate is a little more than 14,650,000.[299] Contrast this to the number of African Americans living in the United States. They arrived only 400 plus years ago, yet their numbers currently top 48 million, more than 3 times the number of Jews worldwide![300] The point here is the Hebrew people should be one of, if not the largest, of communities. But continual persecutions and the fact that they have spent most of their existence without a country of their own have kept their numbers in check.[301] It is remarkable that any are still around, and even more, that the Bible predicts, in the end, God will rule the entire world through them!

Why should this surprise us? Paul told us this is the Lord's modus operandi in bringing salvation to this world. "This foolish plan of God is far wiser than the wisest of human plans, and God's weakness is far stronger than the greatest of human strength. Remember, dear brothers and sisters, that few of you were wise in the world's eyes, or powerful, or wealthy when God called you. Instead, God deliberately chose things the world considers foolish in order to shame those who think they are wise. And he chose those who are powerless to shame those who are powerful. God chose things despised by the world, things counted as nothing at all, and used them to bring to nothing what the world considers important so that no one can ever boast in the presence of God."[302]

The Jewish people now have their own country and are increasing in numbers. So, how did Israel get to its current state? The answer to this question is nothing short of a miracle. When we look at a map of the Middle East prior to AD. 70, we will notice that a Jewish enclave (Judea) still occupied significant territory in and around Jerusalem. A deeper dig into history reveals that a nation called Eretz (land of) Israel was present there until 722 B.C. when the Assyrians captured Samaria, and dissolved the northern kingdom of Israel. So, maps after that time until 1948, an interim period of some 2,700 years, do not include Israel. But get a map created after May 14, 1948, and there it is! That is the birth date of the modern nation of Israel. Overnight the nation was born, yet its conception has a traceable history.

As a result of various expulsions from the land of Israel, Jews tried to assimilate into whatever country they found themselves. What other choice did they have? Yet they were always kept apart because of who they were. Though a small percentage at times would achieve elite status, any collective success was mostly looked upon with even more scorn and consistently rejected.

Consider their treatment from the church and government of Spain in 1492. Christopher Columbus began his diary with this: "In the same month in which their Majesties [Ferdinand and Isabella] issued the edict that *all Jews should be driven out of the kingdom and its territories*, in the same month they gave me the order to undertake with sufficient men my expedition of discovery to the Indies."[303] After they had been in that country for nearly 1,000 years, the Spanish authorities required all Jews refusing to convert to Catholic Christianity just weeks to leave or face annihilation. Estimates of those killed range in the tens of thousands.

Or consider their plight in Russia dating back some 1,500 years. At one time the Russian Empire was home to the largest population of Jews in the world. Beginning in 1791 the Russian government started designating certain territories known as the Pale of Settlement where Jews could have permanent residency. From 1881 to 1884, a backlash of large-scale and deadly protests among the Russian people known as pogroms broke out, targeting the Jewish communities and resulting in widespread raping and killing. Their frustration during this perilous time was illustrated in the 1971 film classic *Fiddler on the Roof* when the Jewish father Tevye says to God, "I know. I know. We are your chosen people. But, once in a while, can't

You choose someone else?"[304] Although it is hard for historians to calculate exactly how many Jewish people perished in Russia, most estimates settle around 60,000–100,000.

The Birth of Contemporary Zionism

This frustration of non-assimilation, persecution, and restricted economic opportunities in foreign lands resulted in the birth of the Zionist Movement which began to eye the possibility of returning displaced Jews to their biblical homeland in Palestine. "The Zionist Movement was fueled by two things: the religious beliefs of the Jewish people regarding a return to their ancient homeland and the waves of anti-Semitism which swept the Jewish world in Europe at the beginning of the 20th century."[305] In 1896 Theodor Herzl, a Hungarian Jew, published a pamphlet called *Der Judenstaat (The Jew's State)*. Before his death in 1904 he formed the World Zionist Organization, and today is considered *"the spiritual father of the Jewish State."*[306] On July 28, 1914, an event began destined to affect the entire world and further propagate the seeds of Zionism. World War I broke out and resulted in a major power shift in Middle East politics. After 400 years of Turkish rule, Britain gained control of the area known as Palestine (modern Israel). In 1917 the British government issued a public statement known as the Balfour Declaration stating that "His Majesty's Government *view with favor the establishment in Palestine of a national home for the Jewish people.*"[307]

The 1930s saw the rise of Nazi Germany under the leadership of Adolf Hitler who personally blamed the Jews for Germany's defeat in the First World War. He sought to reverse that outcome in the Second World War, and once and for all settle what he considered "The Jewish Problem," with "The Final Solution." It was a plan to rid German-occupied Europe of all Jews by either relocating or exterminating them. In Hitler's way of thinking, *"the struggle for world domination will be fought entirely between us, between Germans and Jews. All else is facade and illusion* ... Even when we have driven the Jew out of Germany, he remains our world enemy."[308] In his book *Mein Kampf,* (*My Struggle* or *My Battle*), he wrote, *"the personification of the devil as the symbol of all evil assumes the living shape of the Jew."*[309] Is there any wonder he would conclude, "Therefore, I believe today that I am acting in the sense of the Almighty Creator: *By warding off the Jews I am fighting for the Lord's work."*[310] A naïve world that wanted to brush off the intent of Hitler's words ended up underestimating them. Ninety percent of the Jews in Poland and two-thirds of Jews living in Europe, an estimated six million of them, perished. After reading the account of what took place in the death camp at Auschwitz, Winston Churchill wrote, "There is no doubt this is the most horrible crime ever committed in the whole history of the world."[311]

Could not the message given by the prophet Jeremiah concerning Edom, descendants of Esau and ancient enemies of Israel, also apply here? "As to the terror you cause, your presumptuous heart has deceived you. You who live in the clefts of the rock, *you who occupy the mountain summit, though you elevate your nest like the eagle, even from there I will bring you down."*[312] Is this really prophetic, or just coincidence that Hitler's mountain top retreat situated at 6,000 feet in the Bavarian Alps was called the *Eagle's Nest?*

Re-creation of the Israeli State

In 1945, after World War II ended, 50 countries signed a charter creating the United Nations. One of the first major issues they took up was what to do with Europe's surviving Jewish population. After much debate, on November 29, 1947, the United Nations General Assembly passed the controversial *Resolution 181* giving Jews legal right to parts of their ancient homeland, and permission to establish a Jewish State in the land of Israel. The British set a date of May 14, 1948, to terminate their mandate and end 30 years of rule over the land of Palestine. On the eve of the Jewish Sabbath, on the same day the mandate was to end, representatives of the Jewish Community and delegates of the Zionist Movement secretly assembled in a museum in Tel Aviv and announced "THE ESTABLISHMENT OF A JEWISH STATE IN ERETZ-ISRAEL, TO BE KNOWN AS THE STATE OF ISRAEL."[313]

Within hours United States president Harry Truman signed a personally edited letter that read, "This government has been informed that a Jewish state has been proclaimed in Palestine, and recognition has been requested by the provisional government thereof. *The United States recognizes the provisional government as the de facto authority of the State of Israel.*" [signed Harry Truman, May 14, 1948].[314] Unbelievably, some 2,700 years earlier the Lord had His prophet Isaiah write, "Who has ever seen or heard of anything as strange as this? *Has a nation ever been born in a single day? Has a country ever come forth in a mere moment?* But by the time Jerusalem's birth pains begin, the baby will be born; *the nation will come forth. Would I ever bring this nation to the point of birth and then not deliver it? asks the Lord. No! I would never keep this nation from being born, says your God.*"[315]

But what many had called the "Jewish Problem" did not end there. Instead, it was only the downloading of ancient issues into our modern times. The headline in the *New York Times* for May 14, 1948, read, "ZIONISTS PROCLAIM NEW STATE OF ISRAEL; TRUMAN RECOGNIZES IT AND HOPES

FOR PEACE; TEL AVIV IS BOMBED, EGYPT ORDERS INVASION." The very next day, May 15, 1948, the Arab-Israeli War broke out between the newborn State of Israel and the Arab League comprised of seven neighboring Arab nations. After nearly a year of conflict, the Israel Defense Forces held their ground and the newly declared State of Israel survived its first challenge to its independence and territory.

Verification of a God of Israel requires a State of Israel. Thus, *Israel's existence today is a living testimony to God's existence*. It is one thing to disbelieve such events could happen prior to 1948. It is nothing less than ineptitude in understanding what the Bible is really teaching, or willful ignorance, to dismiss it as factual now. *The return of Jacob sets into motion all things final*. It makes the urgency of our present moment obvious to all who want to see. Looking back over history's timeline we find ourselves not in the days of Abraham, Moses, David, the prophets, or when the Messiah entered His Temple in Jerusalem, or even in the centuries of time when Jerusalem was under the control of Gentile peoples. No, *we stand 70 plus years past the time when Israel (Jacob) officially returned home!* We now view things in reality whereas those living in the periods just mentioned only saw it prophetically, or didn't perceive it at all.

CHAPTER 9

RETURN OF JERUSALEM AND IT'S TEMPLE (TIME OF GENTILES FULFILLED)

"Home sweet home. This is the place to find happiness. If one doesn't find it here, one doesn't find it anywhere."³¹⁶

Many have fond memories of home and their lives there. For others it holds little else but echoes of hurt and bitterness. Their pain sometimes lasts a lifetime, something vividly portrayed in the widely popular film, *Forrest Gump*. When his friend Jenny revisited her childhood home, where she had suffered abuse from her father, she began to hurl rocks at its windows. Watching her fall to the ground, sobbing, Gump's narrative was, "Sometimes I guess there just aren't enough rocks."[317] The Bible commands us to take special notice of such unfortunate souls, because God does. Whether they be orphans, widows, victims of various types of childhood abuse, divorce, or any other issues that deprived them of happiness, their Creator does not overlook their misery. After all, home is the one place He intended to be a safe haven. But sin changed all that. Yet we need not despair. The Lord is recreating a happy home for the family He loves, and all are invited to join it. Jesus told His followers, *"Don't be troubled.* You trust God, now trust in me. *There are many rooms in my Father's home, and I am going to prepare a place for you.* If this were not so, I would tell you plainly. *When everything is ready*, I will come and get you, so that you will always be with me where I am."[318]

Just where is the location of the eternal home that God promises? As we studied earlier, He summoned Abram to leave his earthly home and travel to a land God would show him. His journey led him to Canaan where he "set up camp beside the oak at Moreh. At that time, the area was inhabited by the Canaanites."[319] For the traveler to "set up camp" in those days was another way of saying to "make a home." It was there "the Lord appeared to Abram and said, 'I am going to give this land to your offspring.'"[320] There Abram built the first altar in Canaan to worship his God. Thus, the Lord chose the *land of Canaan as the homeland for His earthly family.*

Sometime later, God again called upon Abram, telling him, "Take your son, your only son—yes Isaac, whom you love so much—and *go to the land of Moriah.* Sacrifice him there as a burnt offering *on one of the mountains, which I will point out to you.*"[321] Just as the Lord had picked out the land for Abram to go to, *He now selects a specific mountain* for him to worship at. But why that particular one?

It was common practice for people of that day to worship and sacrifice to their gods on elevated areas called high places.

Return Of Jerusalem And It's Temple (time Of Gentiles Fulfilled)

There they built altars, erected images, and burned incense to them. The higher the elevation, some must have assumed, the closer one could get to the deity being worshipped. Without question, something about mountain air draws one closer to another world, but it can't make us divine. That concept had passed down from the old Tower of Babel days when the people said, "Let's build a great city with a *tower that reaches to the skies—a monument to our greatness!*"[322] But, curiously, the mountain God chose was not the highest point in the land of Canaan. Mount Hermon is still today the tallest at 7,330 feet, while Mount Moriah is only 2,510 feet.

So, why did God choose a lower elevation? It is a testimony to the Lord's humility. Isaiah defined Him as: "The *high and lofty* one Who inhabits eternity.... The Holy One, says this: 'I live in that *high and holy place with those whose spirits are contrite and humble.*'"[323] That's why when He finally establishes His kingdom on earth "every valley shall be raised up, *every mountain and hill made low.*"[324]

When God commissioned Moses to retrieve His people from Egypt, He told him to bring them to the foot of another mountain called Sinai. "When you have brought the Israelites out of Egypt, you will return here to worship God at this very mountain."[325] It was the nation's first experience at worshiping their Savior. They were ignorant about whom they were revering, or even how to do it, a fact evident when after their visible leader Moses did not immediately return, they fashioned a golden calf and declared it was by its power that they had been brought out of Egypt. Though to be ignorant is nothing to be ashamed of, they were learners, much like people today who first encounter a worship service dedicated to God.

So, the Lord introduced a style of worship designed to teach them not only about who He was, but also what He was like. It took place at a structure termed "the Tabernacle," and since the Israelites did not have a permanent home, it was housed in a large portable tent. The Lord instructed Moses, "I want the people of Israel to build me a *sacred residence where I can live among them*. You must make this Tabernacle and its furnishings *exactly according to the plans I will show you*."[326] Through such a worship model, the people would learn about their God through a sacrificial system administered by an order of priests chosen from the tribe of Levi.

Speaking of those priests and their services, Scripture declares, "They serve in a place of worship that *is only a copy, a shadow of the real one in heaven*."[327] So, through the Tabernacle, their invisible God designed for them an interactive, virtual reality on earth to teach them about unseen heavenly realities. It would be by a ceremonial system of cleansing that the people of Israel would find acceptance with the Lord through a concept called "atonement"—meaning being united with God through sacrifice. Before then, people of faith, such as Noah and Abraham, could offer sacrifices anywhere. But now the Lord commanded they only be brought to the "entrance of the Tabernacle," or they would be "guilty of a capital offense."[328]

The Tabernacle remained with the people during their 40 years of roaming through the Sinai desert. As they prepared to enter their Promised Land, the Lord ordered them, "When you drive out the nations that live there, you must destroy all the places where they worship their gods—*high on the mountains, the hills*, and under every green tree. Break down their altars and smash their sacred pillars. Burn their Asherah poles and cut down their carved idols. Erase the names of their gods from those places. *Do not worship the Lord your God in the way these pagan peoples worship their gods*. Rather, *you must seek the Lord your God at the place he himself will choose* from among all the tribes [of Israel] for his name to be honored. *There you will bring* to the Lord your burnt offerings, your sacrifices ..."[329]

Return Of Jerusalem And It's Temple (time Of Gentiles Fulfilled)

After Israel's arrival in Canaan, they began to settle the land, building homes for themselves, but the Tabernacle (House) of God remained in a tent for some 500 years. King David captured the city of a Canaanite tribe called the Jebusites. Its location was the same hill where Abram had previously gone to sacrifice his son Isaac. David then made it his capital city, calling it *Jerusalem*, or *Zion*.

One day David told the prophet, Nathan, "Here I am living in this beautiful cedar palace, but *the Ark of God is out in a tent!*"[330] God had put it in David's heart to build a permanent dwelling place where the people could meet their God. It, too, would be constructed at a place of divine choosing. The Lord instructed the king to buy a threshing floor from Araunah [Ornan] the Jebusite as the site for the Temple on the same mountain that He had chosen to test Abram's faith through offering up his son Isaac—Mount Moriah in Jerusalem.[331] David's passion for Jerusalem was but a dim reflection of the feeling that God has for it. He inspired the king to write songs about it: "For the Lord has chosen Jerusalem; he has desired it as his home. '*This is my home where I will live forever,*' he said. '*I will live here, for this is the place I desired. I will make this city prosperous ... Here I will increase the power of David; my anointed one will be a light for my people ... he will be a glorious king.*'"[332]

David's son Solomon finally fulfilled his desire to establish the Temple. "So Solomon began to build the Temple of the Lord *in Jerusalem on Mount Moriah*, where the Lord had appeared to Solomon's father, King David. The Temple was built *on the threshing floor* of Araunah the Jebusite, the site that David had selected."[333] It was the world's first permanent structure of worship allocated to monotheism. At its dedication, Solomon declared, "Blessed be the Lord, the God of Israel, who has *kept the promise he made to my father, David.* For he told my father, 'From the day I brought my people out of Egypt, I have never chosen a city among the tribes of Israel as the place where a temple should be built to honor my name. Nor have I chosen a king to lead my people Israel. But now *I have chosen Jerusalem as that city, and David as that king.*"[334]

A Glimpse of Glory

One would think now that the Lord had His chosen people, located in His chosen city, in His chosen country, serving His chosen King, and worshiping at His chosen Temple, the story could end. It was the golden age of Judaism. "So *King Solomon became richer and wiser than any other king in all the earth.* People from every nation came to visit him and to hear the wisdom God had given him."[335] The Bible recalls some of the nation's prosperity during that time. "And Solomon had *forty thousand stalls of horses* for his chariots and twelve thousand horsemen."[336] "And Solomon's provision for one day was thirty measures [dry bushels] of fine flour and threescore [sixty] measures [dry bushels] of meal; ten fat oxen and twenty oxen out of the pastures, and a hundred sheep, besides harts [deer] and gazelles and roebucks and fatted fowl."[337] Scripture sums up this period of peace and plenty for the average Hebrew by stating, "*Judah and Israel dwelt safely*, every man under his vine and under his fig tree ... all the days of Solomon."[338]

Sadly, though, God didn't have the unwavering commitment of the king, nor the people's hearts. "Now King Solomon loved many foreign women ... In Solomon's old age, *they turned his heart to worship their gods instead of trusting only in the Lord his God*, as his father, David, had done ... *On the Mount of Olives, east of Jerusalem, he even built a shrine* for Chemosh, the detestable god of Moab, and another for Molech, the detestable god of the Ammonites."[339]

As one can sense, the story is about to worsen before it gets better. Solomon had made a fatal mistake. He put his nation of Israel ahead of the faith of Israel! By human effort he tried to firmly establish the Lord's earthly kingdom, but had turned a blind eye to the encroachment of paganism upon it. Thus, it now rested upon a shaky foundation not according to the covenant design, so it would be impossible for it to withstand the winds of spiritual testing that would soon sweep its way. Contrast this to when Jesus told Peter, "it is on this [Israel/Christ] rock that I will build my congregation, and the powers of hell will not conquer it."[340]

As goes the king, so goes the nation. Solomon's allowance of idolatry was the beginning of Israel's demise and Jerusalem's disintegration. Upon his death the kingdom split, and succeeding kings in both governments, for the most part, repeated his poor example of leadership. In time the Lord rejected both kingdoms, beginning first when the Assyrians defeated Israel and exiled many.

Then He said, *"I will destroy Judah just as I have destroyed Israel. I will banish the people from my presence and reject my chosen city of Jerusalem and the Temple where my name was to be honored."*[341] The Babylonians devastated the city and its Temple in the sixth century B.C., something foretold by Moses: "The surrounding nations will ask, 'Why has the Lord done this to His land? Why was He so angry?' And they will be told, *'this happened because the people of the land broke the covenant they made with the Lord*, the God of their ancestors, when He brought them out of the land of Egypt. They *turned to serve and worship other gods that were foreign to them* ... In great anger and fury the Lord *uprooted his people from their land and exiled them to another land.'"*[342]

Then came time for the first restoration of Judah. After 70 years of exile the Jews received permission and aid from the Persians, and returned to rebuild the Temple and Jerusalem's walls (a symbol of political statehood). Shortly before the time of Christ, King Herod refurbished the Temple because of its need for repairs, and his need for earthly glory. And then, the Lord Himself, the Messiah, personally paid a visit to His city and Temple.

So, here is a glimpse of some hope, even for us today. Jerusalem's glory days under David and Solomon offer but a brief picture of what will be exceeded in the city's still yet future. What is to come is a reclaiming of all things lost, not just in Jerusalem, but in the homes of all humanity where sin annihilated our sense of happiness and wellbeing. The Lord understands the psychological pain the Jennies of our world go through. He watched His own household of faith become dysfunctional as well. During Jesus' closing hours of His life on earth He displayed God's passion and agony for His people and their sacred city.

The Light of the World

Remember, King Solomon had built altars to pagan gods on the Mountain of Olives located just east of Mount Zion. Olivet (2,710 feet) stands 200 feet taller than nearby Zion (2,510 feet), the mountain chosen by God and where the Temple stood. From Olivet, while looking over at the lights of Jerusalem, Jesus told His people Israel that they were like their city Jerusalem, the "light of the world—*like a city on a mountain*, glowing in the night for all to see."[343] To a world that today dwells in spiritual darkness, the Bible says that Jerusalem and its inhabitants will once again reappear as a guiding light leading them to God.

Jesus later descended Olivet for the purpose of fulfilling what the prophet had predicted that He would do. "Rejoice greatly, O people of Zion! Shout in triumph, O people of Jerusalem! *Look, your king is coming to you.* He is righteous and victorious, *yet He is humble*, riding on a donkey—even on a donkey's colt."[344] He then began making His way to the Eastern Gate for His Messianic entry into Jerusalem.[345] "But as they came closer to Jerusalem and Jesus saw the city ahead, *he began to cry.* 'I wish that even today you would find the way of peace. But now it is too late, and peace is hidden from you. Before long your enemies will build ramparts against your walls and encircle you and close in on you. They will crush you to the ground, and your children with you. *Your enemies will not leave a single stone in place*, because you have *rejected the opportunity God offered you.*'"[346] To a spot called Gethsemane, located at the base of Mount Olivet, He retreated later that evening with His disciples after their last supper to spend the night praying.

There the Temple police arrested and took Him back to Jerusalem for His unjust trial and crucifixion. After His resurrection, it would be from Mount Olivet that He ascended into the heavens.[347] Why is this significant? Because Scripture describes His future return in vivid detail. "On that day *his feet will stand on the Mount of Olives*, which faces Jerusalem on the east. And *the Mount of Olives will split apart, making a wide valley* running from east to west."[348] *Olivet will then no longer tower above Zion,* but will be leveled, reminding us of Isaiah's words: "Listen! I hear the voice of someone shouting, 'Make a highway for the Lord through the wilderness ... *Fill in the valleys and level the hills* ... The glory of the Lord will be revealed, and all people will see it together.' The Lord has spoken."[349]

If anyone wonders why Jesus got so emotional that day, consider what He foresaw would happen to Jerusalem and its people. Once at their Mount Olivet retreat, the disciples asked Jesus what would be the signs of the end of the world. He then predicted the fate of the Jewish people and said that Roman armies would destroy Jerusalem. "They [the Jews] will be brutally killed by the sword or sent away as captives to all the nations of the world. And *Jerusalem will be conquered and trampled down by the Gentiles until the age of the Gentiles comes to an end.*"[350] Because the Bible says to *"pray for the peace of Jerusalem,"* the devil has made sure more human blood has been spilled there than any other city in human history.[351]

It all happened just as Jesus said it would. After His crucifixion unimaginable persecution fell upon the Jewish people. Josephus documents their removal from Jerusalem by the Romans beginning in A.D. 50 when an estimated 30,000 died, and another 40,000 during a later war in A.D. 66. Then, in April A.D. 70 a Roman army of 100,000 troops under the command of Titus besieged Jerusalem, creating a food shortage so severe that Jewish mothers killed, cooked, and ate their own children. When the Romans finally overran the city that following August, an estimated one million Jews perished, while another 97,000 were dispersed to other parts of the empire. Defying orders, a soldier torched the Temple, burning it to the ground. Remember, the politician Herod had refurbished that Temple as a tribute to his glory of wealth and power. God, on the other hand, allowed for its complete destruction as a remembrance to all succeeding generations of His interdependence on anything earthly, and the weakness of humans who think themselves great! Today, the Arch of Titus still stands in Rome with boastful reliefs depicting the general's triumphant return with Jewish slaves and spoils from the Lord's sanctuary.

Sixty-five years later, in A.D. 135, the Roman Emperor Hadrian picked up where Titus left off. His forces put down the last major rebellion by the Jews, killing approximately 580,000 of them. He then ordered the leveling of Jerusalem and a new city called Aelia Capitolina constructed on top of the ruins.[352] Nearly 900 years earlier the prophet Micah wrote, "So because of you [the false religious leaders of Israel], Mount

Return Of Jerusalem And It's Temple (time Of Gentiles Fulfilled)

Zion will be plowed like an open field; Jerusalem will be reduced to rubble! A great forest will grow on the hilltop, where the Temple now stands."[353]

Thus, Jerusalem fell under the control and occupation of Gentiles. The Romans erected a shrine to Jupiter on the former Temple Mount with statues of other mythical gods as an intentional violation of Old Testament Hebrew law. They passed a law forbidding Jews from entering the new city.[354] When Christianity became the official religion of the Roman Empire some two hundred years later, Aelia Capitolina met its own cultural demise with Christ replacing Jupiter as the new god of the Romans.

The Battle for Jerusalem

In the coming centuries, Jerusalem became a desired trophy between Christian armies and the forces of Islam.[355] The fall of A.D. 636 saw it captured by Muslim armies. Construction of the Islamic shrine named the Dome of the Rock finished in A.D. 691/692 on the site where tradition says the Jewish Temple once stood. It collapsed but was rebuilt in A.D. 1022/1023, and today still stands as the world's oldest Islamic monument. In 1099, Jerusalem fell to Christian Crusaders who slaughtered all Muslims and Jews living in the city, including women and children. The Crusaders converted the Dome of the Rock into a Christian church. Eighty-eight years later, in A.D. 1187, Muslims led by the famous general Saladin recaptured the city. Jerusalem and the surrounding area remained under Muslim control for nearly 800 years. Long ago the Lord had told the Hebrews what would happen after their removal from the land: "I will scatter you among the nations.... *Your land will become desolate, and your cities will lie in ruin.*"[356]

Two notable eyewitness accounts depict the condition of

133

Jerusalem during the period of the Jewish absence. The first was Rabbi Moses ben Nachman (Nachmanides). A Spanish Jew, he left Spain in 1267, fleeing persecution from the Christians, and went to Palestine. But, upon his arrival, he said he couldn't even find 10 Jewish men to pray with. In a letter to his son he wrote, "Many are [Israel's] forsaken places, and great is the desecration. The more sacred the place, the greater the devastation it has suffered. *Jerusalem is the most desolate place of all.*" He noted that such stark conditions actually brought him courage, because it was a living testimony of prophecy fulfilled. After quoting Leviticus 26, he recorded that the barrenness of the place "constitutes *a good tiding, proclaiming that during all our exiles, our land will not accept our enemies.* This is a great proof and assurance to us, for in the entire inhabited world one cannot find such a good and large land which was always lived in, and yet is as ruined as it is (today). *For since the time that we left it, it has not accepted any nation or people*, and they all try to settle it, but to no avail."[357]

The American writer Samuel Clemens [aka Mark Twain] documented his 1867 trip to the Holy Land in *The Innocents Abroad*, the book that first brought him fame as a writer. "'Riding on horseback through the Jezreel Valley,' Twain observed, 'there is not a solitary village throughout its whole extent—not for 30 miles in either direction. There are two or three small clusters of Bedouin tents, but *not a single permanent habitation.* One may ride 10 miles, hereabouts, and not see 10 human beings.'"[358]

Jesus prophesied that the Jews would be removed from Jerusalem and remain homeless until *"the age of the Gentiles comes to an end."*[359] As we saw in our previous chapter, the Jews regained control of the land of Israel, officially forming their own country in 1948. But what about Jerusalem?

Between June 5 and 10, 1967, another conflict broke out

between Israel and its Arab neighbors, Egypt, Jordan, and Syria. Known as the Six-Day War, Israeli forces surprised the world with a quick victory in just six days, gaining control of the Sinai Peninsula, the Gaza Strip, the West Bank, the Golan Heights, and, most importantly, the *Old City of Jerusalem.* The *New York Times* headline read "ISRAELIS ROUT THE ARABS, APPROACH THE SUEZ, BREAK BLOCKADE, OCCUPY OLD JERUSALEM."[360]

After capturing Jerusalem, a top Israeli commander wrote to his men, "*For some two thousand years the Temple Mount was forbidden to the Jews.* Until you came—you, the paratroopers— and returned it to the bosom of the nation. The Western Wall, for which every heart beats is ours again. Many Jews have taken their lives into their own hands throughout our long history, in order to reach Jerusalem and live there. Endless words of longing have expressed the deep yearning for Jerusalem that beats within the Jewish heart ... You have been given the great privilege of completing the circle, *of returning to the nation its capital and its holy center ... Jerusalem is yours forever.*"[361]

For the first time in 1,897 years, Jews had jurisdiction over Jerusalem, the city God promised them long ago as an eternal gift to their father David. Great celebration filled the streets among the Jewish people. The words of the Psalmist written some 3,000 years ago came to fruition: "*When the Lord restored His exiles to Jerusalem, it was like a dream! We were filled with laughter, and we sang for joy. And the other nations said, 'What amazing things the Lord has done for them.*"[362] Isaiah's words rang true as well: "*Let the ruins of Jerusalem break into joyful song,* for the Lord has comforted His people, *He has redeemed Jerusalem.* The Lord will demonstrate his holy power before the eyes of all the nations. The ends of the earth will see the salvation of our God.*"[363]

The Gentiles' designated period as overseers of Jerusalem

had come to its end, completing Christ's prophecy given nearly 2,000 years ago. In July 1980 the Israeli government passed the *Jerusalem Law* officially declaring the city as the capital of the state of Israel. In 2018 the United States government recognized this claim by moving its embassy there from Tel Aviv.

God's Capital City and Temple

Can the student of Bible prophecy not discern the things that are being fulfilled in our very day? "This is what the Lord Almighty says: 'My love for Mount Zion is passionate and strong; I am consumed with passion for Jerusalem ... *I am returning to Mount Zion, and I will live in Jerusalem.* Then Jerusalem will be called the Faithful City; the Mountain of the Lord Almighty will be called the Holy Mountain ... *Once again old men and women will walk Jerusalem's streets with a cane and sit together in the city squares. And the streets of the city will be filled with boys and girls at play* ... All this may seem impossible to you now, a small and discouraged remnant of God's people. But do you think this is impossible for me, the Lord Almighty? ... *You can be sure that I will rescue my people from the east and from the west. I will bring them home again to live safely in Jerusalem.*'"[364]

Today people can travel to see it with their own eyes. A flight into Ben Gurion International Airport is one's gateway to melting modern times into the ancient past. Tourists can make reservations at the luxurious *King David Hotel* in Jerusalem! Site tours walk visitors through thousands of years of living history. Enthusiasts can go snow skiing on Mount Hermon, explore the Negev Desert, sunbathe at various Mediterranean, or Red Sea beach resorts, or float in the mineral laden waters of the Dead Sea. Israelis are on the cutting edge of medical technology, and having reclaimed the land, their agricultural practices are among the most advanced in the world.[365] Jerusalem is,

Return Of Jerusalem And It's Temple (time Of Gentiles Fulfilled)

all things considered, relatively peaceful with Jews, Moslems and Christians cohabitating. The Israel Defense Forces (IDF) is one of the best equipped and trained armies on earth dedicated to keeping the country safe in spite of constant threat of attack. In a country about the size of New Jersey, and with a population of approximately nine million, in 2019 Israel welcomed 4.55 million tourists, thus injecting 23 billion NIS (New Israeli Shekel) into its economy.[366]

However, the Bible tells us this is not the end of the story, far from it. Jerusalem has not seen the last of its troubles. While many Jewish citizens focus on Israel's political, economic and territorial gains, others see it only as paving the way for the full restoration of the religious nation. One piece of the Hebrew mosaic remains to be restored to the Jewish people—*the Temple*. Herein lies a major problem: the Dome of the Rock still occupies the site where the Jews believe the first and second Temples stood on Mount Moriah.[367]

Orthodox Jewish organizations both within Israel and around the world have dedicated themselves to seeing the Temple rebuilt. One such organization located in Jerusalem declares in its *Statement of Principles*, "The Temple Institute *is dedicated to all aspects of the Divine commandment for Israel to build a house for G-d's presence, the Holy Temple, on Mount Moriah in Jerusalem.*"[368]

The prophet Ezekiel saw *the glory of the Lord depart from the Temple* in the days of King Jehoiachin prior to Judah's captivity by Babylon.[369] But Ezekiel 43 records that it will return. "And the glory of the Lord came into the Temple through the east gateway ... the glory of the Lord filled the Temple ... And the Lord said to me, 'Son of man, *this is the place of My throne and the place where I will rest my feet. I will remain here forever, living among the people of Israel.* They and their kings will not defile my holy name any longer by their adulterous worship of other gods ... describe to the people of Israel the Temple I have shown you ... describe to them all the specifications of its construction ... *The entire top of the hill where the Temple is built is holy. Yes this [the location on the Temple Mount] is the primary law of the Temple.*'"[370]

Some people say that the building of the Second Temple after the return from Babylon fulfilled the prophecy. But the context is definitely speaking of a time future when both houses of David--Israel and Judah--have regathered.[371] Only remnants of Judah returned from Babylon. Furthermore, when His glory does return, Ezekiel teaches, it will remain with the "people of Israel" "forever." Since the second Temple was again destroyed, clearly the prophecy must be realized in the future, or not at all.

So, if the Jews were to return to Israel, and they have, and rebuild Jerusalem, which they did, is it too farfetched to believe they are going to try to reconstruct their Temple to resume their religious practices of sacrifice? Orthodox Judaism places great faith in Old Testament texts suggesting that it will happen. For example, "In the last days, the *Temple of the Lord in Jerusalem will become the most important place on earth. People from all over the world will go there to worship.* Many nations will come and say, 'Come, *let us go up to the mountain of the Lord, to the Temple of the God of Israel.*'"[372]

Some Christians consider the whole idea about rebuilding the Temple as nonsensical and unnecessary. They bring out texts such as when the woman at the Samaritan well asked Jesus, "'so tell me, why is it that *you Jews insist that Jerusalem is the only place of worship*, while we Samaritans claim it is here at Mount Gerizim, where our ancestors worshiped?' He replied, 'Believe me, the time is coming when *it will no longer matter whether you worship the Father here or in Jerusalem* ... true worshipers will worship the Father in spirit and in truth. The Father *is looking for anyone* who will worship him in that way.'"[373] They believe that when Christ made the ultimate sacrificial blood atonement at Calvary, He provided what the book of Hebrews describes as the "new and living way" for us to have access to God.[374] Not only that, but Paul also told the early believers at Corinth, "Don't you realize that all *of you together are the temple of God* and that the Spirit of God lives in you...*you Christians are that temple.*"[375]

Here we have a dichotomy between faiths. Christians who understand Christ as the Messiah have found the pathway to a relationship with God through the Spirit. Therefore, they say we no longer need an earthly Temple and consider such an idea as absurd and blasphemous. Acts 17:24 states, "since he is Lord of heaven and earth, *he doesn't live in man-made temples.*" Jews, on the other hand, point to biblical references that contextually state a Temple in Jerusalem will be rebuilt before the coming of the Messiah.

The answer to such a conundrum lies in the fact the Jewish people never accepted New Testament teachings that rest on the premise the Messiah came 2,000 years ago in the person of Jesus Christ. Therefore, they still live under an Old Testament interpretation of the Hebrew scriptures and will act accordingly. By the same token, God has promised not to disregard them, or leave them trailing in the dust, but will finish the good work He began in His chosen people by teaching them His way the second time around. And, "Your way, O God, *is in the sanctuary.*"[376] In other words, "the way of God—the true principles of the Divine administration—*are to be learned in the place where He is worshiped.*"[377] For the Jew, one can find God only through the Temple services, the same springboard by which early believers in Christ (who were also Jewish) understood His salvific role as detailed in the book of Hebrews.

The concept of reinstituting animal sacrifices may seem foreign and cruel in the eyes of Gentile believers, but the first covenant that God gave through Moses to the Hebrew people demanded it. "In fact, we can say that according to the law of Moses, nearly everything was purified by the sprinkling with blood. *Without the shedding of blood, there is no forgiveness of sins.*"[378] Of course, those who have accepted the forgiveness principle of the New Covenant believe that "Christ died to set them free from the penalty of the sins they had committed under that first covenant."[379] Because the Jews didn't accept this teaching brought to them by Christ, they still live under an Old Testament mentality that says, "I have given you the blood [of animals] so you can make atonement for your sins. *It is the blood, representing life, that brings you atonement.*"[380]

Now let's think about this. It would be equivalent for Christians to be told that they cannot partake of communion (Eucharist) by which they remember what God has done for them. For all practical purposes, the Jewish people have not had an old-fashioned atonement for the sins of their nation since the destruction of the Temple almost 2,000 years ago! The law was very specific. They were not allowed to sacrifice at locations of their choosing.[381] The Lord had appointed a specific place, and it was the Temple site in Jerusalem.

In the centuries since the destruction of the Temple, many rabbinical teachings have focused on making up for the absence of blood atonement with benevolent acts, citing texts such as Hosea 6:6: "*I want you to be merciful; I don't want your sacrifices.* I want you to know God; that's more important than burnt offerings." Yet, once again it would be similar to Christians trying to make peace with God through their own benevolence. That doesn't work in the Old Covenant any more than it does in the New, because there is no blood. The instruction book told them it must be by means of shed blood. For the New Testament believer that should mean Christ's blood. But Jews don't have that faith yet. This is why Orthodox Judaism has a future expectation of sacrificial atonement that they consider better than Hosea's prescription of being merciful.

The City No Longer Forsaken

If God does have an eternal plan to govern the earth, then in what country will He locate His government if not in Israel? Russia or France? Singapore? Australia maybe, or the United States of America? And, in what city will He rule if not from Jerusalem? Why not Paris, New York, Rome, or Beijing? The answer is obvious. If we really believe the Bible's teaching that the God of Abraham, Isaac, and Jacob is the true Deity, then we have no choice but follow the HIS-STORY of His spiritual footprints in the earth. Study the Bible, and just as the Lord led Abraham and his Old Covenant children to Jerusalem, Israel, so He will guide His New Covenant children to focus their attention on the same location as they await their physical redemption.

"The Lord has sworn to Jerusalem by his own strength: '*I will never again hand you over to your enemies ... Go out! Prepare a highway for my people to return*! Smooth out the road; pull out the boulders; *raise a flag for all the nations to see.*' The Lord has sent this message to every land: '*Tell the people of Israel, Look, your Savior is coming. See, he brings his reward with him as he comes. They will be called the Holy People and the People Redeemed by the Lord. And Jerusalem will be known as the Desirable Place and the City No Longer Forsaken.*'"[382]

To those who think developments in Israel and Jerusalem during the past 70 plus years are unrelated to biblical prophecy, let us just say that nothing concerning Jerusalem escapes God's watchful eye. It is spiritually dangerous to discard what God has clearly stated in His Word: "Anyone who harms you [Israel] harms my most precious possession."[383] "'At that time, *when I restore the prosperity of Judah and Jerusalem,' says the Lord, 'I will gather the armies of the world into the valley of Jehoshaphat. There I will judge them for harming my people, for scattering my inheritance among the nations, and for dividing up my land. ... Then you will know that I, the Lord your God, live in Zion, MY HOLY MOUNTAIN. Jerusalem will be holy forever, and foreign armies will never conquer her again. ... Judah will remain forever, and Jerusalem will endure through all future generations. I will pardon my people's crimes, which I have not yet pardoned; and I, the Lord, will make my home in Jerusalem with my people.'"*[384]

Obviously, such a scenario can only apply to a future occurrence and will be validated by the readjustment of the heights of those hills surrounding Mount Zion. "In the last days *the mountain of the Lord's temple [Zion] will be established as the highest of the mountains; it will be exalted above the hills, and peoples will stream to it.*"[385]

CHAPTER 10
RETURN OF DANIEL (ANTICHRIST REVEALED)

Israel has a spiritual malady that the Lord has promised to heal. Long ago Jeremiah expressed concern at his people's diagnosis. "I weep *for the hurt of my people ... Is there no medicine in Gilead? Is there no physician there? Why is there no healing for the wounds of my people?*"[386] Later, he celebrates the prognosis. "This is what the Lord says: 'Yours [Israel's] is an incurable bruise, a terrible wound. *There is no one to help you or bind up your injury. You are beyond help of any medicine ...* I have wounded you cruelly, as though I were your enemy. For your sins are many, and your guilt is great ... *I will give you back your health and heal your wounds* ... When I bring you home again from your captivity and restore your fortunes, Jerusalem will be rebuilt on her ruins ... *I will establish them as a nation before me,* and I will punish anyone who hurts them.

They will have their own ruler again, and he will not be a foreigner [Gentile] ... You will be my people, and I will be your God... The fierce anger of the Lord will not diminish until it has finished all His plans."[387] Here we see that no human religion or political pact can heal Israel. Their help will come directly from God through a two-part prescription for the restoration of their wellness.

First, the Lord must prepare for the removal of their sins by means of a final round of persecution, because "*the correction of discipline is the way to life.*"[388] His cauterizing technique is known as the "Refiner's Fire," and is designed to forever melt away Israel's earthliness through hardship. Isaiah wrote, "I have refined you in the *furnace of suffering. I will rescue you for my sake ... That way, the pagan nations will not be able to claim that their gods have conquered me. I will not let them have my glory.*"[389] In the context of the coming day of judgment, Malachi asks, "Who will be able to stand and face Him when He appears ... *He will sit and judge like a refiner of silver, watching closely as the dross is burned away*. He will purify the Levites, refining them like gold or silver, so that they may once again offer acceptable sacrifices to the Lord. *Then once more the Lord will accept the offerings brought to him by the people of Judah and Jerusalem, as he did in former times.*"[390]

Now, no responsible surgeon would begin such a procedure without first anesthetizing the patient. Just so, God told Israel, "For the Lord has poured out on you *a spirit of deep sleep*. He has *closed the eyes* of their prophets and visionaries. All *these future events are a sealed book to them.*"[391] When they awaken at the end of time, He will administer the second part of the divine prescription. It is the understanding that, though they suffered much, Yeshua Hamashiach spared them eternal destruction by dying as their sacrificial atonement on Golgotha Hill. They will then realize their salvation is the result of His vicarious life and death. "But *he was wounded and crushed* for our sins. *He was beaten* that we might have peace. *He was whipped*, and we were healed ... But who among the people realized that *he was dying* for their sins—that *he was suffering* their punishment ... Yet when *his life is made as an offering for sin*, he *will have a multitude of children*, many heirs ... And *because of what he has experienced, my righteous servant will make it possible* for many to be counted righteous, for *he will bear all their sins.*"[392] Peter's words will then make better sense to them: "You have been healed by his wounds."[393] As the patient comes around, the physician explains to them what happened while they were unconscious. They will then say, "Come, let us return to the Lord! *He has torn us in pieces; now he will heal us. He has injured us; now he will bandage our wounds.* In just a short time, *he will restore us* [to spiritual health] so we can live in his presence."[394]

Students of Bible prophecy are privileged observers of God's magnificent spiritual procedure. But to understand how it will transpire, we must revisit the book of Daniel which is uniquely qualified to play a role in end-time events. It consists of prophecies foretelling not only incidents and participants, but the historical order in which they occur. Interestingly enough, God told Daniel to "keep this prophecy a secret; seal up the book until the time of the end ... *for what I have said is for the time of the end.*"[395]

What Comes, Then Goes, Then Comes Again?

By now we should recognize a pattern of Hebrew history allowing us to apply the "domino effect." Perhaps we can define it as "a cumulative effect produced when *one event initiates a succession of similar events.*"[396] We have studied the unique composition of all things Israel starting with Jacob and his children; then, their Exodus from Egypt and occupation of the Promised

Land of Israel; next, the establishment of Jerusalem as their capital; finally, the building of the Temple—all of which resulted in them delivering the Jewish Rabbi Jesus Christ as the world's Messiah.[397]

JEW'S RETURN TO LAND > JERUSALEM MADE CAPITAL > TEMPLE BUILT > 1ST APPEARANCE OF MESSIAH

They, of course, did not receive Him as such, and as a result, we saw each aspect of their nation and religion collapse in reverse order like dominos. After rejecting their Messiah, the Temple was destroyed, Jerusalem fell into the hands of the Gentiles, and the Jews were removed from the land by the Romans.

MESSIAH REJECTED > TEMPLE DESTROYED > JERUSALEM DESTROYED > JEWS REMOVAL FROM LAND

Thus, it should come as no surprise that God could again reverse this cursed domino effect to prepare the way for the second appearing of their Messiah. Beginning with the awakening of the descendants of Jacob to the promises given them, the Jewish people have returned to their homeland, and Israel again is a prominent country on the world stage. Next, they regained political control over Jerusalem as their capital, and, still to come, should follow the rebuilding of their Temple and a resumption of their sacrificial system. This, of course, *is all in preparation for delivering the Messiah to the world a second time.*

JEWS RETURN TO LAND > JERUSALEM MADE CAPITAL > TEMPLE REBUILT > 2ND APPEARANCE OF MESSIAH

The following chart provides a more extensive example of this historical pattern.

The Domino Effect

1407 B.C.	1000 B.C.	827 B.C.	827 B.C.
Israel's conquest of Canaan under Joshua.	King David makes Jerusalem capital of Israel.	Solomon builds 1st Jewish Temple.	God's presence fills Temple through Shekinah Glory at dedication.

587 B.C. - 538 B.C.	586 B.C.	587 B.C.	After 622 B.C.
Jews' removal from land to Babylon.	Jerusalem destroyed by Babylonians.	Temple destroyed by Babylonians.	God's Glory departs from Temple after King Josiah's reign.

538 B.C.	457 B.C.	444 B.C. - 349	A.D. 33
Jews' reestablishment in land after Babylonian captivity.	Rebuild of Jerusalem as capital by Ezra.	Jewish 2nd Temple rebuilt by Nehemiah.	God's presence fills Temple with 1st Appearance of Messiah.

A.D. 70 - 134	A.D. 70 - 134	A.D. 70	A.D. 33
Jews' dispersed into world nations.	Jerusalem destroyed by Romans.	2nd Jewish Temple destroyed by Romans.	Rejection of Messiah. Sacrifice of Jesus Christ.

May 14, 1948	1950	Future	Malachi 3:1-4
Israel reestablishment as nation in Palestine.	Jerusalem declared capital by Israeli Knesset.	Future rebuilding of 3rd Temple.	2nd Appearance of Messiah. 2nd Coming of Jesus Christ.

Satan knows all too well it is through the Temple services that God has promised to meet with Israel to give them instruction. Why would it be surprising if he devised a plan to interfere, or intercept, such communication between the Lord and His people at the end of time? And, just what is it going to take for Israel to finally find their own faith in Jesus Christ as their long-awaited Redeemer? Whether the world realizes, or not, the issue will affect every person on earth, because it is the last domino to fall leading to the end of the world as we now know it.

The Bible calls for us to be humble. If honest, all should admit that ideas we once believed to be correct about the future have turned out to be wrong. That is especially true when it comes to Bible prophecy as it presents ever unfolding scenarios. "*Now we see things imperfectly* as in a poor mirror [before events happen], but then [when events do happen] we will see everything with perfect clarity. *All that I know now is partial and incomplete*, but then I will know everything completely."[398]

The best we can now present is a speculative idea of what is to come while lacking exact specifications of times, events, and identities of the players involved. Students of prophecy need to keep one eye on the past and the other on the future in order to understand where they are in the present. They must be willing to adapt as they watch history unfold, and change opinions accordingly without fear of adjusting their previous views.

God declares that only He can tell exactly what will happen going forward. He has asserted *His ultimate goal in allowing history to continue, and what He is waiting for to happen* so that He can usher in a world made new. "And do not forget the things I have done throughout history. For I am God—I alone! I am God, and there is no one else like me. *Only I can tell what is going to happen even before it happens.* For *I am ready to set things right, not in the distant future, but right now! I am ready to save Jerusalem and give my glory to Israel.*"[399]

In light of such a statement, any attempt, however sincere, to suggest that biblical end-time prophecies advance any other religious movement ahead of Israel should be seen for what it is—a Godless, fraudulent prediction. Regarding such soothsayers Isaiah wrote, "Do not think like everyone else does. Do not be afraid that some plan conceived behind closed doors will be the end of you [the Jewish people] ... *I and the children the Lord has given me have names that reveal the plans the Lord Almighty has for His people [Israel].* So why are you trying to find out the future by consulting mediums and psychics ... *Check their predictions against my testimony*, says the Lord. *If their predictions are different from mine, it is because there is no light or truth in them. My people [Israel] will be led away as captives ... Nevertheless, that time of darkness and despair will not go on forever ... Israel will again be great* [and here is why] *... For a child is born to us, a son is given* to us [First Advent]. *And the government [of Israel] will rest upon his shoulders* [Second Advent]. *These will be his royal titles: Wonderful Counselor, Mighty God, Everlasting Father, Prince of Peace. His ever-expanding, peaceful government will never end. He will rule forever with fairness and justice from the throne of His ancestor David. The passionate commitment of the Lord Almighty will guarantee this!*"[400]

There is simply no way around it. To suggest that Daniel would contradict Isaiah's end-time forecast that Israel will become the head of all nations, and that Christ will rule them from David's throne in Jerusalem, *is a major re-writing of Biblical prophecy.* Allowing Israel its rightful place in God's eternal plan *is the master key* that unlocks understanding of all the Hebrew prophecies, including those relating to future events yet to transpire.

God created Israel, but for what purpose? So that when God accomplishes through them what He says He will do, none of the world nations will be able to boast, but everyone will recognize it was all the Lord's doing. That is how He declares He will reveal His glory to the nations. In fact, He views and assesses these same nations through the lens of Israel. "Israel is the only nation created by a sovereign act of God ... When God established the nations of the world, He began with Israel. Israel is the center of the universe in the mind of God. [See Deuteronomy 32:8-10]"[401]

Remember, in Daniel's seventy-week prophecy the angel told him its starting point would be the "command to restore and build Jerusalem," a decree given by the Persian leader in

444 B.C.[402] Then he said the Messiah would appear in Jerusalem at the end of 69 weeks. Considering that in Bible prophecy one day equals a literal year, we calculated back in chapter 6 of this book that from the starting date to the Messiah would be 483 years, bringing us to the year A.D. 33, the year that Jesus rode the donkey into the city, thus laying claim to His Messianic title. As Messiah, He appeared so as to "put down rebellion, to bring an end to sin, to atone for guilt, to bring in everlasting righteousness, to confirm [or fulfill] the prophetic vision, and to anoint the Most Holy Place."[403] It would all have taken place had the collective Jewish people accepted Him as the "Seed" God promised to Eve in the garden, and to their father Abraham when He gave him the covenant.

What Might Have Been

Before we advance into the prophetic future, let's do a bit of *retrospective interpretation.* It means hypothesizing what could have happened in the past if the Jews had accepted Christ as their Messiah. As rumors circulated about a king being born among the Jews, it posed a political threat in King Herod's mind. As a result, he "sent soldiers to kill all the boys in and around Bethlehem who were two years old and under."[404] Jesus escaped when the angel told his parents to flee to Egypt, "because Herod *is going to try to kill the child.*"[405] Here again, Scripture pulls back the curtain, revealing to us things going on in the spiritual world. John recorded that "the dragon stood before the woman [Israel] as she was about to give birth to her child [Messiah], ready to devour the baby as soon as it was born."[406]

If the Jews had accepted Him as their king, the Roman authorities would have seen it as a challenge to their rule in Palestine. In fact, the Jewish religious leaders put political pressure on Pontius Pilate saying, "'If you release this man, you are not a friend of Caesar. *Anyone who declares himself a king is a rebel against Caesar'...* And Pilate said to the people, 'Here is your king!' 'Away with him,' they yelled. 'Away with him—crucify him!' 'What? Crucify your king?' Pilate asked, *'We have no king but Caesar,'* the leading priests shouted back."[407] "And Pilate posted a sign over him that read, *'Jesus of Nazareth, the King of the Jews ...'* Then the leading priests said to Pilate, 'Change it from *The King of the Jews'* to *'he said, I am King of the Jews.'*"[408] Amazingly, Pilate replied as if to spitefully chronicle the truth for future generations, "What I have written, I have written. *It stays exactly as it is.*"[409]

So, if the Jews had proclaimed Jesus as their king, the Romans could have convicted Him on identical crimes of subversion against their government and executed Him. Thus, He would have still offered Himself as a slain sacrifice for the sins of Israel and the world. With this all happening at the beginning of the sixty-ninth week of Daniel's 70 weeks, Israel (through Messiah's ministry) would have confirmed the prophecy well within the probationary period of 70 weeks. The Jewish people would have begun suffering persecution as supporters of the coup attempt against the Roman Empire and at that time gone through their required fires of purification. Days later, Jesus would have been resurrected, the gospel would have very quickly been preached to the Gentiles by means of miracles, and the end of the world would have taken place.[410] Though this may all sound too fantastical, consider that the disciples believed they were then living in the last days. Peter warned, "The end of the world *is coming soon.*"[411] When Jesus went to Galilee and first began His preaching, He referred to the soon expiration of the sixty-ninth week of Daniel's prophecy, the time scheduled for the Messiah to appear, by saying, *"At last the time has come ... The kingdom of God is near."*[412]

Stephen's testimony to the religious leaders equated the Messiah's mission with that of Moses who had attempted to free their forefathers from slavery in Egypt, but they repulsed him. Then he hinted at something most profound: "And *God sent back the same man [Moses] his people had previously rejected ... Moses himself told the people of Israel, 'God will raise up a Prophet like me [Messiah] from among your own people' ... But our ancestors rejected Moses ...* Then God turned away from them and gave them up to serve the sun, moon, and stars as their gods!"[413] Had they accepted Moses the first time, they could have shortened their bondage by 40 years--the interval of time between Moses' first and second appearing in Egypt.[414]

So, Stephen is hinting that in like manner this is what they could now expect from their rejection of the Messianic Deliverer. Because they had spurned Him, the Lord would give them up to their idols *for a stretch of time*, and then He would *resend their Savior to them*. The apostle Peter made a more unambiguous declaration to Israel, saying that the Lord "*will send Jesus your Messiah to you again.*"[415] Where would Peter have gotten such an idea? Was he not present when Jesus spoke to His disciples about going away? And this was well before the Christian movement even began. It was to Peter and other sons of Israel, and not to Christians, that Christ made the initial promise: "If I go and prepare a place for you, I will come again and receive you to Myself."[416] The word "again" implies that He will return to a place and a people He had previously visited. Here, in His own words, *the Messiah promises to come back to His people Israel a second time.*

God Stops the Clock

Though 69 weeks (483 literal years) of prophetic time had expired, the Jewish nation had received 70 weeks (490 actual years) to "confirm the vision," thus leaving them one prophetic week (7 literal years) to accept the Messiah. It was then the Lord did something extremely creative. He called a *"time out,"* thus stopping the ticking prophetic clock. Some theologians call it the "gap theory," because of the nearly 2,000 years between when the clock stopped in A.D. 33 until God begins it again at the end of time. Think of it as a *forbearance agreement* sometimes offered by lenders to help borrowers who are having trouble keeping up with their scheduled payments. Because lenders want to see the borrower succeed in the loan agreement, in lieu of foreclosure they will graciously halt the required payments, adding them to the balance to be paid at the end of the loan. Similarly, the Lord had mercy on Israel by providing them a period of grace that even Daniel couldn't understand in his day.[417] Surely when Israel finally arouses from its slumber, they will say, "Unless the Lord had helped me, *I would soon have died.* I cried out, 'I'm slipping!' and your unfailing love, O Lord, supported me."[418] Who in their right mind, while in their own lives rejoicing in the mercy and grace extended to them by God, would not pray for Israel's full recovery? *"O Israel,* hope in the Lord; for with the Lord there is *unfailing love and an overflowing supply of salvation.* He himself *will free Israel from every kind of sin."*[419]

It sounds somewhat incredible that God should halt prophetic time, but consider He once caused the sun to stand still for one whole day in order for Joshua's army to take revenge upon their enemies, and another time turned back the sundial 10 degrees for King Hezekiah as a sign of His might and power.[420] He is God, and He will do whatever He pleases, even with time. If He altered time out of mercy for Israel of old, is it too farfetched to believe He will do it for Israel in the more present day? Moreover, if He did not stop the prophetic clock from ticking, we have left but two alternatives. Either the Jews' probationary time ran out as scheduled, or the prophecy will never see its complete fulfillment. The Bible teaches neither of these, but instead quotes God as saying, "E*verything I plan will come to pass,* for I do whatever I wish."[421]

What the Bible does teach is that such a gap of time would correspond to the period the Jews would be missing from Jerusalem. That's why the angel told Daniel, "Go now, Daniel, for *what I have said is for the time of the end. Many will be purified, cleansed, and refined by these trials.*"[422] The pause in Israel's existence as a nation, and their present day residence in the same land, is essential to understanding the intermission in Daniel's 70-week time period. As we are about to see, the events that are to transpire in the last week, or seven years, of the prophecy *requires the Jews to be living in Jerusalem along with their restored Temple worship.* Then the stage will be set for the prophecy to resume and meet its culmination.

As explained earlier, if Israel had accepted Christ as Messiah when He appeared in A.D. 33, the 70-week period would then have been subsequently completed. Instead, by their own free will, they fulfilled that part of the prophecy which said, "the Anointed One will be killed, *appearing to have accomplished nothing.*"[423] So, by their rejection, they prolonged the prophecy instead of completing it when they had the divine opportunity. That is what Jesus meant when He said, "I wish that *even today* you would find the way of peace. But now it is too late ... you have *rejected the opportunity God offered you.*"[424] Though they would've, could've, should've, they didn't, so Paul tells us, "God has put them into a deep sleep."[425] Since their disciplinary surgery was lasting longer than the Lord intended, He applied more anesthesia. Remember, He had said, "For *I am ready to set things right, not in the distant future [as to imply He also plans to do this in the distant future], but right now! I am ready to save Jerusalem and give my glory to Israel.*"[426] Yet, the Bible has *good news* to those who are eagerly waiting for an update on the surgery. *The patient Israel is going to survive!* The Great Physician guarantees it. Though it has lasted nearly 2,000 years, they are now awakening. It is time for them to fulfill the seventieth week of Daniel's prophecy.

Referring to the time when the prophetic clock will resume, Jesus said, "No one knows the day or hour *when these things will happen*, not even the angels in heaven or the Son Himself. Only the Father knows. And since *you don't know when they will happen*, stay alert and keep watch."[427]

However, He did not leave us clueless. He instructed us to "now, *learn a lesson from the fig tree*. When its buds become tender and its leaves begin to sprout, you know without being told that summer is near. Just so, *when you see the events I've described beginning to happen, you can be sure that his [Messiah's] return is very near, right at the door*."[428] And just who is the "fig tree," we should be observing and learning from? That's right— it is Israel! The Lord said through Hosea, "*When I found Israel*, it was like finding grapes in the desert; when I saw your ancestors, *it was like seeing the early fruit on the fig tree*."[429]

The Amazing Seventieth Week

Let us now pick up with that final prophetic week, or last seven years of time left in the prophecy.[430] Once again, we are peering through that darkened glass of prophetic understanding in an attempt to elucidate what could still happen. It is a mere prophetical theory that is certainly subject to change as it plays out. While the ending of the 69 weeks brought us to the appearing of the true Christ (Messiah), the same verse introduces the future antichrist. After the prediction of the killing of the Messiah, the very next event foretold was that "a ruler [anti-Christ] will arise whose armies will destroy the city and the Temple."[431] The following verse, Daniel 9:27, describes four things that will transpire when this ruler arrives:

1. He will make a treaty with the (Jewish) people for a period of one week (seven prophetic days, or seven literal years).
2. However, after half this time (three and a half prophetic days, or three and a half literal years) he will put an end to the sacrifices and offerings.
3. Then, as a climax to all his terrible deeds, he will set up a sacrilegious object within the Jewish Temple that causes desecration
4. Until the end when judgment will be poured out upon him.

Though controversial, many Bible scholars teach anti-christ's first task will be to sign a seven-year peace covenant with the modern political state of Israel. That will restart the prophetic time clock to complete the last week or seven years of Jewish probation. The Bible suggests the Jews will agree to it, most likely to avoid possible annihilation by enemy world nations. Such an armistice will offer the Jews that which they have for so long waited—peace in their homeland to worship their God uninterrupted. Part of the treaty could be to allow the religious among them to rebuild their Temple, or some semblance of it, in order to reinstitute their sacrificial ceremonies. In other words, they make what seems to be a reasonable human attempt to switch to another physician who offers them an easy way out, with false hopes of peace and security. But God's assessment is that the new doctor will only offer "*superficial treatments* for my people's mortal wound. They give *assurances of peace when all is war.*"[432]

So again, as He has done throughout history, the Lord will intervene in His chosen people's behalf just as He did when

Balaam tried to change God's plan for Israel. Through Moses, He warned them not to make such contracts with Gentiles. "When the Lord your God brings you into the land ... *Make no treaties with them.*"[433] As Daniel pointed out, the Lord knows that even though this pseudo-savior (antichrist) will seem to be offering peace, his real intention will be to kill many.[434] The King James Version of Daniel 8:25 reads that he "*by peace shall destroy many.*" The Lord recognizes that Israel will have made *a covenant with death and hell*. So, what does He do? He tells them, "You boast that you have *struck a bargain to avoid death* and have *made a deal to dodge the grave ... I will cancel the bargain* you made to avoid death, and *I will overturn your deal* to dodge the grave."[435] This false covenant will then bring us to the mother of all wars. The remainder of Daniel 8:25 tells us that the antichrist "*will even take on the Prince of princes in battle, but will be broken*, though not by human power."[436] Here again, are the same two *princes* as highlighted in Daniel 9:26. And, of course, that first prince, the One with whom the antichrist will have audacity to wage war against, is none other than Jesus Christ the Messiah who came to His people 2,000 years ago, but was killed, appearing to have accomplished nothing.

Some ask the obvious question, why in the world would the devil knowingly engage in a battle with the Lord God Almighty? He has no other option. Similar to a chess game, God has him in *zugzwang*, meaning *any move he now makes is a bad one*, resulting in "checkmate," thus ending his game. Lifting the curtain into the spiritual realm, the book of Revelation says, "Then there was *war in heaven*. Michael and His angels under his command fought the dragon and his angels. And *the dragon lost the battle* and was forced out of heaven. This great dragon—*the ancient serpent called the Devil, or Satan*, the one deceiving the whole world—was thrown down to the earth with all his angels."[437] So, what is the devil's next move? "And when the dragon realized that he had been thrown down to the earth, *he pursued the woman* [Israel] *who had given birth to the child [Messiah]* ... Then the dragon *became angry at the woman [Israel]*, and he *declared war against the rest of her children—all who keep God's commandments and confess that they belong to Jesus.*"[438] Here we see his final campaign against the Jewish people who, through their reinstated religious ceremonies, bring the world's attention back to the God of their forefathers—the God of Abraham, Isaac, and Jacob. Because of Satan's desperation "terror will come on the earth and the sea. For the Devil has come down to you in great anger, and *he knows that he has little time.*"[439]

Which brings us to the second and third things the antichrist will do. Three and a half years into the seven-year agreement he will default by requiring the Jews to stop their sacrificial offerings, and instead set up his own sacrilegious object of worship, demanding that they honor it. Claiming his superiority to the Hebrew God, he will then begin the fiercest campaign of genocide against the Hebrew people the world has ever witnessed. In doing so, he will "defy the Most-High and wear down the holy people of the Most-High."[440] Daniel recorded this period of Judah's history when he reported that "they [the Jewish people] will be placed under his control for a time, times and half a time."[441] This last period of Jewish persecution equates with the remaining three and a half years of their probationary time.[442]

Return Of Daniel (antichrist Revealed)

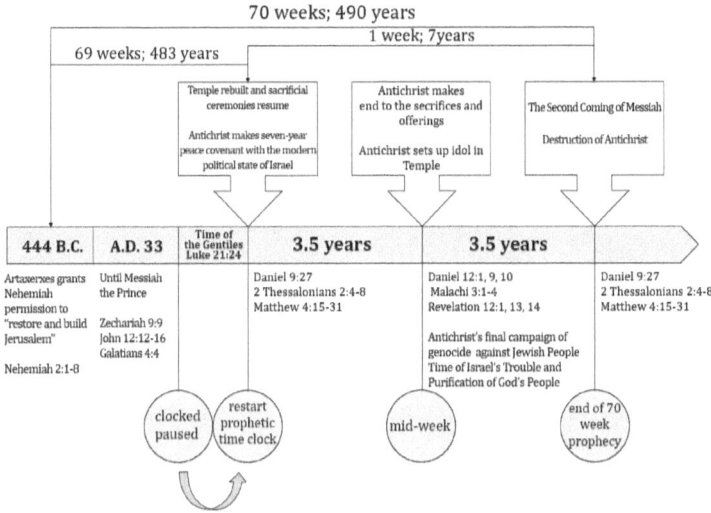

The deal Israel makes with the devil will in turn finally convince them to trust in the covenant that God made long ago with their ancestors. Contracts are only as good as are the parties involved. The contrast here could not be starker. God made His covenant with Israel thousands of years ago through Abraham. He renewed it through Isaac, and then again to Jacob, also known as Israel. Then He eternally confirmed it by sending His Messiah Messenger–Jesus Christ-- to provide the blood atonement needed for its ratification. Contrary to false witnesses today who say His word is no longer good, Daniel's prophecies demonstrate just how committed the Lord is to His people Israel—all the way to the end of the world. Yet this deceiver [Satan through the antichrist] will break his promise to Israel just three and a half years after he makes it. But Jesus told them they would trust such an imposter. Speaking to Israel's leaders He said, "For I have come to you representing my Father, and you refuse to welcome me, even though *you readily accept others who represent only themselves.*"[443] The Lord's testimony through Isaiah should forever put to rest any doubt as to whether God has kept His covenant promise to Israel, or as the spirit of antichrist suggests, canceled it. To His Messiah, the Lord said, "I have given you [Messiah] to my people [Israel] *as the personal confirmation of my covenant with them.* And you will be a light to guide all nations [Gentiles] to Me."[444]

God Purifies His People

Unfortunately, the satanic atmosphere of deceit and betrayal will extend far beyond the devil and his anti-Christian representative. It will live in the very hearts of many Israelites. The prophet Micah gave a most chilling warning to those living during this period. "Your enemies *will be right in your own household.*"[445] With the help of such self-seeking individuals turning on their own kinspeople, Zechariah predicts that when it is all over, "'*two-thirds of the people in the land will be cut off and die*', says the Lord." But *a third will be left in the land. I will bring that group through the fire and make them pure, just as gold and silver are refined and purified by fire.* They will call on my name, and I will answer them. I will say, *these are my people*, and they will say, *the Lord is our God.*'"[446] Here again is the time of Israel's trouble as described by Jeremiah. "In all history, there has never been such a time of terror. *It will be a time of trouble for my people Israel.* Yet in the end, *they will be saved.*"[447]

We now come to a critical juncture in our study. Some ask, "When the Bible speaks of Israel, how can it possibly be referring to ethnic Israel who is today returning to the land of Palestine? Only a small percentage of them practice Judaism, with even a smaller percentage considered to be orthodox."[448] We find the answer in the experience of their archetypal patriarch, Jacob. When returning to Canaan, he engaged in a struggle with God and survived.[449] It was then that he finally *went through a spiritual conversion* wherein the Lord changed his name from the carnal man Jacob to the spiritual man Israel! *This future purification facing ethnic Israel is the anti-typical realization of Jacob's transformation.* Here is the pinnacle moment for Israel which all the prophets saw and tried to describe.

Amos said, "I, the Sovereign Lord, am *watching this sinful nation of Israel*, and I will uproot it and scatter its people across the earth. Yet I have promised that *I will never completely destroy the family of Israel* ... For I have commanded that *Israel be persecuted by the other nations as grain is sifted in a sieve, yet not one true kernel will be lost* ... In that day I will restore the fallen kingdom of David."[450] David's kingdom fell some 3,000 years ago, 200 years before Amos penned his prophecy. So, what Amos is here suggesting will happen must be future as David's kingdom has yet to be restored. Once again, such a cleansing of Israel corresponds with what the angel told Daniel would happen at *"the time of the end. Many will be purified, cleansed, and refined by these trials."*[451]

Thus, unrepentant Israel will become repentant Israel. Malachi adds: "'They will be my people,' says the Lord Almighty. '*On the day when I act*, they will be my own special treasure. I will spare them as a father spares an obedient and dutiful child. *Then you will again see the difference between the righteous and the wicked, between those who serve God and those who do not.*'"[452] Isaiah declares, "'Comfort, comfort my people,' says your God. 'Speak tenderly to Jerusalem. Tell her that her sad days are gone and that *her sins are pardoned.* Yes, *the Lord has punished her in full for all her sins.*'"[453]

It synchronizes with our fourth point of Daniel 9:27—the Judgment. "As I watched, this horn [antichrist] was *waging war against the holy people [Jews] and was defeating them*, until the Ancient One [the God of Abraham] came *and judged in favor of the holy people* [Jews] of the Most-High. Then *the time arrived for the holy people [Jews] to take over the kingdom.*"[454] "At that time Michael, the archangel who stands guard over your nation [Daniel's nation is Israel], will rise. Then *there will be a time of anguish greater than any since nations first came into existence*. But at that time every one of your [Daniel's] people whose name is written in the book will be rescued."[455] This troublesome event will usher in the second appearance of Israel's Messiah—the second coming of Christ—who will then pour out judgment on the final antichrist. *What began as a surgical procedure to save life will actually result in the deliverance of the offspring promised to Eve--and Abraham!* Just as Israel was pregnant and passed through birth pangs of persecution to deliver the Messiah at His first coming, so too will it pass through a painful ordeal to give birth to His second coming.[456] Daniel's revelations will thus realize their prophetic intent, and Christ will establish and begin His earthly reign.

Some scoff at such an interpretation of Daniel's prophecy, claiming it too literalistic to be true. They say the seventieth week is past and cannot be associated with any future events. But, quoting Daniel himself, Jesus places the appearance of antichrist, an event scheduled to take place within the time frame of the seventieth week, *just prior to His second return*. "*The time will come when you will see what Daniel the prophet spoke about: the sacrilegious object that causes desecration standing in the Holy Place*—reader, pay attention ... *For that will be a time of greater horror than anything the world has ever seen or will ever see again*. In fact, unless that time of calamity is shortened, the entire human race will be destroyed. But it will be shortened for the sake of God's chosen ones ... And then, at last, *the sign of the coming of the Son of Man will appear in the heavens*, and there will be deep mourning among all the nations of the earth. And *they will see the Son of Man arrive on the clouds of heaven with power and great glory.* And he will send forth his angels with the sound of a mighty trumpet blast, and they will gather together his chosen ones from the farthest ends of the earth and heaven."[457] Obviously, such an event has yet to happen, which makes a strong case that the seventieth week is still future.

CHAPTER 11
RETURN OF ELIJAH (FINAL CALLING OF GOD'S FAMILY)

Our previous chapter identified the destructive deeds of the antichrist who is yet to come. But what about his identity? There probably exist more opinions in the world about exactly who the antichrist is, or will be, than there are applicants for the job. The Bible doesn't come right out with an identification but instead says we will have to wait for his revealing. Paul wrote, "For that day [the Day of the Lord] will not come until there is a great rebellion against God and *the man of lawlessness is revealed*—the one who brings destruction. He will exalt himself and defy every god there is and tear down every object of worship. *He will even sit in the temple of god,* claiming that he himself is God … And you know what

165

is holding him back, for *he can be revealed only when his time comes*. For this lawlessness is already *at work secretly*, and it *will remain secret until the One who is holding it back steps out of the way*. Then *the man of lawlessness will be revealed*, but the Lord Jesus will kill him with the breath of his mouth and destroy him by the splendor of his coming."[458]

Notice that Paul identifies him by what he will do, not by who he is. Only those who love the truth will receive spiritual discernment to recognize his works of darkness. For those who know Jewish history his desecration of their Temple coupled with intense persecution of the Jewish people should have a ring of familiarity. Earlier we learned, "*Whatever exists today and whatever will exist in the future has already existed in the past. For God calls each event back in its turn.*"[459]

An Old Testament Antichrist

The book of Daniel offers yet another important clue from the past regarding the future and final antichrist. It appears in a vision found in Daniel 8 that took place after the Jews returned from Babylon and rebuilt their Temple. In it, Daniel saw an antisemitic figure who in time would politically control the Mediterranean area, including Jerusalem. One of the rulers of the Greek Seleucid Empire (312-63 B.C.), was Antiochus IV Epiphanes (175-164 B.C.). Bible historians recognize him as "*the Antichrist of the Old Testament*," and a foreshadowing of the New Testament antichrist who will follow after him.[460] Just as there were many individual "types" of Christ prior to His coming--Noah, Moses, Joshua, and David to name a few--there were also "types" of the false Christ. The apostle John said it best: "You have heard that the Antichrist is coming, and already many such antichrists have appeared."[461] Antiochus IV was merely one of the prototypes of the supreme antichrist who shall appear on the world stage at the end of the age. By studying his story, we can better anticipate what the last one will do.

In June 164 B.C. Antiochus IV *came to Jerusalem under a guised mission of a peace covenant* but afterward turned on the Jews, persecuting them. After seizing control of the Jewish Temple, he forbade the priests to perform the evening and morning sacrifices at the Lord's altar. *He then passed laws stopping the Jews from practicing their religious traditions such as Sabbath-keeping, reading the Scriptures, and dietary requirements.* Babies found to be circumcised were thrown from the city walls along with their mothers. Anyone not willing to comply either faced death or exile into slavery. First Maccabees 1:62-63 gives an account of the determination that some Jews had about staying true to the covenant of their fathers: "Many in Israel stood firm and were resolved in their hearts not to eat unclean food. They chose to die rather than to be defiled by food or to profane the holy covenant; and they did die."

During the struggle an estimated 80,000 Jews perished and another 40,000 were sold into slavery. Antiochus then had a statue of the Greek god Zeus set up in the holy Sanctuary along with an altar upon which he ordered Jewish priests to sacrifice swine (an animal considered unclean by Hebrew law). The angel told Daniel this desecration of the Temple would last a period of time equal to 2,300 evenings and mornings. Since there was a sacrifice every evening and morning it required 1,150 literal days to make 2,300 sacrifices. According to Jewish reckoning of a year containing 360 days, it meant Antiochus's idolatry would continue for more than three *years,* which is what happened.[462]

Many Jews refused to follow Antiochus's orders and escaped from Jerusalem into the wilderness where they formed a resistance army. Prominent among them was the Maccabean family. They returned with an estimated 7,000 fighters under the leadership of Judas Maccabee and recaptured Jerusalem along with its Temple grounds. On December 25, 164 B.C., they restored the Temple service to its "rightful place," just as Daniel's prophecy had indicated.[463] It was then discovered that they had only enough oil for the Temple menorah for one day as it required a certain quality of oil prescribed by Levitical law. Miraculously, the lampstand continued to burn for an additional seven days while they waited the preparation of the new oil. Thus, began the Jewish yearly winter celebration called the "festival of lights," or the "feast of dedication," better known as "Hanukkah." It still continues today as "an eight-day Jewish holiday beginning on the 25th of Kislev and commemorating the rededication of the Temple of Jerusalem after its defilement by Antiochus of Syria."[464] Many Christians are surprised to discover the festival closer to their own faith than they realize. John 10:22 states, *"It was now winter, and Jesus was in Jerusalem at the time of Hanukkah."*[465] No doubt He and His disciples joined in the joyous celebration of their ancestors' deliverance some 200 years earlier.[466]

The Coming King of Hell

If one wonders what life may be like in those days of antichrist future, a little use of the imagination might help. Visualize what the world would be like if Adolf Hitler had won World War II. He was also a "type" of antichrist backed by a system of government with the same evil spirit. Mostly noted for his campaign of annihilation against the Jews, he targeted Gentile groups as well, in particular, the Poles, and even killed fellow Germans who resisted his plans.[467]

Thus, it will be with the coming King of Hell who will be but a figurehead of a larger world system of government identified in the Bible as the "beast."[468] This last government will have world authority over all things political, religious, social, and economic. Revelation 13 lists what the antichrist/beast power will do once it gains its desired position:

1. He will "speak great blasphemies against God" (verse 5).
2. He will "wage war against God's holy people [the Jews] and overcome them" (verse 7).
3. He will be "given authority to rule over every tribe and people and language and nation" (verse 7).
4. He will cause "all the people who belong to this world to worship the beast" (verse 8).
5. He will have those who resist "destined for prison to be arrested and taken away," while "those destined for death will be killed," but it will be their "opportunity to have endurance and faith" (verse 10).
6. He will do "astonishing miracles, such as making fire flash down to earth from heaven while everyone was watching" (verse 13).
7. He will "deceive all the people who belong to this world" (verse 14).
8. He will "order the people of the world to make a great statue," and "command that anyone refusing to worship it must die" (verses 14, 15).
9. He will "require everyone—great and small, rich and poor, slave and free—to be given a mark on the right hand or on the forehead. And no one could buy or sell anything without that mark" (verses 16, 17).

The most intriguing part is just how long his system of government will have sway over the earth's inhabitants. "And he was given authority to do what he wanted for forty-two months."[469] Once again, 42 months equals three and a half years. It coincides with the period of time Antiochus reigned down terror on Jerusalem's inhabitants, thus serving as a model to the second half of Daniel's seventieth week when the archfiend, along with his religiopolitical system, breaks his covenant with the Jews and begins to persecute them. Once these end-time world leaders accomplish what they have for so long hoped to do, but haven't been able to because of the Lord's restraint, they will spare none that dare defy their scheme. But this momentous time in earth's history *will arrive according to God's schedule*, not theirs. "For *He has set a day* for judging the world with justice by the man He has appointed [His Messiah]."[470] After their three and half years of self-glory and political triumph, their destruction will quickly ensue.[471] God's appointed hour of judgment will arrive, and it will then be lights out for the world as we know it!

The World's Last Warning

But these things will not transpire without ample warning. *Enter, again, Elijah*! Remember that God raised him up in the days when King Ahab and Jezebel ruled Israel. The union between one of God's chosen (Ahab) and an idolatrous, pagan princess (Jezebel) represents the unholy covenant the Jews will make with antichrist and his corrupt system of political, religious, and economic forces. Political leaders in Israel will forge an illegitimate contract with a Gentile-contrived coalition of political and religious factions promoting world peace and unity. Jesus said the plan will be so craftily designed that "if possible, the very elect would be deceived."[472]

It will open the gate for demons to flood the world. What will happen at the end of time will echo Elijah's confrontation with Ahab and Jezebel. In that same spirit, some, even in the face of economic sanctions and social penalties, including the threat of death, will intervene and unmask this great deception. They will know the true God of Israel, and their actions will be prompted by their understanding.

Not much new exists under the sun. Everything that will take place in the future has a blueprint in the past. Controlling the world through economic sanctions and political strength is one of the oldest and strongest desires of the unregenerate heart. Financial wealth and the inherent political power it can obtain is a most overwhelming lure. Many spend their entire lives pursuing such false security all the while knowing it is not a permanent defense against real, eternal loss. *Here is the secret of the saints.* They take to heart the true definition of wealth that Paul told his young counterpart, Timothy, "*True religion with contentment is great wealth.* After all, we didn't bring anything with us when we came into the world, and we certainly cannot carry anything with us when we die. So if we have enough food and clothing, *let us be content.* But *people who long to be rich fall into temptation* and are trapped by many foolish and harmful desires that plunge them into ruin and destruction. For the love of money is at the root of all kinds of evil. And some people, craving money, have wandered from the faith and pierced themselves with many sorrows."[473]

Just as Elijah was satisfied with sleeping in the wilderness, relying on God to send food by birds and drinking water from a stream, so, too, modern-day Elijah(s) will be content with little. What the world will be offering them is not what they are here for. They cannot be bought, nor will they sell their souls for a temporary seat at Jezebel's table.

Another thing we can know for certain is that Elijah always precedes the Lord's appearing. That day at Mount Carmel, after Elijah had given his warning, "a little cloud about the size of a hand rising from the sea" represented the coming of the

Lord."[474] The cloud brought badly needed rain, thus ending Israel's three *and half years* drought.[475] Concerning the second coming of Jesus Christ, John the Revelator said, "Look! He comes with the clouds of heaven. And everyone will see him."[476] His arrival will end Israel's, and the world's, three and half years of spiritual famine caused by a drought of people lacking true biblical knowledge. "'The time is surely coming,' says the Sovereign Lord, 'when I will send a famine in the land—not a famine of bread or water *but of hearing the words of the Lord*. People will stagger everywhere from sea to sea, searching for the word of the Lord, running here and going there, *but they will not find it*.'"[477] Yet there will be a people living who have a true knowledge of God. While others sought luxury and self-indulgence here on earth, they fed themselves upon the Word of God. Their instruction reads, "you must be patient as you wait for the Lord's return. Consider the farmers *who eagerly look for the rains* in the fall and in the spring. They patiently wait for the precious harvest to ripen. You, too, must be patient. And take courage, for the coming of the Lord is near."[478]

Every passing day makes the spiritual famine more obvious. Preachers are in great abundance but many "are like clouds blowing over dry land *without giving rain*, promising much but producing nothing."[479] They promise much by way of earthly gain in an attempt to increase their following of people who give them money, but do little to prepare them for the coming kingdom. Peter warned about such individuals, declaring, "In their greed *they will make up clever lies to get hold of your money*. But God condemned them long ago, and their destruction is on the way."[480] Would it be shocking to learn that many such shysters are involved in what they call "the Lord's work"? When some do preach the real truth of God's Word, many listeners ask, "Why do we not hear more of this from the pulpit?"

It is such a sad commentary on the superfluous nature of many religious services. Though there be much singing, praising, dancing, prayer, and the doing of good deeds, we hear little mention about God's plan to someday reveal Himself to the world through the hardship He is going to allow to be brought upon His covenantal people. The Bible is crystal clear—the true Israel in these last days will suffer just as their Messiah did.

Today many ignore Jesus' Jewish background. Instead a *Christian version of Christ who is separated from His Hebrew heritage* has been popularized. It offers an ideological view of Jesus that doesn't conform to the Bible's description of Him. Being ignorant of His Hebrew identity, those who thus twist the scriptures do so as they attempt to chart God's future course of end-time events by their own imagination rather than relying on what the Bible outlines. Idolatry did not die with the Old Testament but has become more sophisticated in order to thrive in modern times. Only by a careful search of the entire story, as outlined in both Old and New Testaments, can we detect it. Jesus said, "You search the Scriptures because you believe they give you eternal life. But the Scriptures point to me! Yet you refuse to come to me so that I can give you this eternal life."[481] And here is why we want to create our own version of Jesus: "For I have come to you representing my Father, and you refuse to welcome me, even though you readily accept others who represent only themselves. No wonder you can't believe! For you gladly honor each other, but you don't care about the honor that comes from God alone."[482]

The message of Elijah always negates sin's power within human hearts. It will again bring healing between God and humanity, even unifying the hearts of parents and estranged children. "And *he will persuade many Israelites to turn to the Lord their God.* He will be a man with the spirit and power of Elijah, the prophet of old. *He will precede the coming of the Lord, preparing the people for His arrival. He will turn the hearts of the fathers to their children, and he will change disobedient minds to accept godly wisdom.*"[483] Just as Jacob underwent his transformation from a deceiver to an upright man in God's sight, so, too, will those being purified at the end of time experience similar conversions.

The Old Testament (covenant) closed with a promise of a New Covenant (testament) that was coming to Israel. It was their Messiah. His introduction to the Jewish people would be entrusted to none other than another Elijah spirit. Malachi, the last book of the Old Testament, records, "Look! I am sending my messenger, and *he will prepare the way before Me.*"[484] Just whom was Malachi referring to?

One day the disciples asked Jesus, "'Why do the teachers of religious law insist that Elijah must return before the Messiah comes?' Jesus replied, 'Elijah is indeed coming first to set everything in order. But I tell you, *he has already come, but wasn't recognized*, and he was badly mistreated. And soon the Son of Man will also suffer at their hands.' Then the disciples realized *he had been speaking of John the Baptist.*"[485] Again, the Lord, knowing that corrupt Jewish leadership would conspire and plot with the Roman authorities to oppose the Messiah, sent prior warning to the people as to what would happen. John not only identified the Messiah but also pointed out the sinful behavior of those holding political power at the time. His faithful testimony concerning what was right in life resulted in the loss of his head.[486] Being faithful in explaining God's plan often has negative consequences in this life, but will be compensated for in the world to come.

Just as the spirit of Elijah preceded Christ's first advent, so, too, will it pave the way for His second. "The day of judgment is coming, burning like a furnace. The arrogant and wicked will be burned up like straw on that day ... Look, *I am sending you the prophet Elijah before the great and dreadful day of the Lord arrives.*"[487] People offer differing opinions as to who this Elijah will be. Some guess it will be Elijah himself come down from heaven. Some teach it will be another individual like John the Baptist whom the Lord will commission. And others predict it will be a larger group of people, like the 7,000 God told Elijah hadn't given in to Jezebel's threats. One thing is certain, this end-time force will possess an equal passion, or spirit, to that Elijah had for the Lord's honor. As in the case with the antichrist, the world will probably have to wait for its identification(s), but there will be no mistaking the essence of the message. It will be a calling of all peoples, Jew and Gentile alike, from all nations back to the God of Abraham, Isaac, and Jacob. And it will be the ringing of the dinner bell for all of Abraham's children to join the family reunion during which they will no doubt tell their wonderful stories of how the Lord redeemed them from the corruptness of their personal worlds of sin.[488]

God's Way, or Humanity's Way

If anyone rejects the biblical premise of God's faithfulness regarding His calling of the Hebrew people, then the Bible teaches they will be out of step with the last-day expression of Elijah's spirit. Consider Paul's admonishment to the believers at Rome: "I ask, then, *has God rejected His people, the Jews? Of course not! ... No, God has not rejected His own people, whom He chose from the very beginning.* Do you remember what the Scriptures say about this? *Elijah the prophet complained to God about the people of Israel* and said, 'Lord, they have killed your prophets and torn down your altars. I alone am left, and now they are trying to kill me, too.' And do you remember God's reply? He said, 'You are not the only one left. I have seven thousand others who have never bowed down to Baal.' *It is the same today, for not all the Jews have turned away from God.* A few [translated "remnant"] are being saved as a result of God's kindness in choosing them."[489] No doubt Paul referred here to the same remnant spoken of in Revelation 12:17 whom the devil attacks at the end of Daniel's prophetic seventieth week.

As we have discussed at length in this book, God has His purpose in bringing His Jewish people back to the land of Israel. The devil seeks to hijack those intentions. But like the Maccabeans in their day and John the Baptist in his, the Lord will raise up a resistance force to meet the challenge. They will have the same spirit of Elijah, because they understand that God is eternally committed to staying true to the promises made with His covenant people whom He is working through, and they fear God more than the devil or human beings! That is the real source of their strength. Of them, the Bible states, "And they have defeated him [the devil] *because of the blood* [covenant] of the Lamb and because of their testimony. And *they were not afraid to die.*"[490]

The world order at the time will surely present itself in a way that will appeal to common sense. It might be in the context of saving the planet from a greater threat, a ruse from an old playbook that "the *urge to save* humanity is almost always *a false front* for the *urge to rule*. Power is what all messiahs really seek: not the chance to serve. This is (can be) true even of the pious brethren who carry the gospel to foreign parts."[491] No doubt it will have a religious component as it demands from the world its worship. Though it might at first appeal to the multitudes, a biblical rule will sort it all out, unmasking its real intention: "The one who states his case first seems right *until the other comes and examines him.*"[492] Again from Proverbs, "There is a path before each person that seems right, but it ends in death."[493]

When Elijah arrives, he will show that to conquer or convert the world through a human organization is the way of the Babylonians, Persians, Greeks, and Romans. What individuals would never attempt to do on their own, they often accomplish through committees. Once adopted, the mission then becomes the all-in-all, and nothing is more sacred than its completion, even though it must ruin many lives in the process. The end always seems to justify the means. But God says, "It is not by force, nor by strength, but by my Spirit, says the Lord Almighty."[494] Self-seeking human beings aiming for the stars always end up in the dust. Whereas Abraham's children, who follow his example by seeking a more unpretentious pathway, will turn out to be the unnumbered stars that the Lord promised to their patriarchal father. Herein is revealed the dichotomy of motives between the truly repentant and those who refuse God's way. Do we trust the scheming of some worldly religious or political organization made up of faulty humans to determine the future? Or, do we sincerely seek out how God has told us it will unfold, and then prayerfully try to cooperate with His program? Proverbs 3:6 urges us to "trust in the Lord with all your heart; *do not depend on your own understanding. Seek his will in all you do,* and he will direct your paths."

The world is weary of endless wars and the bloodshed they bring. And for what? So that a few can satisfy their fallen natures by ruling over many? It reminds one of the 1980's song, *Everybody Wants to Rule the World*.[495] But when this thing is over, the one who gets to rule this planet for eternity will be the One who made it to begin with! While powers that now be (whoever they are) are busy devising strategies for world domination, God drew up His plan way back in eternity past. When the two strategies finally collide, it will be a concluding battle between the spirit of antichrist versus the spirit of Elijah. It will divide the whole world into two camps. One will promote a system of worship handed down through the ages from old Babylon that exalts the creature. That is why the Bible identifies it by the number of a man, 666, and warns us that it is not a plan designed by God.[496] The latter will challenge this assertion by introducing a descendant of Abraham and David, who is Himself the Creator of heaven and earth.[497] The spirit of Elijah will make a passionate plea to the world's inhabitants to abandon their false ideas of religion and do as Abraham did by trusting and following the same God he did.[498] One thing is certain--God's end-time witnesses will have both time and truth on their side as the passing of time always makes truth more apparent.

Everyone will have to make a decision. There will be no more sitting on the fence. As God's probationary period of 70 prophetic weeks for the Jewish people expires, so will the world's trial conclude. The plan He revealed to Daniel will be finalized. The ultimate choice will be between God's promise of redemption through the blood of Christ, and an offering of humanistic salvation from Satan. Each side will consist of both Jews and Gentiles—some who have been baptized in the New Covenant blood of Christ, and others who have completely and irrevocably conformed to the world.

Just as the entire earth's inhabitants in Noah's day made an eternal decision, so, too, will the world then find itself required to take a final stand as it hears the spirit of Elijah once again pray, "O Lord, *God of Abraham, Isaac, and Jacob, prove today that you are the God of Israel* and that I [we] are your servant[s]."[499]

CHAPTER 12
RETURN OF DAVID (SECOND ADVENT OF MESSIAH)

Most everyone is familiar with the type of children's puzzle called *Connect the Dots* whereby drawing lines from dot to dot creates a picture previously unseen. As we approach the end of our Bible story, it might be useful to connect some of the dots we have encountered regarding the genealogy of the Messiah:

- Messiah was promised as the offspring of Adam and Eve (Genesis 3:15).
- Messiah was promised as the offspring of Abraham and Sarah (Genesis 12:1-3; 15:4; 17:15-19).
- Messiah was promised as the offspring of Isaac and Rebekah (Genesis 25:23; 26:3-5).

- Messiah was promised as the offspring of Jacob/Israel (Genesis 28:13-15; Revelation 12).
- Messiah was promised as the offspring of Judah as eternal Ruler (Genesis 49:10; Isaiah 9:6, 7).
- Messiah was promised as the offspring of David as eternal Ruler (2 Samuel 7; Isaiah 9:6, 7).
- Messiah was promised as the offspring of Mary, the mother of Jesus, as eternal Ruler (Luke 1:29-35).
- Messiah is promised to return to earth a second time as a descendant of Abraham, Judah, and David to rule the families of the earth for eternity (Revelation 19:11-16; 22:16).

Though Messiah will one day reign as king over all nations, He is best known as the "God of Israel," and "Israel's King, and Redeemer."[500] He has redeemed Israel (by His atoning death at His first coming), and will thereby be glorified through Israel (at His second coming).[501] John F. Walvoord, commenting on the relationship between Israel and the second coming of its Messiah, states, "The second coming of Christ *has a most important relation to Israel as a nation.* At this coming of Christ, *Israel is delivered* from her enemies and persecutions *which characterized the time of Jacob's trouble* which just precede the second advent. It also is the time in which *Israel is brought into the millennial reign*, which is a time of deliverance, glory, and blessing for the nation Israel. This deliverance is indicated in many passages such as Joel 2, Matthew 24-25, Romans 11:26, and Revelation 19:17-21. Zechariah 14:1-3 indicates that *Jerusalem itself* in the midst of military conflict *will be rescued* by the return of the Lord."[502]

King of Kings

"David … knew God had promised with an oath that one of David's own descendants would sit on David's throne as the Messiah."[503] But on what basis did he understand how the promise would be fulfilled? He recognized himself to be a sinner, and that many of his descendants would also disobey the Lord, thereby disqualifying themselves to rule. Yet he also knew by divine promise that one Child from his bloodline would remain steadfast in His obedience to God—the Messiah! So, the promise to David could fail only if the Messiah King did.

Like his fellow human beings, David fell short of God's expectations and received punishment for his transgressions, yet it could never cancel God's promise to him. That would be an impossibility! The Lord clearly laid this out in the Psalms of Ethan the Ezrahite: *"I have found my servant David … I will make him my firstborn son, the mightiest king on earth … my covenant with him will never end. I will preserve an heir for him; his throne will be as endless as the days of heaven.* But if his sons forsake my law … and fail to keep my commands, then I will punish their sin with the rod, and their disobedience with beating. But I will never stop loving him, nor let my promise to him fail. No, I will not break my covenant; I will not take back a single word I said. I have sworn an oath to David, and in my holiness, I cannot lie: His dynasty will go on forever; his throne is as secure as the sun, as eternal as the moon, my faithful witness in the sky."[504]

The Davidic covenant, like that passed down to Israel through Abraham, ultimately rested on the obedience of the Messiah. Paul testified on behalf of Him, saying, "And, in human form, *he obediently humbled himself* even further by dying a criminal's death on a cross. Because of this, God raised him up to the heights of heaven and gave him a name that is above every other name, so that at the name of Jesus every knee will bow, in heaven and on earth and under the earth, and every tongue will confess that Jesus Christ is Lord, to the glory of God the Father."[505] To declare God's covenant promises to Israel through Abraham and David as no longer valid because their offspring were disobedient is to dismiss the obedience of Israel's favorite Son. He is indeed "the [only] hope of Israel."[506]

He came as a human being, was crucified, resurrected, and then ascended to the right hand of His Father's throne in heaven. "But our High Priest offered himself to God as one sacrifice for sins, good for all time. Then he sat down at the place of highest honor at God's right hand. There he waits until his enemies are humbled as a footstool under his feet."[507] Who else but He can say, "Heaven is my throne and the earth, is my footstool?"[508] Does any other human being dare claim the power, or right, to govern the earth? If so, then we need to closely scrutinize their credentials. Psalms 62:11 states, "God has spoken plainly, and I have heard it many times: *Power, O God, belongs to you.*" All political and religious organizations around the world would do well to remember this verse. If they have any political sway at all, it is only because God has allowed it. Never should a human organization seek to use it in a way as to usurp God of His authority to rule the peoples of the earth.

God chose David just as He did Abram, by His divine knowledge, prerogative, and sovereignty. Speaking of him, the Lord declares, "I have installed my King on Zion, my holy mountain."[509] Perhaps we can better understand the future role of David's office through the experience of Hosea and his adulterous wife Gomer. "Then the Lord said to me, 'Go and get your wife again. Bring her back to you and love her, even though she loves adultery. For *the Lord still loves Israel even though the people have turned to other gods*, offering them choice gifts.' *So, I bought her back* ... and said to her, 'You must live in my house for many days and stop your prostitution. During this time, you will not have sexual intercourse with anyone, not even with me.' *This illustrates that Israel will be a long time without a king or prince, and without sacrifices, temple, priests, or even idols. But afterward the people will return to the Lord their God and to David's descendant, their king.* They will come trembling in awe to the Lord, and *they will receive his good gifts in the last days.*"[510]

Just as Jacob is an Old Testament type of modern Israel returning to the Promised Land, so David is an exemplar of Christ returning to earth as "King of kings."[511] At the time of Jesus' birth, the Wisemen arriving in Jerusalem inquired, "Where is the newborn *King of the Jews*? We have seen his star as it arose, and we have come to worship him."[512] It has rightly been said, "Today, wise men still seek Him." As a result of Christ's interview with Nathaniel, the latter said, "Teacher, you are the Son of God—*the King of Israel.*"[513] For Jesus, from this point on it was full-blown kingdom ministry! He "traveled throughout Galilee teaching in the synagogues, *preaching everywhere the Good News about the kingdom.*"[514] Constantly He presented parables about the kingdom, trying to help people with only temporal sight to see spiritual realities. Some did, others did not.

When He stood on trial before the Jewish council, the high priest asked, "'Are you the Messiah [King of Israel], the Son of the blessed God?' Jesus said, 'I am, and you will see me, the Son of Man, sitting at God's right hand in the place of power *and coming back on the clouds of heaven.*'"[515] As Jesus made His triumphant entry into Jerusalem, many in the crowd shouted, "'Bless the *coming kingdom of our ancestor David,*' fulfilling the prophecy '*Hail to the King of Israel! Don't be afraid, people of*

Israel. Look, your King is coming sitting on a donkey's colt.'"[516] The next time He enters the eternal city He will ascend to David's eternal throne, and the true Israel will enter into eternal life through Him.[517]

The apostle Paul made Christ's hereditary connection to David a centerpiece to the gospel when writing, "Never forget that Jesus Christ was a man *born into King David's family* and that He was raised from the dead. *This is the good news I preach.*"[518] The history of David's past earthly kingdom serves as a framework for God's future earthly government that will last forever. If there be any who think God wavers regarding what this kingdom is, where this kingdom is, when this kingdom will arrive, or who its King will be, let them rest assured it was all settled way back in eternity past. To dismiss David's factual calling to God's eternal throne is to dismiss the legitimacy of Christ's coming kingdom!

The Triangular Kingdom

Jacob gave way to Israel; David to the Messiah; and the earthly Jerusalem will someday yield to a New Jerusalem. Inseparably intertwined, they are the dots that when connected show us the grander picture of what the Bible is attempting to portray. Any attempt to advance God's cause on earth must not--will not--ignore this fact. Just as God chose a people and a city, He also chose a king. To say it is anything different is to change what the Bible declares. These three aspects serve as the foundation for the book of Revelation.[519] Regarding that book of the Bible we are warned, "And if anyone adds anything to what is written here, God will add to that person the plagues described in this book. If anyone removes any of the words of this prophetic book, God will remove that person's share in the tree of life and in the holy city that are described in this book."[520]

Satan continually develops narratives and strategies designed to counterfeit or counteract the trinity that makes up the earthly kingdom of God—Israel, Jerusalem, and Messiah David. But should we expect anything less from him? After all, he lies, distorts, bribes, and if necessary, persecutes. Always, he seeks to curse whatever God chooses to bless. We saw this when he prompted Balaam to seek worldly gain from King Balaak in exchange for placing a curse on God's chosen people. In recounting the incident to his people, Moses later wrote, "But *the Lord your God would not listen to Balaam. He turned the intended curse into a blessing because the Lord your God loves you.*"[521] After multiple attempts to change God's mind, Balaam told the king that God had made a covenant with His people, beginning with Abraham, and He would never go back on His word. He said that the Lord, unlike humans, does not lie and does not change His mind. Whatever He has said that He will do, *He will do it!*[522]

Eschatology is a major theme of both Old and New Testaments and a favorite topic of conversation and study among some Christian believers. But here is a question that we must ask ourselves: If God foretold the Jewish people would be removed from Palestine (which happened); would later be regathered to that land prior to Christ's return (which, too, happened), and would reclaim the city of Jerusalem (which also happened), then why would any Christian have a problem acknowledging it as a fulfillment of that covenant promise? And if it is not God's doing, then whose? Satan's? Or just coincidence?

The writer of the book of Hebrews elaborated on this very point: "There was God's promise to Abraham. Since there was no greater one to swear by, God took an oath in his own name, saying: 'I will certainly bless you richly, and I will multiply your descendants into countless millions ...' When people take an oath, they call on someone greater than themselves to hold them to it. God also bound Himself with an oath, so *that those who received the promise could be perfectly sure that he would never change his mind.* So God has given us both his *promise and His oath. These two things are unchangeable because it is impossible for God to lie.* Therefore, we who have fled to him for refuge can take new courage, for *we can hold on to his promise with confidence."*[523]

Again, the issue of God's eternal commitment to those He has handpicked raises the question of His integrity and trustfulness. When God made that covenant with the Hebrews, was He in it for the eternal long haul, or did He somewhere along the way change His mind as Satan suggests through some of today's religious teachings? Scripture faithfully records: "I am the Lord, and *I do not change.* That is why you descendants of Jacob *are not already completely destroyed. Ever since the days of your ancestors*, you have scorned my laws and failed to obey them. Now return to me, and *I will return to you,* says the Lord Almighty."[524] The Lord is way more longsuffering than we humans can comprehend. The long saga of the Hebrew people is not yet over as is evidenced by future references to them in the book of Revelation. Once again, it only goes to prove that if God remains faithful to the promise made to them, then we Gentile converts can with greater assurance believe the promises He has made to us are equally trustworthy, even though we too fall short of His calling. After all, He also had us in mind way back when He made the initial promise to father Abraham, because He loves us no less than He loved him. "God does not show favoritism."[525]

To those who think developments in Israel and Jerusalem during past 70 plus years have no relationship to our discussion, let us just say that nothing concerning Jerusalem escapes God's watchful eye. He is laying His trap for the nations of the earth, and Jerusalem is His bait of choice. "As for you, O Jerusalem, the citadel of God's people, *your royal might and power will come back to you again. The kingship will be restored to my precious Jerusalem ... True, many nations have gathered against you, calling for your blood*, eager to gloat over your destruction. But *they do not know the Lord's thoughts or understand his plan.* These nations don't know that *he is gathering them together to be beaten and trampled like bundles of grain on a threshing floor.*"[526] "As God has said, so shall it be, 'For *my plan is to destroy all the nations that come against Jerusalem.*'"[527] The last-day judgment will occur near the very location of the threshing floor the Lord had David purchase. It is where and when He will separate the good grain from the chaff, the sheep from the goats, good from evil.[528]

Jerusalem will become the most important city in the world, not just to Jews, but redeemed Gentiles as well. "On the holy mountain stands *the city founded by the Lord. He loves the city of Jerusalem more than any other city in Israel.* O city of God, what glorious things are said of you ... And it will be said of Jerusalem, Everyone has become a citizen here. And *the Most High will personally bless this city. When the Lord registers the [Gentile] nations, he will say, 'This one has become a citizen of Jerusalem.'* At all the festivals, the people will sing, '*The source of my life [the Messiah] is in Jerusalem!*'"[529]

The serious Bible student cannot ignore the certainty that Christ will return a second time to Jerusalem as a member of David's royal bloodline to restore His throne. He will keep His new covenant promise with the "House of Judah and Israel" and bring earth its judgment by subjugating the political nations of our world for a period of 1,000 years.[530]

Spiritual Israel Follows Ethnic Israel

"Hogwash!" some say. We cannot take such prophecies literally. Well, if the events predicted for His first coming had literal fulfillments, would those connected with the Second Advent be any different? Take Zechariah, for example. If we believe his statement, "Rejoice greatly, O people of Zion! Shout in triumph, O people of Jerusalem! Look, your king is coming to you. He is righteous and victorious, yet he is humble, riding on a donkey—even on a donkey's colt" was bona fide, then why not accept this ordinary explanation in the same text: *"I will strengthen Judah and save Israel, I will reestablish them because I love them. It will be as though I never rejected them."*[531]

We have all heard the saying, "out of sight, out of mind." Because the Hebrew people have been absent for so long from the land of Israel, it can be a startling concept to think everything the Bible foretold so long ago concerning them can actually be true. Many believers are now waking up to the fact that a restored Hebrew people in Jerusalem is no longer an abstract idea taught in Bible class. No, it is now a reality, just as the Bible predicted it would be. It is the same with David's soon-coming kingdom. The world mistakenly wrote off the nation of Israel, it's capital city of Jerusalem, and David their king as a matter of historical record, never suspecting that they would all three emerge again from antiquity. Now that David's descendants have re-inhabited the land of Israel, and reclaimed Jerusalem as their capital, it is causing some of the world's serious thinkers to reassess their views concerning the second appearance of Israel's Messiah-King.

For example, consider this observation made by a well-known Evangelical minister: "Romans 9-11 has long been the acid test in Pauline exegesis. This awesome pinnacle of theological thought forces us to examine the historical advantages of Judaism, free will, and divine election and to ask ourselves: *What is God doing with Israel today, and why?* As we enter into the twenty-first century, the State of Israel has now been gathered by the mighty right hand of God and flourishes as the only democratic society in the Middle East. How are we to treat the promises of God toward Israel and the Jewish people? *Some evangelicals teach that God has replaced Israel.* This is an anti-Semitic theology that refuses to believe God still has a place in His heart for Israel and the Jewish people. Something that has been replaced vanishes and is no longer heard of. It becomes extinct, just as Sodom and Gomorrah are eternally buried. How can something that's been replaced be functioning with such dynamic force and vitality? *The nation of Israel dominates the news.*"[532]

Perhaps a spiritual principle found in 1 Corinthians 15:45-46 may be helpful: "The first man, Adam, became a living person. But the last Adam—that is, Christ—is a life-giving Spirit. *What came first was the natural body, then the spiritual body comes later.*" Throughout Scripture, we find this principle at work. The natural man always precedes the spiritual man. Commenting on God's revelation to Rebekah that her older son would serve his younger brother, Paul says, "This message proves that *God chooses according to his own plan,* not according to our good or bad works [our plan]. She [Rebekah] was told, '*The descendants of your older [first] son will serve the descendants of your younger son.*'"[533] Jesus applied the identical concept in His story of the Vineyard Workers: "And so it is, that *many who are first now will be last then; and those who are last now will be first then.*"[534]

Consider what Scripture reveals concerning this spiritual order. Cain came before Abel; Ishmael before Isaac; Esau before Jacob; and King Saul before David--yet the latter advanced God's agenda in every case. Samuel, while on a quest to anoint the future king, went through seven of David's older brothers before he recognized God's plan. He understood that "the Lord doesn't make decisions the way you do! People judge by outward appearance, but *the Lord looks at a person's thoughts and intentions.*" When his eyes fell upon David, he knew the youngest son was the one God was calling, and then Samuel got out his anointing oil and fulfilled prophecy.[535]

Though we cannot fully explain or completely understand it, through this one amazing principle we have revealed to us the omniscience of our sovereign and almighty God. Yet in each case the results developed as a product of each character exercising their own individual free will choice. "Oh, what a wonderful God we have! How great are his riches and wisdom and knowledge! *How impossible it is for us to understand his decisions and his methods!* For who can know what the Lord is thinking? Who knows enough to be his counselor? And who could ever give him so much that he would have to pay it back? For everything comes from him; everything exists by his power and is intended for his glory. To him be glory evermore."[536]

We can expand this concept even further. Consider that the appearance of the antichrist will precede that of the true Christ. Furthermore, present-day Jerusalem will someday give way to a new one from heaven right after our mighty Lord replaces our present earth with the pristine habitat that He has waiting for us.[537] It should come as no surprise then, that an unrepentant, ethnic Israel now returning to its holy land *only foreshadows a repentant, spiritual family that is to follow.* A message sent to Israel from the Messiah through the prophet Zechariah reveals a vital part of this new Israel: "Shout, and rejoice, O Jerusalem, for I am coming to live among you. *Many [Gentile] nations will join themselves to the Lord on that day, and they, too, will be my people.* I will live among you, and you will know that the Lord

Almighty sent me to you. The land of Judah will be the Lord's inheritance in the holy land, and *he will once again choose Jerusalem to be his own city.* Be silent before the Lord, all humanity, for he is springing into action from his holy dwelling."[538]

But exactly how will God restore and assemble His people? The answer brings it close to home for all of us. It comes down to the individual believer, regardless of whether we were born Jew or Gentile, to accept the invitation to join the family of spiritual Israel. The strategy never was about saving people by groups, ethnicities, or religions. Instead, God's people at the end of time are to be those who through the ages have made personal decisions to listen to, and follow, that still, small voice of God as it speaks to their consciences. Such individuals, despite their dissimilar backgrounds, share one thing in common—they seek to give priority to the things of God instead of securing their personal gain in a world that is passing away.[539] It makes them, spiritually speaking, free indeed![540] All such will experience varying degrees of persecution, because "You, brothers and sisters, are children of the promise like Isaac. Furthermore, at that time *the son who was conceived in a natural way persecuted the son conceived in a spiritual way. That's exactly what's happening now.*"[541] Many will find themselves cast out of families, churches, and countries just because they dare to be different. Others who may profess, but do not share in a love of the truth, will go along with the world around them even though they may once have been convicted differently.

The Jewish teacher Nicodemus is a fitting example. Something within was troubling him to find the truth even though he had grown up in a culture that claimed to have it. Secretly, he sought Jesus out, hoping to find some answers. Jesus told him that "the truth is, *no one can enter the Kingdom of God without being born of the water and the Spirit. Humans can reproduce only human life, but the Holy Spirit gives new life from heaven.* So don't be surprised by my statement that you must be born again. Just as you can hear the wind but can't tell where it comes from or where it is going, *so you can't explain how people are born of the Spirit.*"[542]

An Appeal

This book would not be worth the paper it is printed on if I did not make an appeal to each individual reader to consider carefully the unseen reality of Christ's coming kingdom, and whether or not you are ready for its arrival. Have you personally received God's plan for salvation by accepting Christ as the Messiah King regardless of what kind of difficulty it puts you in here on earth? You say, "Yes, I want it," but don't know exactly how to get it? Pray for it, and wait for God to answer. It is available to all who ask, believing that He will answer. Its realization may take a while, perhaps a lifetime, but if it is a sincere prayer of faith, it will happen, and you will see eternal life! Then you will be one of those "stars" God promised to give Abraham as children. When the Messiah King returns to fulfill David's hopes, He can say to you, "Here comes an honest man [person]—a true son [offspring] of Israel."[543]

A life journey with God is possible for all who will wholeheartedly follow their conviction. That's what our Father Abraham did. No doubt such a resolution can be scary, because we don't know where it might lead, but neither did he. But, if you think about it, even the richest person on earth can't predict what even tomorrow may bring, much less arrange their eternal destiny. The best any earthling can do is to make the wisest choice possible, for without accepting our coming King, all earthly decisions result only in temporary gains. Every reader, *at this very moment, has an opportunity* to make an eternal decision. It need not be done before a large congregation, for it is a most private matter between each sinner and their Redeemer. It might cost everything we have on this earth, but it will be traded for a share in Christ's eternal inheritance.

The choice is ours personally. No one else can make it for us. "But," some say, "my sins are too great to be forgiven!" That idea is one of the most insidious misconceptions ever created by the devil. God would have us examine His people Israel's past behavior of rejecting Him. Consider the fact their King David was an adulterer, a liar, and even a murderer. Yet God neither cast Israel or their king aside forever, because when they saw their waywardness and understood His tremendous plan to save them, they repented. Let it never be doubted, "Because the Lord is just and righteous, *the repentant people of Jerusalem will be redeemed*. But all sinners will be completely destroyed, for they refuse to come to the Lord."[544] "'Come now, let us argue this out,' says the Lord. *'No matter how deep the stains of your sins, I can remove it*. I can make you as clean as freshly fallen snow. Even if you are stained as red as crimson, I can make you as white as wool. *If you will only obey me and let me help you*, then you will have plenty to eat. But *if you keep turning away and refusing to listen*, you will be destroyed by your enemies. I, the Lord, have spoken.'"[545]

It seems like a hard choice. Perhaps that's why so few ever make it. But Jesus never promised us a rose garden this side of Eden restored. No, the roses here are full of piercing thorns. And so was that earthly crown thrust upon His head. So, He says to all earth's inhabitants, "If any of you wants to be my follower, *you must put aside your selfish ambition*, shoulder your cross, and follow me. *If you try to keep your life for yourself, you will lose it*. But if you give up your life for me, you will find true life. And *how do you benefit if you gain the whole world but lose your own soul in the process*? Is anything worth more than your soul? For I, the Son of Man, will come in the glory of my Father with his angels and will judge all people according to their deeds."[546]

We were all born blind, spiritually speaking. Through His written Word, given primarily to explain His dealings with Israel, the Holy Spirit promises to restore our sight. An incident that occurred during Christ's ministry brings out this spiritual reality. "As they approached Jericho, a blind beggar was sitting beside the road. When he heard the noise of a crowd going past, he asked what was happening. They told him that Jesus of Nazareth was going by. So, he began shouting, *'Jesus, Son of David, have mercy on me!*' The crowds ahead of Jesus *tried to hush the man, but he only shouted louder,* 'Son of David, have mercy on me!' When Jesus heard him, he stopped and ordered that the man be brought to him. Then Jesus asked the man, 'What do you want me to do for you?' 'Lord,' he pleaded, 'I want to see!' And Jesus said, 'All right, you can see! Your faith has healed you.' Instantly the man could see, *and he followed Jesus*, praising God. And *all who saw it* praised God, too."[547]

It will be the same with the redeemed in the end. They will connect the dots and see the picture! Only then will they recognize that they have been spiritually blind, and sick, and are in need of the Great Physician, and then cry out to be healed. Others, who are equally as sick, if not sicker, who either don't know it or won't admit it, will try to repress the attention the Lord's followers are directing to the Messiah. Remember Jesus said, "Healthy people don't need a doctor–sick people do. *I have come to call sinners, not those who think they are already good enough.*"[548] But those realizing their sinfulness through contrition provide *the one sacrifice God will never turn away*. "The sacrifice you want is a broken spirit. A *broken and repentant heart*, O God, you will not despise."[549] *"The Lord is rebuild-*

ing Jerusalem and bringing the exiles back to Israel. He *heals the broken-hearted*, binding up their wounds ... His power is absolute! His understanding is beyond comprehension! The Lord *supports the humble*, but he brings the wicked down into the dust."[550]

Anyone involved in the Lord's ministry will confess that one of the most painful, yet wonderful things ever beheld by anyone, is that of a sinner getting right with God! Years of repressed guilt, shame, and hatred for both God and fellow human beings come gushing forth as a mountain stream during a spring thaw. Yet that is what each member of Jacob's family known as Israel must go through. It is what he went through. Only then can we become one of those stars God showed to Abraham, each representing a child re-born into his spiritual family. As the Psalmist acknowledged, "He ... counts the stars and *calls them all by name*."[551]

Messiah David

The connection between David and Christ goes way deeper than it appears on the surface. "Jesus further confounded the Scribes and Pharisees by asking them to explain the meaning of this very title: how could it be that the Messiah is the son of David when David himself refers to Him as 'my Lord' (Mark 12:35-37; cf. Psalms 110:1)? The teachers of the Law couldn't answer the question. Jesus thereby exposed the Jewish leaders' ineptitude as teachers and their ignorance of what the Old Testament taught as to the true nature of the Messiah, further alienating them from Him. Jesus' point in asking the question of Mark 12:35 was that the Messiah is *more* than the physical son of David. If He is David's Lord, He must be greater than David. As Jesus says in Revelation 22:16, 'I am the Root and the Offspring of David.' That is, He is both the Creator of David and the Descendant of David. Only the Son of God made flesh could say that."[552]

Just as the political and religious leaders back then felt their authority threatened by Jesus' claim to David's kingship, so future world leaders will also put up a fight when the Son of David returns. Words the Psalmist himself penned thousands of years ago will someday prove true. "Why do the nations rage? *Why do the people waste their time with futile plans? The kings of the earth prepare for battle; the rulers plot together against the Lord and against his anointed one.* 'Let us break their chains,' they cry, 'and free ourselves from this slavery [to God].' But the one who rules in heaven laughs. The Lord scoffs at them. Then in anger, he rebukes them, terrifying them with his fierce fury. For the Lord declares, *'I have placed my chosen king on the throne in Jerusalem, my holy city.'* The king proclaims the Lord's decree: The Lord said to me, 'You are my son. Today I have become your Father. *Only ask, and I will give you the nations as your inheritance, the ends of the earth as your possession.* You will break them with an iron rod and smash them like clay pots.' *'Now then, you kings, act wisely! Be warned, you rulers of the earth! Serve the Lord with reverent fear, and rejoice with trembling. Submit to God's royal son, or he will become angry, and you will be destroyed in the midst of your pursuits*—for his anger can flare up in an instant. *But what joy for all who find protection in him!*'"[553]

The Jews were warned about rejecting the Messiah at His first coming, and received their judgment for it. So, too, the Bible equally warns the Gentile world concerning the reality of His second advent. Will they not face a similar fate if they spurn Him, just because it doesn't conform to their desired earthly hopes? Zionism is now leading Jews back to the land of

Israel in preparation for what they call the "Messianic Age." In other words, they believe they are returning to meet their Messiah. It is in keeping with what Peter explained to their forefathers: "And he [the Lord] *will send Jesus your Messiah to you again.* For *he must remain in heaven until the time for the final restoration of all things,* as God promised long ago through his prophets."[554] And Jesus Himself, having concern for Jerusalem as a mother hen does her brood, foretold both the destruction of that city and His future return by saying, "And now look, your house is left to you, empty and desolate. For I tell you this, *you will never see me again until you say, 'Bless the one who comes in the name of the Lord.'*"[555]

Israel is now being set on exhibit in God's display case for the entire universe to see. **Jerusalem** is again becoming like a lighted city on a hill, situated where all can view it. Soon, the Bible declares, the **Son of David, the Messiah**, will return there, and "everyone will see him."[556]

CHAPTER 13
RETURN OF MOSES (SHAKING OF THE LAWGIVER)

We have spent a great deal of time discussing the covenants that God gave to Israel, particularly the ones made through Abraham and David. As we now examine Christ's anti-typical fulfillment of the prophet Moses, we must turn our attention to the covenant God made with the children of Israel as He delivered them from Egyptian bondage. It is commonly known as the law covenant, one consisting of 613 ordinances as recorded in the Torah (first five books of the Hebrew Scriptures). The centerpiece of this covenant was the Ten Commandments presented in Exodus 20:1-17. The mediator of it was Moses as stated in John's Gospel: "For the law was given through Moses."[557] Israel received it at Mount Sinai, located outside the boundaries of Israel. The blessings of this covenant, too, were based on the people's obedience, which after promising it, they failed to comply.

It is vital we recognize the parties involved in the agreement. It did not include the fathers of the Hebrew faith—Abraham, Isaac or Jacob. No, instead God made it with the people at the time of its presentation, and to all future generations of Israel. "Moses called all the people together and said ... 'While we were at Mount Sinai, the Lord our God made a covenant with us. *The Lord did not make this [law] covenant long ago with our ancestors, but with all of us who are alive today.*'"[558] Again he told them, "The Lord your God is *making this [law] covenant with you who stand in his presence today* and also *with all future generations of Israel.*"[559]

Another people group not included in the covenant was the Gentiles. "He has revealed his words to Jacob, his principles and laws to Israel. *He has not done this with any other nation; they do not know his laws.*"[560] In his letter to the Romans, Paul tried to explain the practicality of the law as it relates to both Jew and Gentile. "God will punish the Gentiles when they sin, even though *they never had God's written law*. And he will punish the Jews when they sin, *for they do have the law.*"[561] He goes on to explain, "For it is not merely knowing the law that brings God's approval. Those who obey the law will be declared right in God's sight. Even when Gentiles, *who do not have God's written law, instinctively follow what the law says, they show that in their hearts they know right from wrong. They demonstrate that God's law is written within them, for their own consciences either accuse them or tell them they are doing what is right.* The day will surely come when God, by Jesus Christ, *will judge everyone's secret life.*"[562] Here Paul describes the effects of the New Covenant as displayed in the lives of Gentile believers. The Jews stood amazed at the Gentiles as their lives became morally upright upon acceptance of the gospel message of Christ.

A New Covenant

God still has plans for what He will do for His people Israel when He awakes them from their spiritual slumber.[563] He says, "This is the new covenant I will make with my people on that day, says the Lord: *I will put my laws in their hearts so they will understand them*, and I will write them on their minds so they will obey them."[564] Then the prophet added, "They will stop polluting themselves with their detestable idols and other sins, for I will save them from their sinful backsliding. *I will cleanse them [their consciences]*. Then they will truly be my people, and I will be their God. My servant David will be their king, and they will have only one shepherd. They will obey my regulations and keep my laws. They will live in the land of Israel where their ancestors lived, the land I gave to Jacob."[565]

The issue of the law has always been at the center of theological debate. It certainly became a major point of contention as believers first began to preach the gospel among the Gentiles. Some of the Jews who had accepted Jesus as Messiah were adamant that any Gentile seeking salvation would need to observe the Jewish codes of law. Paul argued fiercely that salvation was something obtained apart from the keeping of the law. He pointed to the fact that Abraham found favor with God 430 years before God presented the law at Sinai. Therefore, believers were to find salvation the same way—through faith in the covenant promise the Lord had made with Abraham, and not by the covenant given at Sinai.[566] Paul continued his argument, "Well then, why was the law given? *It was given to show people how guilty they are. But this system of law was to last only until the coming of the child to whom God's promise was made.*"[567] "The law was our guardian and teacher to lead us until Christ came. So now, through faith in Christ, we are made right with God. But now that faith in Christ has come, *we no longer need the law as our guardian* ... And now that you belong to Christ, you are the true children of Abraham. You are his heirs, and now all the promises God gave to him belong to you."[568]

Interestingly, the children of Israel did not enter the Promised Land under the leadership of Moses, who in many ways represented the law. Because of his mishandling of the incident with providing water for Israel, he died without actually stepping foot on it.[569] Instead, the leadership of Yeshua (Joshua) brought them into the land, because they believed God had promised it to them in His covenant with Abraham. Both Moses and Joshua were pre-figures of the Messiah. Jesus said that He came to fulfill the law of Moses.[570] In order to meet the law's full requirement, it was necessary that He die, as did Moses, but also like his predecessor He was resurrected. Then, He fulfilled the role of Joshua (His name in the Hebrew is Yeshua Hamashiach) and entered into heaven through promise. He now offers us the same promise of eternal life through faith in what He did.

It all comes into greater focus as we contrast the law covenant with the covenant of grace that had previously been in place in the days of Abraham and before the giving of the law. Yes, the Lord did indeed present the law through Moses, but "God's unfailing love and faithfulness came through Jesus Christ."[571] It happened just as Malachi said it would some 400 years before the appearance of Jesus. "Then the Lord you are seeking will suddenly come to his Temple. The messenger of the covenant, whom you look for so eagerly, is surely coming."[572] In contrast to Moses' role, Jesus entered the Temple as the messenger of the New Covenant, died within the land of promise, was resurrected, and is now the mediator of that same covenant. "You have come to Jesus, the one who mediates the new covenant between God and His people."[573] After

His arrival, humanity no longer needed human intercession to find divine approval. In fact, Jesus is the very embodiment and actualization of the New Covenant. Succinctly stated, Jesus is the New Covenant.

"And there is this further difference [between the two covenants]. God gave His laws to angels to give to Moses, who was the mediator between God and the people. Now a mediator is needed *if two people enter into an agreement,* but *God acted on his own when he made his promise to Abraham.*"[574] Remember, Abraham was asleep when God walked through the bloody pathway, committing Himself to an eternal oath.[575] Likewise, spiritually speaking, humanity was asleep when Christ offered Himself as a sacrifice for our sins. We did not do anything to earn our place in God's spiritual family any more than we had anything to do with being born into our earthly family.

The early believers held a council in Jerusalem to decide what they should expect of the Gentiles when it came to the matter of them observing Jewish law. Acts 15 summarizes its conclusions. The committee's mandate came down to what we could rightly label as *Rules for Gentiles,* presented in a letter from the apostles and elders: "For it seemed good to the Holy Spirit and to us to lay no greater burden on you than *these requirements.* You must abstain from eating food offered to idols, from consuming blood or eating the meat of strangled animals, and from sexual immorality. If you do this, you will do well. Farewell."[576]

Over time Gentile Christians sought to distance themselves from the Jews and their laws. Some took the message of salvation by faith alone to an unhealthy position of antinomianism.[577] By isolating themselves from Israel's moral law they also lost sight of the chosen people's role in God's plan to bring salvation to the world. Even today, if Israel is an abstract concept, then Gentiles can continue to live in the wild, wild west of behavior, but if Israel is anchored to a definitive place, and to a definitive people, then the God of Israel can better rein the Gentiles in. Remember, Israel is the hook the Great Fisherman has set in the mouth of the Gentile world, and He is about ready to reel in His catch.

A New Law

Well, enough of the theological wrangling. The truth is that when one enters into a personal relationship with Christ they are under "the law of Christ."[578] They begin learning to live by the "law of the Spirit."[579] Different from the one given at Sinai, it "is full of living power. It is sharper than the sharpest knife, *cutting deep into our innermost thoughts and desires. It exposes us for what we really are.* Nothing in all creation can hide from him. Everything is naked and exposed before his eyes. This is the God to whom *we must explain all that we have done.*"[580] While some feel guilty after committing adultery, those under Christ's law feel castigated even thinking about it. Though human law can only judge someone after they have committed murder, the law of Christ convicts someone at the very first feelings that would lead to such a crime. In short, it is the awakening of the human conscience from its spiritual slumber. Then the sinner's desire is to "*try to find out what is pleasing to the Lord.*"[581]

Confused, you say? Just wish God would come Himself and explain exactly what He expects of us? Well, help is on the way! Confusion regarding how the Lord wants His people to live will not continue forever. Change is on the horizon. Isaiah provides a glimpse of what we can expect after Christ returns and establishes His earthly kingdom. "In the last days, the Temple of the Lord in Jerusalem will become the most important place on earth. People from all over the world will go there to worship. Many nations will come and say, 'Come, let us go up to the mountain of the Lord, to the Temple of the God of Israel. *There he will teach us his ways, so that we may obey him.*' For in those days the Lord's teaching and his word will go out from Jerusalem."[582] The *American Standard Version* of Isaiah 2:3 reads: *"for out of Zion shall go forth the law."*

Then, and only then, will genuine peace exist in the world. No more wars, killing, stealing, or cheating. "For the Lord is our judge, our lawgiver, and our King."[583] As lawgiver He will make the laws; as judge, He will interpret and determine how they should be applied; and as King He will enforce the laws for the protection of everyone. It will be a new and glorious time! Then Genesis 49:10 will realize its completion: "The scepter will not depart from Judah, nor the ruler's staff from his descendants, until the coming of the one to whom it belongs, *the one whom all the nations will obey.*" During His first earthly visit, Jesus sought to provide some clarity to the law from Sinai in His exposition of it at His Sermon on the Mount. Any theological conundrums regarding the transfer of current laws to new life in the millennial kingdom the Lawgiver Himself will clearly explain when He lays it out from Mount Zion.

Until then honesty is the best policy. In other words, don't engage in secretive schemes designed to get the best of someone in order to advance one's self. Sure, that may be how the world operates, but such gain is something that is by nature only temporal. While we may brag about our ability to deal sharply and how we have fleeced others, the damage we may do to them could have external ramifications. Jesus said it best: *"Do for others as you would like them to do for you."*[584] We should seek to be as transparent as possible when it comes to dealing with others. "Again, you have heard that the law of Moses says, 'Do not break your vows; you must carry out the vows you have made before the Lord.' But I say, don't make any vows ... *Just say a simple, 'Yes, I will,' or 'No, I won't.' Your word is enough.* To strengthen your promise with a vow shows that something is wrong."[585]

Today we live in a world of meaningless contracts. Indeed, we have come to a sad time when a person's word is not enough security for their promised actions. Human laws often accommodate and encourage the worst attributes of sinful human nature. Envy, jealousy, and greed lead to the betrayal of friends, business partners, and even family members for the purpose of personal gain and advancement. The most intimate covenants get broken with little consideration of the consequences in the lives of those affected. Paul warned that a society of people who do not keep their word will be a mark of the final days of our present world. "In the last days there will be very difficult times. *For people will love only themselves and their money.* They will be boastful and proud, scoffing at God, disobedient to their parents, and ungrateful. *They will consider nothing sacred [covenant breakers].* They will be unloving and unforgiving; they will slander others and have no self-control; they will be cruel and have no interest in what is good. *They will betray friends*, be reckless, be puffed up with pride, and love pleasure rather than God. *They will act as if they are religious, but they will reject the power that could make them godly.*"[586]

Our world operates on a principle of social injustice. For the most part, money, power, and position determine what kind of existence one can enjoy. The less faith we have in a better world to come, the more we want of the one we now live in. That is what those who belong to this earth seek after, and are tempted to sell their eternal inheritance for it. It is that important to them. To such the world invites to become part of the "buddy" system that decides what is right or wrong. If you have enough money and know the right people, you stand a good chance of getting away with anything--or so we think.

Yet a higher power watches and documents all such behavior. His court has yet to convene. When it does, He will rule the earth through a government based on laws that offer true equality and social justice. He will right all the wrongs and hold the offending parties accountable. Do we really think He takes no notice of our trickery and deceit? "Help, O Lord, for the godly are fast disappearing! The faithful have vanished from the earth! Neighbors lie to each other, speaking with flattering lips and insincere hearts. May the Lord bring their flattery to an end and silence their proud tongues. They say, 'We will lie to our heart's content. Our lips are our own—who can stop us?' The Lord replies, 'I have seen violence done to the helpless, and I have heard the groans of the poor. Now I will rise up to rescue them, as they have longed for me to do.' The Lord's promises are pure, like silver refined in a furnace, purified seven times over. Therefore, Lord, we know you will protect the oppressed, preserving them forever from this lying generation, even though the wicked strut about, and evil is praised throughout the land."[587]

Who among us has lived such a life so as to pass the Lord's judgment? The book of Romans tells us that "all people, whether Jews or Gentiles, are under the power of sin ... No one is good—not even one."[588] It goes on to add, "For no one can ever be made right in God's sight by doing what his law commands. *For the more we know God's law, the clearer it becomes that we aren't obeying it.* But now God has shown us a different way of being right in his sight—not by obeying the law but by the way promised in the Scriptures long ago [to Abraham]. We are made right in God's sight when we trust in Jesus Christ to take away our sins. And we all can be saved in this same way, no matter who we are or what we have done."[589] Here is the only defense we need to face God's judgment. Though Satan stands before God "day and night," "accusing" those who want to do right, the Lord has appointed us an ample state attorney. "My dear children, I am writing this to you so that you will not sin. But if you do sin, there is someone to plead for you before the Father. He is Jesus Christ, the one who pleases God completely. He is the sacrifice for our sins ... Those who say they live in God should live their lives as Christ did."[590]

Certainly, we do not want to take the devil's position by using the law of God in a way as to accuse or condemn others. "Don't speak evil of each other ... If you criticize each other and condemn each other, then you are criticizing and condemning God's law. *But you are not a judge who can decide whether the law is right or wrong. Your job is to obey it.* God alone, who made the law, can rightly judge among us."[591] Bringing a person into harmony with God's will is something that only God can do. The Holy Spirit illuminates our consciences, thereby communicating to us what is right and wrong. It is a private work done within each individual, because we all arrive at different convictions at different awakenings during our spiritual journeys.

Using examples such as what dietary choices, or what day one should observe as sacred, Paul wrote, "Who are you to condemn God's servants? They are responsible to the Lord, so *let him tell them whether they are right or wrong. The Lord's power will help them do as they should.*"[592] But, in the same text, Paul also counsels, "But it is wrong to ... do anything else if it might cause another Christian to stumble. You may have the faith to believe that there is nothing wrong with what you are doing, but keep it between yourself and God. *Blessed are those who do not condemn themselves by doing something they know is all*

Return Of Moses (shaking Of The Lawgiver)

right. But if people have doubts about whether they should eat something they shouldn't eat it. They would be condemned for not acting in faith before God. *If you do anything you believe is not right, you are sinning.*[593] The law of the Spirit is a matter of individual conscience. It protects us from being strong-armed into following the convictions of others, yet holds us accountable to the One who has our eternal destiny in His hands. God does not desire a family of robots, but children who think for themselves and don't just go around merely reflecting the thoughts of others that too often wind up as church rules. Yet their consciences will be fine-tuned to the Spirit's influence. They understand that *"it is a sin to know what you ought to do and then not do it."*[594]

"This should be your ambition: to live a quiet life, minding your own business and working with your hands."[595] No doubt there may be times when God specifically calls on us to reprove sin in another person's life. That is biblical.[596] Especially is it the case if one is involved in spiritual leadership. However, we can know if it is the Spirit of God prompting us to do such--or a different spirit. If we are eager to reprove those obviously living destructively, the directive most likely is not from the Lord. When the Lord does place such a burden upon us, we will feel like Jonah did when called to warn the city of Nineveh as told in the biblical book of Jonah. That's right, we will want to run the other way. Yet, if it really is the Lord calling us to duty, He will not remove the divine compulsion from our soul until the deed is done.

We must remember that we only see most people through a window of time during their lives. Do we really possess enough knowledge to size them up in such a brief period? Few people are as annoying as those who think they know what is best for everyone else. And, especially if people are young in faith, they will need to be handled with kid gloves. Spiritual birth is similar to physical birth. Sometimes it is hard to tell in the early stages if spiritual conception has occurred. But we can apply a pregnancy test. *In their spirit do they really want to do what pleases the Lord?* If so, then before we expect too much, we must understand that newborns of all creatures must first be fed milk and be allowed to take baby steps. It is the same with those born again by faith. We must be careful not to interfere between the spiritual children being called, and Him who is calling them.

Here is another simple test regarding which law we are to live by. The Old Testament law can cause us to judge others for what they should, or should not, be doing. The New Covenant law of the Spirit encourages us to be introspective as to how we interact with others. While it is designed to protect us from the condemnation of others, it also shields them from our own criticism. Israel acquired a reputation for being very judgmental toward Gentiles, and now that Gentiles have had their opportunity, they are, sad to say, reciprocating the same wrongful attitude. Disputes over biblical law have separated Jew from Jew; Jew from Gentile; and Gentiles from Gentiles. Such debates are nothing short of wasted arguments. "But don't have anything to do with stupid arguments about ancestors. And stay away from disagreements and quarrels about the law of Moses. Such arguments are useless and senseless."[597] God's law *is a living Spirit* that seeks to guard us from the judgmentalism of one another, thereby bringing us all in the unity of the faith.[598]

Warnings from Mount Zion

Hebrews 12 assures us that as God spoke His law to the Hebrew people from atop Mount Sinai, He will deliver His law to both Hebrews and Gentiles from Mount Zion when He returns to deliver them from the bondage of the present world. It will be a law adapted for a new millennial age. The profession of all will be revealed when those who have determined not to follow the Lord will depart from those who will.

Moses' warning to Israel from Mount Sinai went unheeded, and the world has been eyewitnesses to their suffering the consequences.[599] The future of Israel foretold to them happened exactly as pronounced. And why did Scripture record their failings and punishments? "These events happened as a warning to us, so that we would not crave evil things as they did or worship idols as some of them did.... *All these events happened to them as examples for us. They were written down to warn us, who live at the time when this age is drawing to a close.*"[600] The King James Version of the verse reads, "These ... things are written for our admonition, upon whom *the ends of the world are come.*"

What can we expect if we refuse to obey God who speaks to us from Mount Zion?[601] "You have not come to a physical mountain ... as the Israelites did at Mount Sinai when God gave them his laws ... No, you have come to Mount Zion, to the city of the living God, the heavenly Jerusalem, and to thousands of angels in joyful assembly. You have come to the assembly of God's firstborn children [His true church], whose names are written in heaven. You have come to God Himself, who is judge of all people. And you have come to the spirits of the redeemed in heaven who have now been made perfect. You have come to Jesus, the one who mediates the new covenant between God and people.... *See to it that you obey God, the one who is speaking to you [your conscience].* For if the people of Israel did not escape when they refused to listen to Moses, the earthly messenger, how terrible our danger if we reject the one who speaks to us from heaven! When God spoke from Mount Sinai his voice shook the earth, but now he makes another promise: 'Once again I will shake not only the earth but the heavens also.' This means that the things on earth will be shaken, *so that only eternal things will be left.* Since we are receiving a Kingdom that cannot be destroyed, let us be thankful and please God by worshiping Him with fear and awe. For our God is a consuming fire."[602]

Here we see revealed the real Mover and Shaker of the universe! Any human claims of power, influence, authority, and wealth are no match to Him to whom we must all give answer. Hebrews 12 contrasts the warnings for disobedience to the covenants—the Old Covenant law from Mount Sinai, and the New Covenant law spoken from Mount Zion when Christ returns as Supreme Law Giver. The point the writer is trying to get across is this: if we think the penalties for disobedience to the Old Covenant were severe, they pale in comparison to what shall happen if we disregard the instruction given in the New Covenant. *Here is, the most serious warning given in the entire Bible.* Hebrews 10:26-29 explains: "Dear friends, if we deliberately continue sinning after we have received *a full knowledge of the truth* [concerning the Messiah and His relationship to the biblical covenants], there is no other sacrifice that will cover these sins. There will be nothing to look forward to but the terrible expectation of God's judgment and the raging fire that will consume his enemies. Anyone who refused to obey the law of Moses [old covenant] was put to death without mercy on the testimony of two or three witnesses. *Think how much more* terrible the punishment will be for those who have trampled on the Son of God and *have treated the blood of the covenant [new covenant] as if it were common and unholy.* Such people have insulted and enraged the Holy Spirit who brings God's mercy to his people."

People often inquire "what is the unpardonable sin?" Here we have it. Jesus said, "Every sin or blasphemy can be forgiven—except blasphemy against the Holy Spirit, *which can never be forgiven.* Anyone who blasphemes against me, the Son of Man, can be forgiven, *but blasphemy against the Holy Spirit will never be forgiven, either in this world or in the world to come.*"[603] That's why Scripture admonishes, "But never forget the warning: '*Today you must listen to his voice [as the Spirit speaks to your conscience].* Don't harden your hearts against him as Israel did when they rebelled.'"[604] The Holy Spirit offers us eternal life through the blood covenant of Christ, and if we reject it there is nothing more that even God can do to save us. When He returns, we will still by choice be bound to our sinfulness and will cease to exist before His holy presence of consuming fire. We will be like the fallen angels who once walked in the mercy of the Holy One, but spurned His ways. "And I remind you of the angels who did not stay within the limits of authority God gave them but left the place where they belonged. God has kept them chained in prisons of darkness, waiting for the day of judgment."[605] That is why the demons, when confronted with the presence of Christ at His first coming, "began screaming at him, 'Why are you bothering us, Son of God? You have no right to torture us before God's appointed time.'"[606] These things are real, dear reader! God forbid that any of us place ourselves in such a hopeless position.

The shaking brought forth in Hebrews 12 represents the irreversible day of God's judgment.[607] The gospel offer will have gone to all living humanity, and all decisions are final. Then the Judge of all will say, "Let the one who is doing wrong continue to do wrong; the one who is vile, continue to be vile; the one who is good, continue to do good; and the one who is holy, continue in holiness. See, *I am coming soon*, and my reward is with me, to repay all according to their deeds. I am the Alpha and the Omega, the First and the Last, the Beginning and the

End."[608]

CHAPTER 14
RETURN OF ABRAHAM (UNITING OF GOD'S FAMILY)

Family reunions can be interesting gatherings, especially if a lengthy period of time has passed since the last get-together. Younger members meet cousins for the first time while older ones reminisce about days gone by and remember those who have passed on. Such periods of reflective interaction sometimes bring healing to torn relationships. Issues that divided in the past often don't seem quite as important as they used to, and when reassessed for the breakups they caused, seem even less significant. Old wounds heal and new friendships form. When it's over, everyone leaves with a better sense of wellbeing—as if a heavenly spirit had hosted the event. Surely the Psalmist got it right when he penned a song for his generation as they ascended to Jerusalem for a family reunion: "How wonderful it is, how pleasant, when brothers live together in harmony."[609]

There will be a such future reunion among the members of Abraham's spiritual family. And, yes, there have been many divisions among them that have brought untold pain to our planet, but someday all will live in harmony. Jesus observed that "a kingdom at war with itself will collapse. A home divided against itself is doomed."[610] Another way of saying this is that *everyone involved must unify and function together or it will simply not work out.*

Let's all be clear on this point. God is not going to allow eternal division to doom His household of faith! He has way too much invested in His family to allow it to disintegrate because of human pride, jealousy, and lust for dominance. In this clan, those who seek to be first shall be last, and the humble will be exalted. All who would try to bring dissension to the family reunion will not be allowed in. It was what Jesus was trying to tell the religious bigots of His day. Their attitude was that they inherently had rights to the promises just because they were blood descendants of Abraham. And the Gentiles? Well, they were just flat out of luck. But Jesus told the Jewish religious leaders, "I tell you this that *many Gentiles will come from all over the world and sit down with Abraham, Isaac, and Jacob at the feast* in the Kingdom of Heaven. But *many Israelites—those for whom the Kingdom was prepared—will be cast out* into outer darkness, where there will be weeping and gnashing of teeth."[611] Who exactly is it that will find themselves denied entrance to the eternal city? "Outside the city are ... all who love to live a lie."[612]

One of the biggest lies told today is that God has replaced Israel in His plan with a different religious group. It distorts the truth concerning His stated intention to use ethnic Israel to organize His spiritual family from diverse peoples from all around the world. Any such deception should be called out for what it is—unbiblical propaganda designed to advance personal, or more corporate, agendas. Thus, it has absolutely no basis in Scripture. Anyone who willingly, or knowingly, tries to thwart God's authoritative right to organize His human family, and who seek to rule it themselves by their own political and religious schemes, will have no place in His eternal kingdom.

Unfortunately, the world is full of divisions. Political divisions between nations, and even within nations themselves. Religious divisions between Jews, Muslims, Christians, and the myriad of other religious identities, even within such groups themselves. They have saturated the earth's soil with blood for millennia. But someday soon God will say, "No more!"

All in One Accord

In the earthly reunification of Abraham's family, undoubtedly many issues of disagreement may linger, but there will be an eternal assent on at least three points. First, they will agree on the covenants given to Abraham and David. Two, agreement on the identity of the promised Seed—the Messiah. For example, Christians believe He is Jesus Christ of Nazareth. Jews hold that the Messiah must be a descendant of David yet to appear. Messianic Jews are ethnic Jews who believe Jesus, or "Yeshua" in Aramaic, will be that recognizable descendant of David when He returns again to earth. Thirdly, and the point we want to now focus on, agreement by each individual family member on what their appointed role is in God's design, and their willingness to be content and faithful to that assignment.

When something or somebody gets chosen, it is a selection intended to perform a certain task.[613] We select a soup spoon over a fork for obvious reasons. A team picks a quarterback as the chief player to lead the rest to victory. In democratic societies an elected official is thought the best available choice to carry out the desires of a constituency. But it doesn't take a genius to see how this can provide the perfect environment for our fallen natures to produce jealousy, envy, and hatred. It happens as deep in our hearts we become discontent with our own role and desire one given to someone else. When an offensive lineman, whose main purpose is to protect his quarterback, instead tries to get the ball to throw the game-winning pass, the team cannot expect to win many championship games.

This concept of interdependence is crucial in executing God's plan as well. It is vital for each party, or individual, to find their God-ordained role and seek to carry it out faithfully. A premier principle in discovering our role is how we read the instruction book—the Bible. Instead of approaching it objectively, for what it is clearly saying, we often interpret it subjectively, trying to insert the part we see ourselves as playing. For example, Saul of Tarsus subjectively saw himself as a defender of Abraham's religion. One could say he was already blinded by his faith when he set out for the gates of Damascus to deliver what he thought was divine justice to early believers in Christ. It was then God knocked him off his horse, thereby providing him a more objective view of His eternal plan. Paul the apostle later recounts during his testimony before King Agrippa that the Lord said to him, "It is hard for you to fight against my will ... Now stand up! For I have appeared to you to appoint [choose] you as my servant and my witness. You are to tell the world about this experience... I was *not disobedient* to that vision ... I teach nothing except *what the prophets and Moses said would happen*—that the Messiah would suffer and be the first to rise from the dead *as a light to Jews and Gentiles alike.*"[614] The question we must ask, therefore, is "Where exactly did Moses, or any of the prophets, say it was God's will for a religion of non-Jews to assume the role given to the Hebrews? Or, where did Jesus, or the writers of the New Testament, ever document God disenfranchising His Hebrew family from their initial eternal calling?" The biblical record simply cannot substantiate such ideas.

We must emphasize just how important it is to find our true calling, then humbly accept it with joy and thanksgiving instead of always desiring someone else's role. If not careful, we run the risk of being like Judas Iscariot, who, blinded by his own ambitious zeal, missed what God had planned for him. Jesus selected him along with the other eleven disciples, but he ended up betraying Him as a result of his wrong decisions. Deep down he must have known something wasn't right about selling out the Lord in an attempt to have a greater leading role in His ministry, but after it was too late, he couldn't reverse what he had done.[615]

And don't forget Esau whose physical appetite was more important to him than his place in God's family. While Judas aspired a role he wasn't assigned, Esau discounted the one he had been handed. If either man had truly been diligent seekers of truth, they may have realized the role they were about to act out on the prophetic stage. God has forewarned each of us, "Try to live in peace with everyone [and what they have been chosen of God to do] and… look after each other so that none will miss out on the special favor [calling] of God. Watch out that no bitter root of unbelief [jealousy or envy] rises up among you, for whenever it springs up, many are corrupted by its poison. Make sure that no one is immoral or godless like Esau. *He traded his birthright [calling] as the oldest son for a single meal.* And afterward, when he wanted his father's blessing, he was rejected. It was too late for repentance, even though he wept with bitter tears."[616]

When sin entered the world, it distorted everything, including, and especially, the human heart. It made us self-seeking and envious. James 4:1-3 provides insight into the depraved nature of humanity: "What is causing the quarrels and fights among you? Isn't it the whole army of evil desires at war within you? You want what you don't have, so you scheme and kill to get it. You are jealous for what others have, and you can't possess it, so you fight and quarrel to take it away from them. And yet the reason you don't have what you want is that you don't ask God for it. And even when you do ask, you don't get it because your whole motive is wrong – you want only what will give you pleasure."

We see such selfishness on display in the Gospel account of the mother of the sons of James and John, two of Jesus' disciples, who along with her came to Jesus asking for a favor. She said, "'In your Kingdom, will you let my two sons sit in places of honor next to you, one at your right and the other at your left?' But Jesus told them ... 'I have no right to say who will sit on the thrones next to mine. *My Father has prepared those places for the ones he has chosen.*' When the ten other disciples heard what James and John had asked, they were indignant [jealous]. But Jesus called them together and said, 'You know that in this world kings are tyrants, and officials lord it over the people beneath them. *But among you it should be quite different.* Whoever wants to be a leader among you must be your servant, and whoever wants to be first must become your slave. For even I, the Son of Man, *came here not to be served but to serve others*, and to give my life as a ransom for many.'"[617]

Here we see it is God, and He alone, who chooses and positions His children according to His divine will and knowledge. He is determined to order His household of faith according to His wisdom, and no power on earth is going to stop Him from His resolution. And, *God chose Israel as a model nation to teach the rest of the world that He is the one and only true God.* "'But you are my witnesses, O Israel!' says the Lord. And you are my servant. *You have been chosen to know me, believe in me, and understand that I alone am God. There is no other God; there never has been and never will be.* I am the Lord, and there is no other Savior. First, I predicted your deliverance; I declared what I would do, and then I did it—I saved you. No foreign god has ever done this before. *You are my witnesses that I am the only God,'* says the Lord. From eternity to eternity I am God. *No one can oppose what I do. No one can reverse my actions.*"[618] All Gentiles must come to grips with Israel's appointed purpose before they can discover their true position before God.

Regarding Israel's relationship with other nations, God told them that if they would perform their role by obeying Him and not pursue foreign gods, "the Lord *will make you the head and not the tail,* and you will always have the upper hand … But if you refuse to listen to the Lord your God and do not obey … *They [the Gentile nations] will be the head, and you will be the tail.*"[619] Here we see a temporary glitch in God's plan—not that His plan isn't perfect, because it is. In fact, it is so perfect it deals with human rebellion and resistance by mysteriously using it to aid in its success. For some strange reason Israel has always sought to be the tail, and the Gentiles desire to be the head. The Bible teaches that this difficulty will someday get worked out, and when it does, both Jew and Gentile will finally realize God's purpose.

Israel's Purpose Realized

Here is the central intent of Israel's sacred calling. By means of their blessings for obedience and curses for rebellion, they are to show people in our lost world the way back to the Father's house. The calling of the Hebrew people pre-exists the founding of the Christian Church by some 2,000 years. Thus, it is preposterous for the latter to stake a claim as their replacement. It would be something similar to a child claiming to go back to the time of their conception and act as a surrogate parent to itself. In other words, when viewed objectively, the belief is utter nonsense. In the past God has gone on biblical record stating that He has, and will again in the future, reveal Himself to every other people group through the Hebrew race. Any person, church, or nation that seeks a god without giving serious consideration to this sacred history can only expect to discover a deity different from the one who first called Abraham to the world's notice.

Instead of being appreciative, past nations who did not know God sought to cut Israel down, hoping to rid the earth of its existence. "Israel will remain a stump, like a tree that is cut down, *but the stump will be a holy seed that will grow again.*"[620] In spite of such persecution, the Lord continues to advance His divine will through His chosen people. "'I, the Sovereign Lord, am watching this sinful nation of Israel, and *I will uproot it and scatter* its people across the earth. Yet *I have promised that I will never completely destroy the family of Israel,*' says the Lord. 'For I have commanded that *Israel be persecuted by the other nations as grain is sifted in a sieve, yet not one true kernel will be lost.*'"[621] As it happened in the past, so will it be in the future. The modern state of Israel is only 70 years old, and already much of the international community wants to either limit its rights as a sovereign nation or completely annihilate it. But that opposes what the Lord has clearly revealed. "I have made Israel for myself, and *they will someday honor me before the whole world.*"[622]

To this day the Hebrew people are an enigma to the average Gentile. Perhaps it's because some who now claim to be the spiritual progeny of the Hebrew ancestors have written their legitimate birth children (ethnic Israel) off centuries ago. Consider, however, some of the spiritual lessons we can learn from understanding the history of God's Old Covenant people: "The Holy One praised be He said to Israel: I set My love upon you because even when I grant you greatness you make yourselves small [i.e. humble] before Me. I gave greatness to Abraham, and he said, 'Behold, I am dust and ashes' [Gen. 18; 27]; to Moses and Aaron, and they said: 'But what are we?' [Ex. 16:7]; to David, and he said 'I am a worm, not a man' [Ps. 22:7]. But the other nations of the world are not like you. I gave greatness to Nimrod, and he said 'Let us build for ourselves a city and a tower with its top in the heavens …' [Gen. 11:4]; to Pharaoh and he said 'Who is the Lord?' [Ex. 5:2] … to Nebuchadnezzar and he said 'I will ascend above the heights of the clouds; I will make myself like the Most-High. [Isa. 14:14].'"[623]

This has always been the big test for the Gentile nations—how they choose to relate to Israel in light of God's relationship with it. Going forward, some will support His choice of Israel. Others, however, will repeat the mistakes of nations and empires before them by opposing God's chosen from a sense of superiority because of Israel's faulty past. Yet, they will be just as powerless as were the world powers before them to halt the plan that God has set into motion and will likewise receive devastating punishment for their resistance. Sliding into disbelief regarding the Israeli covenants by thinking the Lord has turned His back on Israel, they see its disobedience in rejecting Christ as an unpardonable sin for the nation. But in denouncing Israel because of its unbelief, they unwittingly pass judgment upon themselves. As a result, they miss one very important biblical principle that will come into play when "the Lord, will judge the godless nations! *As you have done to Israel, so it will be done to you.*"[624]

"But as for you, Israel my servant, Jacob my chosen one, descended from my friend Abraham, I have called you back from the ends of the earth so you can serve me. *For I have chosen you and will not throw you away.* Don't be afraid, for I am with you ... *Anyone who opposes you will die ... They will all be gone ...* Despised though you are, O Israel, don't be afraid, for I will help you. I am the Lord, your Redeemer, I am the Holy One of Israel."[625] We wonder, *Why Israel?* It was the Gentiles whom God sought to save from the very beginning! Before Abraham, the whole world was Gentile. Israel didn't even exist until the time of his grandson Jacob, and then it was the creation of the Almighty merely for the purpose of bringing salvation and eternal order to the world. Lost under the spell of sin, the world was completely helpless to find its way back to an understanding of just who God really is.

Thus, the concept of Israel was a divine plan designed to retrieve us from sin and the death it brings. Yet amazingly, much like a drowning person, many seek to fight off the rescuer that God sent to save them, because they somehow believe subsequent religious systems derived by mankind are enough to deliver them. That is no different than the old pagans who fashioned and then trusted their idols of wood and stone. Seriously, it is an issue we need to forever settle in our minds. If all the wonderful predictions concerning Israel's glorious destiny are untrue, then God again lied when He told His prophet, "I have made Israel for myself, and *they will someday honor me before the whole world.*"[626] The only way Gentiles can get around it is to redefine Israel and make it appear in the likeness of their own religious conceptions (images).

When we judge Israel for its disobedience, offering no grace, we do not realize that is exactly how we will in turn be judged. "God's decision to set His affection on Israel was *in no way determined by their performance* or national greatness *but rather by His free will and sovereign purposes ... the full outworking of God's purpose through Israel will not depend on their faith-*

fulness."[627] Once we understand this, we can begin to appreciate Scripture's revelation of God's eternal plan in a way that we never before dreamed possible. If God did not choose Israel based on its performance, then neither could it be disqualified by it. The various contractual relationships He made with it-- the contract with Abraham; the contract at Mount Sinai; the contract with David-- were all conditional, yet *the people were never able to meet those conditions.* Which is why there is a need for a culminating contract. God thus uses a New Covenant to validate all prior covenants, resulting in His people receiving all the blessings He has offered them. That New Covenant is embodied in the holy birth, sinless life, atoning death and eternal resurrection of the Messiah Jesus Christ. When in the future He again appears to Israel, they will accept Him as their New Covenant.

Israel Accepts Its God

God says He will make a "new covenant *with the people of Israel and Judah.*"[628] The Bible never says that He establishes it directly with Gentiles, although they, too, will be saved by its provisions of grace. Think about it. Christians teach that through the vicarious life and death of Christ they receive forgiveness for their shortcomings. If God forgives them for their past rebellion, who among them will place limits by saying that He can't apply this same gospel principle to the faithful remnant of a nation—Israel? We must never forget that it was to *a group of twelve Jews* that Jesus gave a cup of wine and said, "Each of you drink from it, for this is my blood, *which seals the covenant between God and His people [Israel]* ... I will not drink wine again until the day I drink it new with you in my Father's Kingdom."[629] The world is waiting on its Hebrew brothers and sisters to acknowledge this New Covenant toasting of Christ as the Messiah, which the prophets predict they will do just prior to His return in Jerusalem the second time to establish God's eternal kingdom.[630]

They will then realize the contrast between the two covenants as demonstrated in the story of Abraham's two wives and sons. "The Scriptures say that Abraham had two sons, one from his slave-wife and one from his freeborn wife. *The son of the slave-wife was born in a human attempt to bring about the fulfillment of God's promise. But the son of the freeborn wife was born as God's own fulfillment of His promise.* Now these two women *serve as an illustration of God's two covenants.* Hagar, the slave-wife, represents Mount Sinai where people first became enslaved to the law. And now Jerusalem is just like Mount Sinai in Arabia, because she and her children live in slavery. But Sarah, the freewoman, *represents the heavenly Jerusalem.* And she is our mother."[631]

If the reader thinks this book is trying to say that the Jews are now returning to their homeland, Israel, just to set up shop as usual by following the prescriptions of the Mosaic laws and customs, he or she has missed the entire point. To the contrary, the Jews will now have an experience with God that will usher in for all of us an entirely new world order of heavenly realities! People fighting today over territorial rights to Jerusalem and its surrounding regions fail to comprehend God's broader goal. The Jews can no more fulfill the promise of God by their efforts, religious or political, than Abraham could when siring a son by his wife's slave, or Jacob when he tried to obtain the birthright by stealing it from his brother, or when Moses failed at his first attempt to deliver his people from Egypt by his fighting skills. Yes, modern Israel will try to fulfill God's prophetic promises by their own wisdom and human design. That's why they will enter into a contract with the antichrist. But it will not work for them anymore than it did for their predecessors. No, as studied earlier concerning Daniel's seventieth week prophecy, God will cancel their deal with the devil and Himself achieve His own promises through them when He leads them to accept by faith the Promised Son–their Jeshua Hamashiach.

That is what excited and inspired the prophets when they penned such words as, "For the Lord will cause something new and different to happen—*Israel will embrace her God.*"[632] "*But the Lord will save the people of Israel with eternal salvation. They will never again be humiliated and disgraced throughout everlasting ages.*"[633] "'Thus, I will make known my holy name among my people of Israel. I will not let it be desecrated anymore. *And the nations, too, will know that I am the Lord, the Holy One of Israel.* That day of judgment will come,' says the Sovereign Lord. '*Everything will happen just as I have declared it. ... Then my people will know that I am the Lord their God—responsible for sending them away to exile and responsible for bringing them home. ... And I will never again turn my back on them, for I will pour out my Spirit upon them,*' says the Sovereign Lord."[634] "'Yes,' says the Lord, 'I will do mighty miracles for you, like those I did when I rescued you from slavery in Egypt. *All the nations of the world will stand amazed at what the Lord will do for you. They will be embarrassed that their power is so insignificant... Where is another God like you, who pardons the sins of the survivors among his people... You will show us your faithfulness and unfailing love as you promised with an oath to our ancestors Abraham and Jacob long ago.*'"[635] "Then I will pour out a spirit of grace and prayer *on the family of David and on all the people of Jerusalem.* They will look on me *whom they have pierced* and mourn for him as for an only son."[636] Here we have Israel's quintessential repentance. They will finally recognize and accept their God!

This is the central theme of Scripture—God's unfailing commitment to His people Israel through His chosen Messiah Messenger by whom He also extends His eternal grace to all peoples of the earth! In attempting to separate the Messiah from His commitment to the Hebrews, the latter inadvertently reject their own eternal life support. "All of us are sinners who deserve nothing but death. God's relationship with Israel is a demonstration of His grace—a manifestation of unmerited love. And in that regard, *the Jewish people to this day remain a witness of what it means to have a relationship with God.* Thus, from their history, we can see that when we are faithful, He blesses. When we are unfaithful, He disciplines. And when we repent, He forgives and forgets and begins to bless again."[637] The only way we Gentiles ever conceived of a forgiving God was by observing the mercy He extends to His chosen Hebrew people.

"Concerning the calling of the Gentiles, God says in the prophecy of Hosea, 'Those *who were not my people*, I will *now call my people.*'"[638] Gentile believers are indeed chosen of God, *but not as a replacement for Israel.* Like the lineman who protects his quarterback, they should be tenacious in defending the sacred calling of their Hebrew spiritual relatives. Their calling is to advance the divine plan to parts of the earth the Jew can never reach. Though we cannot be Abraham, Moses, King David, Elijah, Peter, Paul, or Mary the mother of Jesus, we can follow their examples of remaining faithful to our own calling.

Lessons from the Past

Throughout this entire book, we have been following God's incredible plan that He first revealed to Abraham and through which He intends to save the world. We have seen a central component of it was the Lord's calling, or choosing, of Abraham's offspring through his grandson Jacob—or Israel.

The focus of our discussion has been whether or not God is still on course with His program of working through Israel, or has He abandoned it and replaced it with another people or religion?

Today we have a unique advantage point in understanding His intent. Unlike many who have gone before us, we can look back on a greater scope of historical events and grasp a better revelation of divine purpose. Scripture and secular history record the deliverance of Abraham's descendants from Egyptian bondage and their reception of the law covenant at Mount Sinai; their conquest and settlement of the Holy Land; the establishment of the Davidic kingdom; its division into north (Israel) and south (Judah); the expulsion of Israel from the land by the Assyrians; the removal of Judah by the Babylonians along with the destruction of Jerusalem and the first Temple; the return of the Jews to the land and the rebuilding of the Temple and city of Jerusalem; the birth, ministry, and death of the promised "Seed"—the Messiah; the rejection of the Messiah by His own people; the acceptance of Christ by a core group of Jewish followers whose witness, in turn, laid the groundwork for the establishment of the Christian Church; the destruction of the Second Temple, along with Jerusalem, and the scattering of the Jews throughout the nations of the earth; their persecution in foreign lands; and finally, the return of the Jewish people to the same land God promised to them through Abraham. In more recent years we have witnessed the re-establishment of the government of Israel. The nation today finds itself at the forefront of both political and religious discussions the world over. The emblem they fly on their flag is none other than the Star of David! Watching God call ethnic Israel back to their earthly home should encourage His followers around the world to also return there in their own spirits.

Yet the most amazing part is that the prophets foretold all this history and it is on record as a witness to divine guidance. With an understanding of God's unfolding providence in the past, we can better discern the exciting events about to transpire in the future. They, too, have been predicted. God is about to wrap up His agenda on planet earth! We have no excuse for not knowing, and no justifiable reason to plead ignorance. Scripture has laid it all bare. If we miss out, it will only be because we didn't want to accept God's way, but rather our own. So, let's now focus on how the Bible predicts the Lord will culminate His master plan.

It would be impossible for all the end-time prophecies to be fulfilled if the Lord had not already brought the Hebrew people back to Palestine and established them in Jerusalem. Now He is in the process of reuniting the broken family ties between them, thereby laying the framework for healing the divisions between world nations. Then the prediction made by Paul will be realized: "And this is his plan: *At the right time he will bring everything together under the authority of Christ*—everything in heaven and on earth."[639] Obviously, that will be the uniting of spiritual Israel (consisting of both Jews and Gentiles) under the blood-stained banner of our everlasting covenant—the Lord Jesus Christ.

First, He is to heal the division between the family members of Jacob that occurred during the time of Solomon's son Rehoboam. Notice the healing occurs as the Lord returns His people to their ancestral land under the banner of David—the modern Israeli state. "'Then *the people of Israel and Judah will join together*,' says the Lord, '*weeping and seeking the Lord their God. They will ask the way to Jerusalem and will start back home again. They will bind themselves to the Lord with an eternal covenant that will never again be broken.*'"[640] "I will strengthen Judah and *save Israel*; I will establish them because I love *them*.

It will be as though I had never rejected them, for I am the Lord their God, who will hear their cries."[641]

But that will not happen without resistance. Many Gentile nations will form a coalition to overthrow Israel's right to possess the land of Palestine and Jerusalem. "I will make Jerusalem and Judah like an intoxicating drink to all the nearby nations that send their armies to besiege Jerusalem. On that day I will make Jerusalem a heavy stone, a burden for the world. None of the nations who try to lift it will escape unscathed."[642] The jealousy and hatred that the world nations still harbor toward Jews will provide opportunity for antichrist to broker an apparent peace agreement to save the world. But it will fail because again it is just another attempt to fulfill God's purposes by human effort. Then, Christ, who is the "Prince of Peace," will step in and "rule forever with fairness and justice from the throne of His ancestor David."[643] To those nations who sought to interfere with His plan, He will say, "*Yes, you nations will drink and stagger and disappear from history, as though you had never even existed. ...* And the people of Israel will come back [to Jerusalem] to reclaim their inheritance ... The exiles of Israel will return to their land ... The captives from Jerusalem exiled in the north will return to their homeland and resettle the villages of the Negev. Deliverers will go up to Mount Zion in Jerusalem to rule. And the Lord Himself will be King."[644]

Many will assume they are doing a great work for God in seeking to save the world by their own devices. Paul, however, gives a dire warning about this very point: "*they refuse to believe the truth* that would save them. So God will send great deception upon them, and *they will believe all these lies.*"[645] "All these lies" relate to a different plan than the one revealed by the God of Abraham, Isaac, and Jacob. It is a worldview not derived from Scripture but rather one created in the minds of those seeking their own power and world dominion. God's plan will be the only thing standing in their way, and as we have seen, His design has always been for Israel to live in the land He promised to Abraham and his descendants. Jealous of Israel's calling, godless nations will form a coalition to make one last attempt to rid the earth of Hebrew blood. Thirsty for world power, they do not realize they are really playing their part in God's plan.

The groundwork is already being laid for the world to believe the big lie. Today, multitudes of false ministers, so-called shepherds, take advantage of people's ignorance and fleece the flock. Jesus described them as "false prophets who come disguised as harmless sheep, but are really wolves that will tear you apart."[646] Being ignorant themselves of what the Scriptures really teach, they spiritually abuse sincere people to gain power and money in order to prop up their own brands of religion. One thing they have in common is they usually promote Gentile-derived religions as a substitute for God's choice of Israel.

Out of this mayhem, God will miraculously orchestrate *"peace between Jews and Gentiles* by creating in himself *one new person from the two groups."*[647] "The Lord says, 'Shout and rejoice, O Jerusalem, for I am coming to live among you. *Many nations will join themselves to the Lord on that day, and they, too, will be my people.* I will live among you, and *you will know that the Lord Almighty sent me to you.* The land of Judah will be the Lord's inheritance in the holy land, and *he will once again choose Jerusalem to be his own city.* Be silent before the Lord, *all humanity*, for he is springing into action from his holy dwelling.'"[648] After much blood and destruction during a time known as "Jacob's [Israel's] Trouble," a new nation will emerge—God's new Israel. The Messiah will then visit Jerusalem a second time to take His rightful place upon David's throne.[649]

"But the Lord will have mercy on the descendants of Jacob. Israel will be his special people once again. He will bring them back to settle once again in their own land. And *people from many different nations will come and join them there and become a part of the people of* Israel."[650] God will then throw a great feast for His family of redeemed children. Scripture even tells us what will be on the menu. "In Jerusalem, *the Lord Almighty will spread a wonderful feast for everyone around the world*. It will be a delicious feast of good food, with clear, well-aged wine and choice beef. In that day *he will remove the cloud of gloom, the shadow of death that hangs over the earth*. He will swallow up death forever! The Sovereign Lord will wipe away all tears. He will remove forever all insults and mockery against his land and his people. The Lord has spoken!"[651]

Why Israel? Because when people attend family gatherings it is often hard for them to hide their true feelings about others. Though intended for the family's enjoyment, often things can get tense and nasty with everyone leaving just thankful the event is over. Before we get to the reunion of God's spiritual family, we must, and will, lay aside all animosity. He is now giving us the opportunity to see what's in our hearts, and He is using Israel to do it. The Lord seeks to test the Gentiles for jealousy by once again acknowledging the Jews just as He tested the Jews when turning to the Gentiles. Antisemitism is still a very real thing, a deeply rooted spiritual sentiment that exists throughout our world. To hear something positive about the Jewish race evokes instant negative emotions within the hearts of many. As for the Jews, they must give up any feelings of spiritual pride and superiority, and commit to a serious inquiry into the validity of the messianic claim made by Jesus and his followers.

That's why those present at Abraham's family get-together are so special. By the grace of God, they were able to set aside their earthly territorialism and embrace each other as family.

CONCLUSION

The apostle John sought to explain the nature of God when he wrote, "God is love."[652] I really believe that is what the Lord is trying to say to every one of us regardless of our ancestry, our past history, or our present condition. I regard this as the Bible's major lesson. I also believe that the most effective way God could teach His love to us in our darkened understanding is through a show-and-tell story. It is HIS-STORY, and it reads like a passionate love novel complete with desire, romance, betrayal, and forgiveness. At times it seems like an illusional fantasy, but then we realize its reality is well documented by history.

It is a tale about an all-powerful king who falls in love and chooses a woman who is helpless and enslaved.[653] Giving her freedom and taking her away from her life of degradation, he seeks to make her his own. After buying her a city on a hill, he builds her a beautiful home, protected by a high wall from anything or anyone that might harm her. He promises always to love her and assures her that he will never, ever leave her. Intensely affectionate, he writes her songs and crafts the most seductive, romantic prose in an attempt to woo his sweetheart into returning the love he has for her. Only a fool would seek to steal her away from him or to break up his happy home.

But all is not well in an otherwise picturesque love story. She does not reciprocate his love. Instead, restless from being all wrapped up in a fairy tale life of secured luxury, she feels that she is missing out on something more exciting. So, she begins to seek lovers whom she doesn't even know. Time and again she cheats on her husband, only to have him forgive her with an even more profound love. Although she bears the king a son, the heir to his throne, she rejects her own flesh and blood in favor of continuing her adulterous lifestyle, even allowing strangers to kill him. Finally, the king has no choice but to let her go her own way and be mistreated by multitudes who only use her to satisfy their own self-interests. She wanders from house to house, even in foreign lands, sometimes by choice but mostly by force, destitute of a place to call home. Her subsequent offspring, though confused as to their real identities, still have some inner awareness that their mother once belonged to a special person in a special place.

The king will now do everything possible to get her back. But it must be different this time. She must finally come to her senses and desire him in the same way that he does her. That's what the readers are waiting for, isn't it? What the world is waiting for? For you see, the man in the story represents God; the woman His people Israel; the city on that beautiful hill Jerusalem; their house the Temple of the Lord; their child the Seed promised to her father Abraham, *the Mashiach*, the Lord Jesus Christ; her lovers the phantom gods who told her she could have anything her heart desired, only to empty her of all that made her truly happy; and the readers of this wonderful love story is the Gentile world.

Then one day, like the prodigal in the parable, the woman (Israel) awakes from her delusional dream and discovers the nightmare she has plunged herself in.[654] Like Eve, she realizes her nakedness and embraces her shame.[655] She feels a strange yet wonderful longing to return home and be made one with her husband (God). So, she goes back to the place (Jerusalem) where God had loved her so deeply. Remembering her firstborn son (Messiah) whom she despised and rejected, she now weeps for him.[656] With repentance that can only come from a truly regretful heart, she seeks forgiveness. And guess what? The king accepts her back and loves her even more than if she had never left! That's because she always has been, and always will be the "apple of His eye," His most precious possession, and He refuses to exist without her.[657]

As she returns home, she brings with her the offspring of many nations (Gentiles) whom the King adopts as His own! They, too, now share all the inherited privileges with the firstborn Son! For you see, it was never about our individual ethnicities. We were all included in God's original plan. Israel is just the model student chosen to illustrate to the entire class how God decided to deal with the human race that had plunged itself into sin. That's why in the Christian tradition we as children memorize what John continued to teach us concerning God's love, "For God so loved the world that he gave his only Son, *so that everyone who believes in him will not perish but have eternal life.*"[658] It's also why we learn the simple song, "Jesus loves the little children, all the children of the world; Red, and yellow, black and white, they are precious in His sight; Jesus came to save the children of the world."[659]

We Gentiles owe Israel a debt of gratitude. They did not pick their role in world history--God did it for them. They are like Balaam's donkey in that for millennia they have been carrying the world's heavy load, and when the world whipped them, we were blind to the fact they were but shielding us from the direct retribution of the Almighty.[660] In this, they were but acting as another type of Messiah whom their ancestral line bore for us. He, too, stands between us and God, interceding in our behalf as a divine firewall.[661]

But the time of the Gentiles is drawing near its close. God is about ready to judge the nations, and as the Bible inquires, "For the great day of their wrath has come, and who will be able to survive?"[662] "For we must all stand before Christ to be judged. We will each receive whatever we deserve for the good or evil we have done in our bodies."[663] Oh, God, how we need that shield of His protective grace!

Why have I repeatedly asked, *Why Israel?* Because God wants us to overcome our sinful tendencies of envy, jealousy, and hatred. He set up a plan designed to allow the human race to manifest its real nature of hate to itself, so that it could later look back and see the pain, suffering, sorrow, and destruction such evil causes. Then He offers us a better, more sane choice, "God showed how much he loved us by sending his only Son into the world so that we might have eternal life through him. This is real love … Dear friends, since God loved us that much, we surely ought to love each other. No one has ever seen God. But if we love each other, God lives in us, and his love has been brought to full expression through us."[664]

Though I know that some, if not many, will misinterpret it, I did not write this book motivated by any political agenda. I am a Gentile with nothing personal to gain by pointing out the Bible's support for Israel. If Scripture had stated it differently, then I would have done likewise. Current-day conflicts between Jews and Palestinians concerning their border disputes only indicate that human hearts are still hard on both sides. I once heard it stated that the Bible does not hold out a blueprint for peace in the Middle East. Maybe not in the short term, but eternally speaking that is exactly what it does. Peace between the bitterest of enemies is possible when the Spirit of

God enters the picture by filling the human heart with understanding that leads to forgiveness. The Bible is indeed a book of global reconciliation. My book is a mere attempt to reflect that same spirit. It has not tried to make the Bible say something it doesn't in order to create a narrative to advance any earthly political or religious organization.

While the world fights over earthly boundaries, God is planning to someday give the meek the entire earth. It's a hard teaching, but it's true, "Any man who makes it his object to keep his own life safe, will lose it, but whoever loses his life will preserve it."[665] While those with political ambition jockey for control of an earthly Jerusalem, God is preparing His family a New Jerusalem to be drop-shipped someday to our planet from heaven.[666] God will eventually Himself draw the borders, and people from all backgrounds will inherit the expanded boundaries that encompass the entire earth. Just as God once portioned off the Promised Land to the original tribes of Israel, He is to do the same with spiritual Israel after He conquers the nations who presently occupy the earth.[667]

Why do I ask, *Why Israel?* Because to remove ethnic Israel from its intended role in the world's storyline is to strip the Bible of its true meaning. Its nothing short of an attempt to rewrite the divine script, and we can be assured that God will not let that happen. Like the lion of Judah that He is, He is crouched and ready to spring into action to protect His territory and people. No group, political and/or religious, will ever succeed in such a foolish endeavor. What part of "the earth is the Lord's, and everything in it. The world and all its people belong to Him" do we not comprehend?[668]

But the story is not over. We haven't gotten to the part in which they all lived happily ever after. But we soon will even though before the dawn the world must pass through its midnight. Antisemitism is again to raise its ugly head in a big way, but it will be for the final time. As predicted, the antichrist's last-ditch effort will make all prior pograms and holocausts look like warm-up practice. Antichrist is the fool who tries to come between the King and His woman. He is arousing her (Israel's) former lovers (the world nations) to form a coalition to re-enact The Final Solution—to uproot the Jews from their homeland and rid them from the face of the earth. It will be a serious re-enactment of the book of Esther. Though Esther's story happened long ago, the Jewish people still remember it annually through their Festival of Purim.

And it will all be in preparation for the King to return, save the woman, and usher in His eternal kingdom. "It will be a time of trouble for my people Israel. Yet in the end, they will be saved."[669] Zechariah's vision will finally meet its reality as the Messiah makes His second appearance on earth. "On that day, *his feet will stand on the Mount of Olives*, which faces Jerusalem on the east."[670] That, of course, will be the fulfillment of what the angels told the disciples at His ascension from that same spot: "Jesus has been taken away from you into heaven. And someday, *just as you saw him go, he will return*."[671] The establishment of *His millennium kingdom on earth* will set the stage for events such as the resurrection of the dead; the final judgment of the Lake of Fire; the renovation of the earth; the descent of the New Jerusalem; and finally, the shepherding of the world into pastures of eternal bliss.[672]

Now comes the best part—and they lived happily ever after. "In that day the wolf and the lamb will live together; the leopard and the goat will be at peace. Calves and yearlings will be safe among lions, and a little child will lead them all. The cattle will graze among bears. Cubs and calves will lie down together. And lions will eat grass as the livestock do. Babies will crawl safely among poisonous snakes. Yes, a little child will put its hand in a nest of deadly snakes and pull it out unharmed. *Nothing will hurt or destroy in all my holy mountain.* And as the waters fill the sea, so the earth will be filled with people who know the Lord. *In that day the heir to David's throne will be a banner of salvation to all the world.* The nations will rally to him, for the land where he lives will be a glorious place. In that day the Lord will bring back a remnant of his people for the second time, returning them to the land of Israel … *He will raise a flag among the nations for Israel to rally around.* He will gather the scattered people of Judah from the ends of the earth. Then, at last, the jealousy between Israel and Judah will end. *They will not fight against each other anymore."*[673]

However, it is not only the Gentiles who struggle with taking God at His word concerning His vow never to forsake Israel. Throughout the ages, the Jews have disbelieved it as well. Nearly 3,000 years ago the prophet wrote, "Zion [the Jews] say, 'the Lord has deserted us; the Lord has forgotten us.' Never! Can a mother forget her nursing child? Can she feel no love for a child she has borne? But even if that were possible, I would not forget you! See, *I have written your name on my hand.* Ever before me is a picture of Jerusalem's walls in ruins. *Soon your descendants will come back, and all who are trying to destroy you will go away* … This is what the Sovereign Lord says: 'See, I will give a signal to the godless nations. They will carry your little sons back to you in their arms; they will bring your daughters on their shoulders. Kings and queens will serve you. They will care for all your needs. They will bow to the earth before you and lick the dust from your feet. *Then you will know that I am the Lord… All the world will know that I, the Lord, am your Savior and Redeemer, the Mighty One of Israel.'"*[674]

The God of Abraham, Isaac, and Jacob has staked proof of His existence on the fact He would not only maintain the

Hebrew people until the end of the world, but *they would end up being the "head" and not the "tail" among the political nations of the earth.* The Lord sealed the guarantee at Calvary when He tattooed their name in His own body, thus signifying with those scars of crucifixion that they will be with Him throughout eternity. Yet it is amazing how many among the Jewish people today, who have such a rich spiritual heritage, dismiss their special calling, or are even unaware of it!

Once again, I ask, *Why Israel?* Because, Hebrews do not look to Christian history to find their origin of faith, but Christians must look to the Hebrew's past to find any evidence of theirs. If that is true, then how can any Gentile say with a straight face that God has forgotten the people He originally chose? How in the world can various sects of Christians who profess to believe what the Bible teaches accept the idea they were chosen to replace Israel when the concept of a Christian didn't evolve until some 2,000 years after God called Abraham? Those who advocate such theology face real difficulties when presented with Old Testament writings that clearly explain God's relationship with the Hebrew people, even to this day. They have only two choices to make: (1) dismiss Old Testament history entirely by saying that the New Testament made it obsolete by teaching that the church replaced Israel. Yet, the New Testament record itself presents the same challenges to this theory in passages such as Romans 9-11. (2) or they can accept the Old and New Testaments as they read and give Israel its rightful place in God's master plan for saving the human race.

The answer to such a dilemma is this: Gentiles from all backgrounds are also chosen of God *if it is understood in the context of being adopted into the Hebrew family* that God started with Abraham. We Gentiles have absolutely no need to try to secure a place in God's kingdom ourselves. The Lord has already considered us and has not overlooked us. He had Isaiah write, *"And my blessings are for Gentiles, too, when they commit themselves to the Lord. Do not let them think that I consider them second class citizens ... I will bring them also to my holy mountain of Jerusalem* and will fill them with joy in my house of prayer ... For the Sovereign Lord, who brings back the outcasts of Israel, says: *'I will bring others, too, besides my people Israel.'"*[675] Genesis 17:4 makes it crystal clear that from the initial calling of Abraham he understood the covenant was designed to make him the father "of many nations," not just Israel. Yet, though still gentile those nations will be "counted" as being a part of Israel. It is in this context that the Bible portrays how Gentiles become incorporated as "the new people [Israel] of God."[676]

We must allow God to arrange His family as He sees fit! He specifically told Abraham how the family of faith was to be ordered. "Do not be upset ... Do just as Sarah says, *for Isaac is the son through whom your descendants will be counted."*[677] We need to understand that "everything has already been decided. *It was known long ago what each person would be [Jew or Gentile]. So there's no use arguing with God about your destiny."*[678] Every Gentile has the right to claim their part of Christ's inheritance through "adoption" into Abraham's family of faith, or else choose to go the way of all the great world empires who tried to restructure the world on their own terms--and who no longer exist. Are we Gentiles content with our God-appointed role as being part of the tail, and giving up our quest to be the head? Are we willing to humble ourselves by accepting our appointed position in God's family plan as a wild branch grafted into original Hebrew stock?

Gentiles today are being tested as was the woman who came

begging Jesus to heal her demon-possessed daughter. "*Since she was a Gentile ... Jesus told her, 'First I should help my own family, the Jews. It isn't right to take food from the children and throw it to the dogs.' She replied, 'That's true, Lord, but even the dogs under the table are given some crumbs from the children's plates.'"* I just love the response Jesus gave her: "'Good answer!' he said, 'And because you have answered so well, I have healed your daughter.'"[679]

What a privileged role and high calling it is to have any degree of participation with Christ in "bringing salvation to the farthest corners of the earth."[680] How painful, yet wonderful, to decrease in our own spiritual self-assessment so that God's overall purpose in the earth can increase. *How humbling it is to recognize if it were not for God's work through the Hebrew race all Gentiles, Christians included, would never have heard of Jesus the Messiah and would still be worshiping the pagan gods of our ancestors.*

Finally, we get to the real query. Would we Gentiles really want it any other way? After the Jews rejected Christ, God turned and gave the gospel to us through revelations from Hebrew history that taught us the truth about Christ—the New Covenant Messiah. We didn't do anything to deserve this, and we only know what we do because God woke us up to tell us. Now the Jews are asleep. If we could advise God on what He should do, what would we tell Him? Let His chosen people continue on sleeping as eternal punishment for their sins, or be merciful to them just as He was to us?

I think Paul gave us the clear, unmistakable answer: "*I am saying all of this especially for you Gentiles.* God has appointed me as the apostle to the Gentiles. *I lay great stress on this*, for I want to find a way to make the Jews want what you Gentiles have [faith in Christ], and in that way, I might save some

Conclusion

of them. For since the Jew's rejection [of Christ as Messiah] meant that God offered salvation to the rest of the world, how much more wonderful their acceptance will be [as if to imply it is certain to happen]. *It will be life for those who were dead.*"⁶⁸¹

Prayerfully, this book will realize it's intended purpose, and the next time the reader hears the name *Israel*, they will better understand *Why!*

ENDNOTES

AUTHOR'S PREFACE

1 https://nowthinkaboutit.com/2012/06/why-the-bible-is-the-true-best-seller/
2 See Genesis 3:19; see also Romans 5:12*
3 See Genesis 3:14, 15 and Romans 5:17-19*
4 Genesis 3:20
5 Genesis 4:1-16
6 Genesis 4:25*
7 Oxford Dictionary
8 See Isaiah 46:9-10
9 Genesis 3:14-15*
10 Revelation 12:9
11 Revelation 12:1-5*; The fact this symbolism refers to Israel is best understood through Joseph's dream in which the sun, moon, and 12 stars represent Jacob and his offspring of 12 sons who headed the 12 tribes of Israel. See Genesis 37:9, 10
12 Revelation 17:14
13 Obadiah 15
14 Obadiah 16*
15 Revelation 5:9, 10*
16 Romans 2:10, 11
17 2 Peter 3:9

[18] Scripture quotations are taken from the Holy Bible, New Living Translation, copyright © 1996. Used by permission of Tyndale House Publishers, Inc. Wheaton, Illinois 60189. All Rights Reserved.

*bracketed material supplied to clarify context

Chapter 1

[19] Genesis 12:1-3
[20] See Genesis 12:10-17
[21] Hebrews 11:8-10
[22] Genesis 13:14-17
[23] Genesis 15:2-8
[24] See Genesis 15:9-12
[25] Genesis 15:13-18. Fire is a biblical metaphor used to describe the divine presence as here demonstrated by the smoking pot and flaming torch. God alone walked through the covenantal pathway while Abram slept, thus demonstrating it was to be a unilateral agreement.
[26] Genesis 17:5-8
[27] Genesis 17:15-22. Regarding God's blessing of Abraham's son Ishmael by creating a "great nation" from him, it happened this way. After arriving in Canaan, Abraham went into Egypt as a result of a famine (Genesis 12:10). It was there his wife Sarai acquired as a servant "an Egyptian woman named Hagar," who bore Abraham his son Ishmael (Genesis 16:1-6). When he was older, Ishmael's "mother arranged a marriage for him with a young woman from Egypt" (Genesis 21:21). The Bible provides a brief history of Ishmael and his offspring in Genesis 25:12-18. He had 12 sons who became the founders of today's Arab nations.

[28] Genesis 21:1-3

[29] Genesis 21:10-14

[30] Genesis 22:7-14; God is sometimes thought of as cruel in that He really intended that Abraham kill his son, yet nothing could be farther from the truth. It is a false witness to His nature. This was later brought out when the Lord gave His laws to His people at Mount Sinai. "Do not give any of your children as a sacrifice to Molech, for you must not profane [debase or degrade] the name [character] of your God. I am the Lord" (Leviticus 18:21*).

Again, later the Lord rebuked the people of Judah when they disobeyed His command. "They have built the pagan shrines of Topheth in the valley of the son of Hinnom, where they sacrifice their little sons and daughters in the fire. I have never commanded such a horrible deed; it never even crossed my mind to command such a thing!" (Jeremiah 7:31). No, what God was doing with the situation with Abraham was demonstrating how He is different from the pagan gods of Abraham's past. Moreover, He was teaching him the principle of the substitutionary sacrifice that He was preparing to make for the world by giving His own Son to die in our place.

[31] See Isaiah 53:7

[32] Genesis 22:17, 18

[33] Genesis 24:16

[34] Genesis 24:60, 61

[35] Genesis 24:67

[36] Genesis 26:2-4; also see verses 23, 24

[37] See Genesis 21:12 and Hebrews 11:18

[38] Genesis 15:6

[39] See Hebrews 11:17-19

[40] See James 2:23

* bracketed material supplied to clarify context

Chapter 2

[41] See Genesis 25:7-9
[42] Genesis 25:5
[43] Genesis 25:23*
[44] Genesis 25:29-34
[45] Genesis 27:29
[46] Genesis 27:31-38
[47] See Romans 8:25
[48] Genesis 27:41-45
[49] Genesis 28:3-4
[50] Genesis 28:13-15
[51] Genesis 29:17
[52] See Genesis 30:25-43; 31:1-21
[53] Genesis 32:26-28
[54] Jeremiah 29:13; Berean Study Bible
[55] 1 John 5:4, 5*
[56] Genesis 3:16; The story of Jacob building his family appears in Genesis 29 and 30. The account of Rachel's death is in Genesis 35:16-26.
[57] See Genesis 35:28-29
[58] See Genesis 37
[59] Genesis 39–50
[60] Hebrews 11:35
[61] Genesis 50:19, 20
[62] Exodus 1:8, 9
[63] See Genesis 15:13-16

[64] Genesis 50:24-26

[65] Hebrews 11:22; Joseph's dying wish was honored when the Lord brought His people out of Egypt. "Moses took the bones of Joseph with him, for Joseph had made the sons of Israel swear that they would take his bones with them when God led them out of Egypt – as he was sure God would" (Exodus 13:19).

* bracketed material supplied to clarify context

Chapter 3

[66] Isaiah 49:22, 23

[67] Josephus, Antiquities of the Jews 9:2

[68] See Exodus 1:22

[69] Acts 7:22

[70] Hebrews 11:24-27*

[71] Exodus 3:1-15; The name by which God identifies Himself both Jesus and Peter invoke in New Testament times. See Mark 12:26, 27 and Acts 3:13

[72] Deuteronomy 4:23, 24

[73] Hebrews 12:28, 29

[74] 2 Thessalonians 2:7, 8*

[75] Revelation 20:15

[76] See Exodus 13:21, 22

[77] See 2 Kings 6:8-23

[78] See Daniel 3

[79] 2 Peter 3:10

[80] 1 Corinthians 3:11-15*

[81] 2 Corinthians 4:18, New International Version

[82] Deuteronomy 32:47
[83] Exodus 4:22, 23*
[84] Exodus 11:4-9
[85] Exodus 6:2-8
[86] 1 Corinthians 5:7, 8; World English Bible
[87] Exodus 12:35, 36
[88] Isaiah 60:1-22
[89] Exodus 14:28-30
[90] Exodus 12:37, 38
[91] Exodus 19:18
[92] Exodus 20:2-5
[93] Romans 1:21-25
[94] Exodus 24:17, 18
[95] Exodus 32:4
[96] Exodus 32: 13, 14
[97] Arthur Hertzberg, Judaism (George Braziller, 1961), p. 30
[98] Deuteronomy 9:5, 6
[99] Deuteronomy 12:29-31
[100] Exodus 34:15
[101] Deuteronomy 23:12, 13; The book of Leviticus details the instructions given to the Israelites through Moses.
[102] Ephesians 2:12, Contemporary English Version
[103] Isaiah 43:1-3
[104] Deuteronomy 1:8
[105] Numbers 13:31-33*; see Numbers 13 and 14 for the entire account.
[106] Exodus 13:21, 22

*bracketed material supplied to clarify context

[107] Genesis 28:15

Chapter 4

[108] See Deuteronomy 1:2-3
[109] See Numbers 27:12-22
[110] Joshua 1:6
[111] Numbers 24:9
[112] Joshua 23:14-16
[113] Joshua 24:14-15*
[114] See Genesis 3:15 and Revelation 12:1-5
[115] Judges 2:1
[116] Judges 2:11, 12
[117] Judges 21:25
[118] 1 Samuel 8:5-9
[119] 1 Samuel 8:19, 20
[120] 1 Samuel 12:18, 19
[121] 1 Samuel 12:20-22
[122] 1 Samuel 18:6-9
[123] 1 Samuel 22:2
[124] 1 Samuel 22:23
[125] 1 Samuel 24:20; Though Saul put David on his most wanted list, their relationship was much closer than one might think. David had married Saul's youngest daughter, Michal (1 Samuel 18:20-29). Also, Saul's eldest son, Jonathan, was David's closest friend. First Samuel 18:1 tells us that "Jonathan became one in spirit with David, and he loved him as himself" (New International Version). Jonathan would try to reconcile the two men, but to no avail. Though Jonathan was heir to Saul's throne, when one reads the entire story it is quite

obvious that he supported David. When Jonathan later died along with his father in battle, David, upon hearing the news lamented for both: "I grieve for you, Jonathan my brother; you were very dear to me. Your love for me was wonderful, more wonderful than that of women. How the mighty have fallen! The weapons of war have perished!" (2 Samuel 1:26, 27; New International Version). Saul's character flaws were obvious, and because of this, biblical scholars have long viewed him as an enemy to Israel. Some in the Hebrew tradition, however, offer a different assessment. Renowned Jewish historian Joan Comay observes, "The career of the first Hebrew king thus ended in a noble last stand against hopeless odds. Intent on stressing David's role, the later biblical chroniclers may have done Saul less than justice. He had been tragically unstable – moody, superstitious and liable to fits of violence. But he emerges as a brave and honourable man and a redoubtable general. He had accustomed the tribes to the overriding authority of a collective ruler, stimulated their emerging sense of nationhood, united their fighting men under a single command, and for some two decades held their external foes at bay. His reign had ended on Mount Gilboa in defeat and death; but the foundations had been laid on which David would build an empire" (Joan Comay, The Hebrew Kings [William Morrow And Company, Inc.; New York, 1977], p. 31).

[126] 1 Samuel 25:28

[127] 1 Samuel 25:39-44

[128] Psalm 89:3; also see 2 Samuel 7

[129] 2 Samuel 23:5

[130] Genesis 49:10

[131] See 1 Samuel 13:13, 14

[132] The dramatic story of David's great sin and God's even

greater forgiveness appears in 2 Samuel 11 and 12. David's experience reveals not only the sinfulness of our human natures, but the wickedness of our hypocrisy as well. The condemnation we so willing impose on others while ignoring the fact that we have done the same, or worse, God will not tolerate. The good news is that God does forgive, so why should we not freely take advantage of it as David so wisely and sincerely did.

[133] Revelation 5:5; 3:7
[134] See Genesis 12:3 and Galatians 3:8
[135] 2 Samuel 5:4
[136] 1 Chronicles 12:23-40
[137] 1 Chronicles 12:23
[138] 1 Chronicles 11:1, 2
[139] 1 Kings 11:10-13*
[140] 1 Kings 12:16-20*
[141] 1 Kings 12:24
[142] Luke 1:31-33
[143] Luke 1:68-73
[144] Matthew 27:37
[145] Acts 13:23-41*

* bracketed material supplied to clarify context

Chapter 5

[146] See 1 Kings 12, and 2 Chronicles 10 and 11
[147] Joan Comay, The Hebrew Kings, pp. vii, viii; William Morrow and Company, Inc.; New York, 1977; copyright 1976 by Joan Comay
[148] Psalm 105:6-11
[149] Nehemiah 9:31

150 1 Kings 16:30-33
151 See 1 Kings 21
152 1 Kings 21:25
153 See Matthew 17:1-8
154 1 Kings 17:1-4
155 1 Kings 17:12-16
156 See 1 Kings 17:17-24
157 Hebrews 11:13-16, New International Version
158 1 John 4:17, 18*
159 1 Samuel 17:26
160 1 Samuel 17:46, 47
161 Judges 6:12
162 Gideon's story appears in Judges 6-8.
163 Mark 14:36
164 1 Peter 3:13, 14
165 Psalm 23:4*
166 Isaiah 8:13
167 Proverbs 9:10
168 Romans 8:15-17
169 1 Kings 18:1
170 1 Kings 18:17-40*
171 1 Kings 18:44, 45
172 1 Kings 19:3
173 1 Kings 19:18
174 See 2 Kings 9 and 10

* bracketed material supplied to clarify context

Chapter 6

[175] Arthur Hertzberg, Judaism (George Braziller, 1961), p. 15.
[176] See Genesis 3:15
[177] Amos 3:2
[178] 2 Kings 8:18, 19
[179] Daniel 4:25
[180] Daniel 6:26, 27
[181] Daniel 9:2
[182] Jeremiah 29:10-14*
[183] See Daniel 9 and Leviticus 26
[184] Daniel 9:15-19
[185] Ezekiel 4:5, 6
[186] Daniel 9:25; Study Bible
[187] Isaiah 45:13
[188] Galatians 4:4, Holman Christian Standard Bible
[189] As can be expected there are varying opinions regarding the dating of events in the seventy sevens prophecy. Biblical chronology is a can of worms with many different interpretations and assignments of dates. While here we begin with the 444 BC decree, some date it to 445 BC. Reputable scholars place the death of Christ variously in AD 30, 31, and 33. For those interested in this arcane subject, a useful tool is a book by the noted evangelical scholar Jack Finegan, Handbook of Biblical Chronology. Revised ed. Peabody MA: Hedrickson Publishers, 1998.
[190] See Zechariah 9:9 and John 12:12-16
[191] John 8:53-58
[192] Mark 8:27-31

193 Luke 24:19-21
194 Isaiah 53:1-3
195 Daniel 9:26*
196 Psalm 118:22-23; see also Matthew 21:33-46 and Acts 4:8-12
197 John 1:10-13*
198 Luke 24:26-27; An excellent website provides 353 Messianic prophecies fulfilled by Jesus. https://www.accordingto-the-scriptures.org/prophecy/353prophecies.html
199 Romans 1:2-4*
200 John 8:51;
201 See 1 Corinthians 15:17-19
202 2 Peter 1:16
203 There has been, and continues to be, an ongoing debate as to whether or not the Antichrist will be of Jewish or Gentile descent. The most convincing evidence supporting his Gentile heritage appears in Daniel 9:27. Commenting on this verse, one Bible student states, "Fourthly, the Bible not only teaches that Antichrist will be Gentile, but it also tells us he will be of Roman descent. This is understood from Daniel 9:27 where the one cutting a covenant with Israel is said to represent the revived Roman Empire, since it was the Romans who destroyed Jerusalem and the Temple in A.D. 70." Thomas D. Ice, "The Ethnicity of the Antichrist" (2009). Article Archives. Paper 93. http://digitalcommons.liberty.edu/pretrib_arch/93
204 See Revelation 13:8
205 Hebrews 9:16-28*
206 Romans 8:31-32
207 John 11:25-26
208 The word "testament" is synonymous with "covenant," so the Bible consists of the Old and New Covenants.

[209] Daniel 10:14*
[210] Daniel 12:9-10
[211] Daniel 12:13*
* bracketed material supplied to clarify context

Chapter 7

[212] Isaiah 45:18-23*
[213] Romans 1:20
[214] Amos 3:2-7
[215] Deuteronomy 4:26, 27
[216] Deuteronomy 32:21
[217] See Romans 10:19
[218] Romans 9:4
[219] Ephesians 2:11-13*
[220] Romans 15:8-10
[221] Mark 1:17
[222] Ronald E. Diprose, Israel and the Church, pp. 16, 17.
[223] Romans 9:6-8; see also Genesis 21:12
[224] Galatians 3:22-29
[225] Romans 11:2-8*; see also Isaiah 29:10
[226] Romans 11:15; 25-27*; This is in keeping with Isaiah 59:20, 21 in which God promises to "buy back those in Israel."
[227] Romans 11:28, 29
[228] Ephesians 3:8, 9
[229] Ephesians 3:6,10, 11
[230] Isaiah 49:6
[231] Ephesians 2:14, 15
[232] See Ephesians 1:5; 2:19; and Galatians 3:29*

233 Isaiah 56:3
234 Ephesians 2:18
235 Ephesians 4:2-5
236 Ephesians 4:14
237 1 Corinthians 3:21*
238 See Matthew 13:44
239 Hebrews 8:11
240 Hebrews 12:23
241 1 Corinthians 10:32
242 Romans 8:10
243 2 Corinthians 5:6, 7
244 1 Corinthians 1:18-25*
245 Luke 4:25-27*
246 Luke 4:28-30
247 Luke 2:30, 31
248 Luke 24:46, 47*
249 Ronald E. Diprose, Israel and the Church, pp. 10, 11, 17.
250 Galatians 6:14-16*; Many Christians use this passage in an attempt to prove that the Christian Church has replaced Israel as the new "Spiritual Israel." However, when employed in such a manner, it must first be wrested from its context. Paul is referring here to an invisible body of believers comprised of both Jews and Gentiles, not a visible religious establishment.
251 See 2 Corinthians 5:17; Revelation 21; Isaiah 66:22; 2 Peter 3:13
252 Dr. Renald E. Showers, What on Earth Is God Doing, p. 59.
253 Acts 4:27, 28*
254 See Acts 3:12-25
255 Acts 15:16 also Amos 9:11, 12

[256] Acts 26:6, 7*
[257] Acts 1:6, 7*
[258] Jeremiah 33:24-26; see also Jeremiah 31:35-37
[259] Acts 26:17, 18
[260] See Deuteronomy 7:6
[261] Amos 8:7; see also 2 Chronicles 7:14
[262] Deuteronomy 4:30,-31; This promise is reiterated to Israel in numerous other scriptures such as Deuteronomy 31:6-8; Joshua 1:5; 1 Kings 8:57; Psalm 37:28; and Psalm 94:14.
[263] See Hebrews 13:5
[264] Numbers 23:19
[265] See Luke 23:34
[266] Jude 11
[267] Romans 11:17-24*
* bracketed material supplied to clarify context

Chapter 8

[268] Daniel 12:1
[269] Jeremiah 30:7-11*
[270] Matthew 24:21,22
[271] See Jeremiah 30:7
[272] Deuteronomy 29:28
[273] Deuteronomy 30:3-5
[274] Zechariah 10:9, 10
[275] Isaiah 43:5, 6
[276] Ezekiel 11:16, 17
[277] Jeremiah 16:14, 15; also see Zechariah 10:11
[278] Ezekiel 37:3

[279] Ezekiel 37:10-14
[280] Ezekiel 37:15-28
[281] Revelation 7:9
[282] Ezekiel 37:13
[283] Ezekiel 37:28
[284] Exodus 5:2
[285] See Luke 18:1-8*
[286] See Jeremiah 30:10-11 and Amos 9:14-15
[287] Clarence Larkin, Dispensational Truth or God's Plan and Purpose in the Ages (Martino Publishing, 1918), p. 63
[288] 1 John 4:1-3*
[289] John F. Walvoord; The Nations in The Millennium and The Eternal State; January 2008; www.walvoord.com
[290] Isaiah 14:1
[291] webstersdictionary1828.com/Dictionary/mercy
[292] See Exodus 30:6
[293] James 1:1; 2:13
[294] Isaiah 14:1-2*
[295] Some people argue that because the Jewish bloodline has become so mixed with the other races over time, today it is impossible to determine who is really Jewish, and therefore this somehow discredits the reliability of the biblical prophecies concerning their return to Israel. Well, positive identification didn't seem to interfere with Hitler making a determination of Jews in Europe just some 90 plus years ago. Not only did he target them, but also their sympathizers.

Is it really necessary that we have a technical definition of Jewry before we accept the reality of the prophecies? First, we need to recognize as we discuss Judaism that we are not just speaking of an indigenous group, but a religious belief. Judaism is designed not just to call the world's attention to a people with a particular physical heritage, but that these same people will direct the world's attention to a specific God – the God of Abraham, Isaac, and Jacob.

For those who are really that concerned about their potential Jewish heritage, or desire to convert to the religion itself, then modern technology has made it easier. DNA tests are now available claiming the ability to trace one's biological connection through their mother's ancestry (Judaism considers its heritage as passed on through the mother). The internet reveals myriads of opinions of what is required for one to become part of the Jewish faith. It will most likely require male circumcision, or the ceremonial drawing of blood for those who have already had the procedure. In addition, it will require numerous lifestyle changes as it relates not only to religious practices such as sacred observance of the weekly Saturday Sabbath and other annual holy days, but other issues such as prescribed health and dietary habits. Furthermore, it will also need to be acknowledged by a "bone fide Orthodox beit din (ecclesiastical court)" according to Rabbi Menachem Posner.1 (https://www.chabad.org/library/article_cdo/aid/3408865/jewish/How-Do-I-Know-If-I-Am-a-Jew.htm)

All such discussion takes us back to arguments being made when the Lord first began taking the gospel to the Gentiles. What exactly should be expected of those wanting to accept Israel's Messiah? Once again, the Jerusalem council of early church leaders settled on having them abstain from eating the meat of animals sacrificed to false gods; sexual immorality; and ingesting the blood of animals (Acts 15:19, 20).

Paul provided his listeners with even greater insight of exactly whom the Lord considers to be a Jew. He said we become an Israelite not by the works of the law given to their ancestors at

Mount Sinai, but by believing in the covenant given to Abraham, Isaac, and Jacob. The apostle told the Galatians that the patriarchs found and followed the true God centuries before the giving of the law (see Galatians 3:16-18). Thus, he was adamant that "the Scriptures looked forward to this time when God would accept the Gentiles, too, on the basis of their faith. God promised this good news to Abraham long ago when he said, 'All nations will be blessed through you.' And so it is: All who put their faith in Christ share the same blessing Abraham received because of his faith... Through the work of Christ Jesus, God has blessed the Gentiles with the same blessing he promised to Abraham, and we Christians received the promised Holy Spirit through faith" (Galatians 3:8-14).

Paul continued, "So Christ has really set us free. Now make sure that you stay free, and don't get tied up again in slavery to the law. Listen! I, Paul, tell you this: If you are counting on circumcision to make you right with God, then Christ cannot help you. I'll say it again. If you are trying to find favor with God by being circumcised [or by obeying any other requirements of the law] you must obey all of the regulations in the whole law of Moses [or Mitzvot]. For if you are trying to make yourselves right with God by keeping the law, you have been cut off from Christ! You have fallen away from God's grace" (Galatians 5:1-4*).

The apostle became even more definitive in his letter to the Romans. "For you are not a true Jew just because you were born of Jewish parents or because you have gone through the Jewish ceremony of circumcision. No, a true Jew is one whose heart is right with God. And true circumcision is not a cutting of the body but a change of heart produced by God's Spirit. Whoever has that kind of change seeks praise from God, not from people" (Romans 2:28, 29). However, as new believers by faith, we shouldn't be surprised when we find ourselves mysteriously desiring to put into practice things contained in God's law. It is tangible evidence of a new Spirit who sits enthroned within our hearts!

We must take extreme caution when we consider prophecies relating to events foretold to happen just prior to the Messiah's return. Just as there is a physical return of the Jewish people to the ancient land of Israel, more importantly, there will be a spiritual return to the God of Israel in the hearts of all true believers, regardless of their physical heritage. That is what really counts!

[296] https://www.jewishvirtuallibrary.org/law-of-return*

[297] https://www.jewishvirtuallibrary.org/jewish-and-non-jewish-population-of-israel-palestine-1517-present

[298] Exodus 12:37, 38

[299] https://www.jewishvirtuallibrary.org/jewish-population-of-the-world

[300] https://blackdemographics.com/population/

[301] https://www.quora.com/How-many-Russian-Jewish-people-were-killed-in-pogroms

[302] 1 Corinthians 1:25-29

[303] https://www.jewishvirtuallibrary.org/the-spanish-expulsion-1492

[304] Fiddler on the Roof, a book by Joseph Stein about a Jewish family and their community located in the Pale of Settlement of Imperial Russia near the turn of the twentieth century. It made its Broadway debut in 1964. The 1971 film adaptation is a musical with music written by Jerry Bock, and lyrics by Sheldon Harnick. The story ends with authorities dissolving the Jewish community of Anatevka, Ukraine, and its citizens dispersing, some to Israel and others to America. Still hoping

to find their Promise Land, it depicts the massive migration of Jewish people that took place to both America and their biblical homeland Israel during the late 19th and early 20th centuries.

[305] https://www.jewishhistory.org/the-zionist-movement/

[306] https://mfa.gov.il/mfa/foreignpolicy/peace/guide/pages/declaration%20of%20establishment%20of%20state%20of%20israel.aspx

[307] https://www.history.com/this-day-in-history/the-balfour-declaration

[308] Rauschning, Hitler Speaks, p. 234

[309] Mein Kampf (Houghton Mifflin Company, 1939), p. 447.*

[310] Ibid., p. 84.

[311] http://www2.gvsu.edu/walll/Churchill%20and%20the%20Holocaust.htm

[312] Jeremiah 49:16., Holman Bible

[313] https://mfa.gov.il/mfa/foreignpolicy/peace/guide/pages/declaration%20of%20establishment%20of%20state%20of%20israel.aspx

[314] www.trumanlibrary.gov/library/online-collections/recognition-of-state-of-israel

[315] Isaiah 66:7-9

* bracketed material supplied to clarify context

Chapter 9

[316] Quote by M. K. Soni.

[317] Forrest Gump, screenplay written by Eric Roth based on the 1986 novel by Winston Groom.

[318] John 14:1-3

[319] Genesis 12:6
[320] Genesis 12:7
[321] Genesis 22:2
[322] Genesis 11:4
[323] Isaiah 57:15
[324] Isaiah 40:4, New International Version
[325] Exodus 3:12
[326] Exodus 25:8, 9
[327] Hebrews 8:5
[328] Leviticus 17:1-3
[329] Deuteronomy 12:2-6*
[330] 2 Samuel 7:2
[331] See 1 Chronicles 21 and 22; also 2 Samuel 24
[332] Psalm 132:13-18; see more songs about Jerusalem in Psalm 120-134
[333] 2 Chronicles 3:1
[334] 2 Chronicles 6:4-6; see also 2 Samuel 7
[335] 1 Kings 10:23, 24
[336] 1 Kings 4:26, American Standard Version
[337] 1 Kings 4:22-23*, American Standard Version
[338] 1 Kings 4:20, American Standard Version
[339] 1 Kings 11:1-8
[340] Matthew 16:18*, International Standard Version; In some Christian quarters the thinking here is that Jesus is building His church upon Peter whom He refers to as a rock. Other scriptural texts such as Ephesians 2:20 clarify this confusion, lumping Peter and the other apostles with all believers, "You are like a building with the apostles and prophets as the foundation and with Christ as the most important stone" (Con-

temporary English Version). Peter himself testified, "Come to Jesus Christ. He is the living stone [rock] people have rejected, but which God has highly honored. And now you are living stones being used to build a spiritual house ... It is just as God says in the Scriptures, 'Look! I am placing in Zion [Jerusalem] a choice and precious cornerstone. No one who has faith in this one will be disappointed" (1 Peter 2:4-6*, Contemporary English Version). Zechariah informs us that "the cornerstone will come from Judah" (Zechariah 10:4, Berean Study Bible). The Bible gives us no clear indication exactly what tribe Peter was from, but again and again it does confirm that Jesus Christ was from Judah.

[341] 2 Kings 23:27
[342] Deuteronomy 29:24-28
[343] Matthew 5:14
[344] Zechariah 9:9
[345] See Luke 19:28-40
[346] Luke 19:41-44
[347] Acts 1:9-12
[348] Zechariah 14:4
[349] Isaiah 40:3-5
[350] Luke 21:24
[351] See Psalm 122:6; "Throughout its long history Jerusalem has been attacked 52 times, captured and recaptured 44 times, besieged 23 times, and destroyed twice." (Do We Divide the Holiest Holy City? Moment Magazine, June 3, 2008, According to Eric H. Clines tally in "Jerusalem Besieged.")
[352] Clarence Larkin, Truth or God's Plan and Purpose in the Ages (Martino Publishing, 1918, reprinted 2015), p. 61.
[353] Micah 3:12*

354 https://www.britannica.com/place/Aelia-Capitolina

355 An excellent history regarding the struggle between Christian and Islamic forces after the Jews' removal from the region can be found in the book Sword and Scimitar (Fourteen Centuries of War Between Islam and The West) by Raymond Ibrahim (2018).

356 Leviticus 26:33

357 https://www.aish.com/h/9av/j/48956656.html*

358 https://www.jpost.com/Opinion/Unto-the-nations-505760

359 See Luke 21:24; Some versions translate this as "time of the Gentiles."

360 New York Times; June 8, 1967; Many historians consider such military conflicts as part of an ongoing war between the Arabs and Israelis that started the moment Israel achieved its statehood. Encyclopedia Britannica defines the Arab-Israeli wars as a "series of military conflicts between Israeli and various Arab forces, most notably in 1948–49, 1956, 1967, 1973, 1982, and 2006." (https://www.britannica.com/event/Arab-Israeli-wars)

361 Israeli Commander Motta Gur to his brigade upon their recapture of Jerusalem's Old City; http://www.sixdaywar.org/content/ReunificationJerusalem.asp

362 Psalm 126:1, 2

363 Isaiah 52:9, 10

364 Zechariah 8:1-8

365 https://www.factsaboutisrael.uk/agriculture-in-israel/; https://mfa.gov.il/mfa/innovativeisrael/agriculture/Pages/default.aspx?WPID=WPQ3&PN=2

Old Testament prophecies predicted that when the Lord removed the Hebrew people from their land it would become desolate and unproductive (Deuteronomy 29:22, 23). Yet it also predicted the return of the land's usefulness would coincide with the return of the Hebrews to it. When the Jews began returning to the land of Israel in the latter part of the nineteenth century it was a malaria infested wasteland. The first Kibbutz was founded in 1909 and a more organized work of reclaiming the land's agrarian treasures began. Ezekiel spoke of this time by writing "The fields that used to lie empty and desolate – a shock to all who passed by – will again be farmed. And when I [the Lord] bring you back, the people will say, 'This god-forsaken land is now like Eden's garden! The ruined cities now have strong walls, and they are filled with people! Then the nations all around ... will know that I, the Lord, rebuilt the ruins and planted lush crops in the wilderness. For I, the Lord, have promised this, and I will do it'" (Ezekiel 36:34-36*). Through Isaiah the Lord proclaimed what He would do for his people when He reinstated them to their land: "I will open up rivers for them on high plateaus. I will give them fountains of waters in the valleys. In the deserts they will find pools of water. Rivers fed by springs will flow across the dry, parched ground. I will plant trees – cedar, acacia, myrtle, olive, cypress, fir, and pine – on barren land. Everyone will see this miracle and understand that it is the Lord, the Holy One of Israel, who did it" (Isaiah 41:18-20).

[366] Jerusalem Post; Israel Welcomes Record Breaking 4.55 Million Tourists in 2019; By Eytan Halon; December 29, 2019.

[367] There is some debate as to the exact location of the former Temples. While tradition teaches that they stood in the exact spot where the Dome of the Rock now resides, there is a theory they were actually located closer to the Gihon Spring. The theory extrapolates that the current "Wailing Wall" in Jerusalem is

actually the foundation of the Antonia Fortress, the fort which housed the 10th Roman Legion whose duty it was to guard Herod's Temple, and police Jerusalem and the surrounding area. Proponents see possible significance in this because if it proves to be true, the Jews could begin rebuilding their Temple without disturbing the Dome of the Rock, the destruction of which has the potential to cause a major world-wide conflict. Two books on the subject are The Temples That Jerusalem Forgot, by Ernest L. Martin; and Temple, by Bob Cornuke.

368 https://www.templeinstitute.org/statement.htm

369 See Ezekiel 10

370 Ezekiel 43:4-12*

371 See Ezekiel 37:15-28; Jeremiah 50:4

372 Isaiah 2:2, 3; The significance and restoration of the Temple to the Hebrew people provided them continual hope of connecting their past with their future during the two millennia they were absent from Jerusalem. "It [the Temple] gave tangible expression to the covenant God had made with David, giving the divine blessing to his dynasty, and therefore to the institution of kingship that was, for Israelites, still new and in some quarters dubious. Its existence made Jerusalem not only the capital city but the Holy city. Long after the final destruction of the Temple, its memory would remain for a scattered people the symbol of their future return." (Joan Comay, The Hebrew Kings [New York: William Morrow and Company, Inc., 1977], p. 66). Now that they have returned and regained political power over Jerusalem, it can only be a matter of time before they attempt to fulfill their long-awaited dream.

373 John 4:20-23

374 Hebrews 10:20, New International Version

375 1 Corinthians 3:16, 17

376 Psalm 77:13, New King James Version
377 Barnes' Notes on the Bible
378 Hebrews 9:22
379 Hebrews 9:15
380 Leviticus 17:11*
381 Deuteronomy 12:5-7
382 Isaiah 62:8-12
383 Zechariah 2:8*
384 See Joel 3
385 Micah 4:1*, New International Version
* bracketed material supplied to clarify context

Chapter 10

386 Jeremiah 8:21, 22
387 Jeremiah 30:12-24*
388 Proverbs 6:23
389 Isaiah 48:10, 11
390 Malachi 3:2-4
391 Isaiah 29:10, 11
392 Isaiah 53:5-11
393 1 Peter 2:24
394 Hosea 6:1, 2*
395 Daniel 12:4-10
396 Merriam-Webster
397 See Revelation 12:4, 5
398 1 Corinthians 13:12
399 Isaiah 46:9-13
400 Isaiah 8:11-20 and 9:6, 7*; The name Isaiah means "The

Lord will save." The prophetic names of his children are Shear-jashub, or "a remnant will return," and Maher-shalal-hash-baz, or "swift to plunder and quick to spoil." What Isaiah is saying in Isaiah 8:18 is that the meanings of his and his children's names are prophetic revelations of "the plans the Lord Almighty has for his people [Israel]."

401 John Hagee; Earth's Final Moments (Charisma Media/Charisma House Book Group, 2011), pp. 92, 93.

402 See Daniel 9:25 and Nehemiah 2:1-8

403 Daniel 9:24*

404 Matthew 2:16

405 Matthew 2:13; Jesus' trip with his parents into Egypt, and afterward returning to Palestine, was yet another anti-typical fulfillment of the link to His Hebrew ancestors who had spent time in Egyptian servitude only to return to the land promised them by God. Hosea 11:1 says, "When Israel was a child, I loved him, and out of Egypt I called my son" (New International Version). Again, we see the synonymity of the nation Israel and their Messiah.

406 Revelation 12:4*; Revelation 12:9 defines the dragon as the devil and Satan. His obsession with the killing of Hebrew babies is of course an attempt to eradicate the promised Seed, something throughout Hebrew history he has sought to do as evidenced by the king of Egypt during the time of Moses (Exodus 1:15-22).

407 John 19:12-15

408 John 19:19-21

409 John 19:22

410 Consider the miraculous story of Philip disappearing after teaching the gospel to the Ethiopian Eunuch in Acts 8:26-40.

411 1 Peter 4:7

412 Mark 1:15

413 Acts 7:35-42*

414 Israel had the free-will decision to enter the Promised Land 40 years earlier than they did, but failed because of their "unbelief." Read Hebrews 4:6. They learned from that previous mistake and took advantage of their second opportunity, occupying the land under the leadership of Joshua. Scripture indicates there will be a replication of this pattern as it relates to their initial rejection, but later acceptance, of their Messiah which will result in the inheritance of their eternal homeland.

415 Acts 3:20

416 John 14:3, New King James Version

417 See Daniel 8:27

418 Psalm 94:17, 18

419 Psalm 130:7, 8

420 See Joshua 10:12-14; Isaiah 38:1-7

421 Isaiah 46:10

422 Daniel 12:9, 10

423 Daniel 9:26

424 Luke 19:42-44

425 Romans 11:8

426 Isaiah 46:13*

427 Mark 13:32, 33

428 Mark 13:28-30*; Commonly known as the "Fig Tree Prophecy," it teaches that just as the green shoots on the fig tree indicate that summer is approaching, so will Israel and Judah's return to their homeland in Palestine, after their diaspora among the world nations, serve as evidence that the end of the world is nearing. How near? Proponents of the prophetic

theory focus on Mark 13:30. It reads, "I assure you, this generation will not pass from the scene until all these events have taken place [notably, Christ's second coming]." Some interpret it to mean the generation of people living who saw the Jews return to their homeland in 1948 will also witness the second return of Christ. Assuming 1948 is the correct starting date to enter into this prophetic equation, we are now some 70- plus years past that time as of this book's publication. Others dispute over exactly what amount of time constitutes a "generation." Perhaps a more pragmatic approach to understanding what Jesus meant by "this generation" is that this cycle of Jews returning to the land of Israel will be the last one. They are now there to stay even though the forces of darkness will again try to remove them. The Bible does not predict a third diaspora of the Hebrews. In other words, it will be this generation of God's chosen people who will remain in Jerusalem to witness the Parousia of the Hebrew Messiah.

In Luke 13:6-9 Jesus gave His listeners an illustration of a barren fig tree. "A man planted a fig tree in his garden and came again and again to see if there was any fruit on it, but he was always disappointed. Finally, he said to his gardener, 'I've waited three years, and there hasn't been a single fig! Cut it down. It's taking up space we can use for something else.' The gardener answered, 'Give it one more chance. Leave it another year, and I'll give it special attention and plenty of fertilizer. If we get figs next year, fine. If not, you can cut it down.'"

In another place He sternly warned the leaders of His chosen people, "'You brood of snakes!' he exclaimed. 'Who warned you to flee from God's coming judgment? Prove by the way you live that you really have turned from your sins and turned to God. Don't just say, 'We're safe – we're the descendants of Abraham.' That proves nothing. God can change these stones here into children of Abraham. Even now the ax of God's judgment is poised, ready to sever your roots. Yes, every tree that does not produce good fruit will be chopped down and thrown into the fire" (Matthew 3:7-10).

In time Christ's warnings saw their fulfillment as the Romans cut down the fig tree of Israel to a stump in A.D. 70, and A.D. 135 when they plowed Jerusalem like a field. But Isaiah had predicted it as part of Israel's purification process. The Lord instructed him to bring a rebuke to Israel, thus hardening their hearts. When he asked how long he should do this, God replied, "Until their cities are destroyed, with no one left in them. Until their houses are deserted and the whole country is an utter wasteland. Do not stop until the Lord has sent everyone away to distant lands and the entire land of Israel lies deserted" (Isaiah 6:11, 12). Then the Lord predicted something truly amazing. He said, "Israel will remain a stump, like a tree that is cut down, but the stump will be a holy seed that will grow again" (verse 13).

Not only have the Jewish people again taken root in the land of Israel, they are now shooting forth verdant greenery. Today, the nation of Israel is a living and vibrant society as it pertains to the physical world. If anyone doubts its rejuvenation, just take a vacation to the modern city of Tel Aviv, Israel's second most populated city. The Bible never mentions Tel Aviv, because it wasn't founded until 1909. Now the man who owns the garden (God) is waiting in great expectation for Israel's spiritual figs to produce!

[429] Hosea 9:10, New International Version; see also Jeremiah 24
[430] Read again Daniel 9:24-27
[431] Daniel 9:26
[432] Jeremiah 6:14
[433] Deuteronomy 7:1, 2

434 See Daniel 8:25
435 Isaiah 28:15, 18
436 Daniel 8:25
437 Revelation 12:7-9
438 Revelation 12:13-17*
439 Revelation 12:12
440 Daniel 7:25
441 Daniel 7:25*
442 This period of three and a half years when the antichrist persecutes the Jewish people is well established in many Scriptures in various calculations:

- Daniel 9:27*— "And he shall make a strong covenant with many [Jews] for one week [7 literal years], and for half of the week [3.5 literal years] he shall put an end to sacrifice and offering."
- Daniel 7:24, 25*—"He shall speak words against the Most-High, and shall wear out the saints of the Most High [Jews] … and they [Jews] shall be given into his hand for a time [1], times [2], and half a time [.5]." Added together this equals 3 and a half literal years.
- Daniel 12:7*— "It would be for a time [1], times [2] and half a time [.5], and that when the shattering of the power of the holy people [Jews] comes to an end all these things would be finished." Again, a period of 3 and a half literal years.
- Revelation 11:2*— "For it [the court outside the Temple] is given over to the [Gentile] nations, and they will trample the holy city [Jerusalem] for forty-two months. And I will give authority to my two witnesses, and they will prophesy for 1,260 days, clothed in sack-

cloth." Forty-two months divided by 12 months per year equals 3.5 prophetic years. 1,260 days divided by 360 [days per year] equal 3.5 literal years.

- Revelation 12:6*— "And the woman [the Jewish people] fled into the wilderness, where she has a place prepared by God, in which she is to be nourished for 1,260 days." 1,260 days divided by 360 [days per year] equal 3.5 literal years.
- Revelation 12:13, 14*— "And when the dragon saw that he had been thrown down to earth, he pursued the woman [the Jewish people] who had given birth to the male child [Christ the Messiah]. But the woman was given the two wings of the great eagle so that she might fly from the serpent into the wilderness, to the place where she is to be nourished for a time [1], times [2] and half a time [.5]." Again, a period of 3.5 literal years.
- Revelation 13:5*— "And the beast was given a mouth uttering haughty and blasphemous words, and it was allowed to exercise authority for forty-two months ... And the beast was allowed to make war on the saints [the Jewish people and those who support them] and to conquer them." 42 months divided by 12 months per year equals 3.5 literal years.

[443] John 5:43
[444] Isaiah 42:6*
[445] Micah 7:6
[446] Zechariah 13:8
[447] Jeremiah 30:7
[448] http://www.jcpa.org/dje/articles2/howrelisr.htm
[449] See Genesis 32:22-32
[450] Amos 9:8-11

451 Daniel 12:9, 10
452 Malachi 3:17, 18
453 Isaiah 40:1, 2
454 Daniel 7:21, 22*
455 Daniel 12:1*
456 See Micah 5:1-4
457 Matthew 24:15-31
* bracketed material supplied to clarify context

Chapter 11

458 2 Thessalonians 2:3-9*; Some translators have interpreted this text as talking about a future time when professed Christians fall away from believing in the covenants given to Abraham, Isaac, Jacob, and their Hebrew descendants. For example, The Amplified Bible renders the passage as such: "Let no one in any way deceive or entrap you, for that day will not come unless the apostasy comes first [that is, the great rebellion, the abandonment of the faith by professed Christians], and the man of lawlessness is revealed, the son of destruction [the antichrist, the one destined to be destroyed]."

459 Ecclesiastes 3:15

460 Larry Cockerham, Antiochus IV Epiphanes: The Anti-christ of the Old Testament, p. 1.

461 1 John 2:18

462 See Daniel 8:13, 14

463 See Daniel 8:14, English Standard Version

464 Merriam Webster

465 John 10:22

466 Commenting on the fate of this man who compared him-

self to God, the angel Gabriel told Daniel, "He will be broken, but not by human power?" (Daniel 8:25) History records that "in the same year Antiochus IV, who was busy fighting another campaign, heard about the Jewish uprising and determined to return and end it. But something happened as he was making his way back to Jerusalem. He commanded his chariot to be driven, without stopping in his journey, the judgment of heaven urging him forward because he had spoken so proudly, that he would come to Jerusalem, and make it a common burying place of the Jews. But the Lord God of Israel, that seeth all things, struck him with an incurable and an invisible plague. For as soon as he had ended these words, a dreadful pain in his bowels came upon him, and bitter torments of the inner parts … being filled with pride, breathing out fire in his rage against the Jews, and commanding the matter to be hastened, it happened as he was going with violence that he fell from the chariot so that his limbs were much pained by a grievous bruising of the body. Thus he that seemed to himself to command even the waves of the sea, being proud above the condition of man, and to weigh the heights of the mountains in a balance, now being cast down to the ground, was carried in a litter, bearing witness to the manifest power of God in himself: So that worms swarmed out of the body of this man, and whilst he lived in sorrow and pain, his flesh fell off, and the filthiness of his smell was noisome to the army. And the man that thought a little before he could reach to the stars of heaven, no man could endure to carry, for the intolerable stench. And by this means, being brought from his great pride, he began to come to the knowledge of himself, being admonished by the scourge of God, his pains increasing every moment. And when he himself could not now abide his own stench, he spoke thus: It is just to be subject to God, and that a mortal man should not equal himself to God" 2 Maccabees 9:4-12

467 https://www.jewishvirtuallibrary.org/non-jewish-victims-of-the-holocaust
468 See Revelation 13
469 Revelation 13:5
470 Acts 17:31*
471 Revelation chapters 14-18
472 Matthew 24:24
473 1 Timothy 6:6-10
474 1 Kings 18:44
475 See James 5:17, 18
476 Revelation 1:7
477 Amos 8:11-14
478 James 5:7, 8
479 Jude 12
480 2 Peter 2:3; The apostle Paul also had dealings with false ministers who were trained and eloquent speakers, but taught a different gospel about a different Jesus than the one the Bible certifies. See 2 Corinthians 11:1-15
481 John 5:39, 40
482 John 5:43, 44
483 Luke 1:17
484 Malachi 3:1
485 Matthew 17:10-13
486 See Matthew 14:1-12
487 Malachi 4:1-5
488 It is the author's opinion this modern-day Elijah spirit, and the confrontation it is to have with the forces of evil, Revelation 11:1-13 portrays through the imagery of the "Two Witnesses." As one reads this passage of Scripture in light of similar

past biblical accounts, it suggests a strong connection between these two witnesses to Moses and Elijah. Remember, the Lord through Moses turned the waters of the Egyptian river Nile into blood (Exodus 7:14-21), and used Elijah to prevent rain or dew from falling to earth for three and a half years (1 Kings 17:1; James 5:17, 18). This is the same period of time (3.5 years; 42 months; 1,260 days) that these two witnesses will testify on the Lord's behalf as foretold in Revelation 11.

[489] Romans 11:1-5*

[490] Revelation 12:11*

[491] H.L. Mencken, Minority Report, Published August 28th 2006 by Johns Hopkins University Press (First Published 1997)*

[492] Proverbs 18:17, English Standard Version

[493] Proverbs 14:12

[494] Zechariah 4:6

[495] A song written by producer Chris Hughes, Roland Orzabal, and Ian Stanley. The latter two, along with Curt Smith, comprised the English Pop Rock Band Tears For Fears who recorded the song. Its original title was Everybody Wants To Go To War. Smith commented that the themes of the song were "quite serious – it's about everybody wanting power, about warfare and the misery it causes." "1985 – Tears For Fears' 'Songs From The Big Chair' Hits #1". RTTNews. Accessed June 22, 2014.

[496] See Revelation 13:16-18; 14:8

[497] See Colossians 1:16

[498] See Revelation 18

[499] 1 Kings 18:36*

* bracketed material supplied to clarify context

Chapter 12

[500] Psalm 72:17-19; Isaiah 44:6
[501] See Isaiah 44:23
[502] https://walvoord.com/article/107
[503] Acts 2:30; Only God knows how history will unfold. In the case of Him choosing David's family to reign over His eternal kingdom, the Bible implies that the sons of Israel expected Joseph and his offspring to be the chosen royal family. Remember he had those dreams recorded in Genesis 37:5-16 in which the family of Jacob bowed before him. The dreams proved true when from Egypt Joseph saved them from the famine. But whether the devil, or anyone else, assumed God would pick Joseph's family for His kings, they were wrong. Instead, God threw the proverbial curveball in Genesis 49:10 by choosing Judah's family to hold the reins of kingly authority. Psalm 60:7 unequivocally states that "Judah will produce my Kings." Just where does God go to find someone with such princely qualities? "But he rejected Joseph's descendants; he did not choose the tribe of Ephraim. He chose instead the tribe of Judah, Mount Zion, which he loved … He chose his servant David, calling him from the sheep pens. He took David from tending the ewes and lambs and made him the shepherd of Jacob's descendants–God's own people, Israel. He cared for them with a true heart and led them with skillful hands" (Psalm 78:67-72). Of course, this was simply a paradigm pointing to the eternal rule of the real King of kings–Jesus Christ, the Messiah, "the Lion of the tribe of Judah, the heir to David's throne" (Revelation 5:5). That is why the Lord told his prophet in Jeremiah 33:20, 21, "If you can break my covenant with the day and the night so that they do not come on their usual schedule, only then will my covenant with David, my servant, be broken.

Only then will he no longer have a descendant to reign on his throne."

504 Psalm 89:19-37
505 Philippians 2:8-11
506 Jeremiah 17:13*
507 Hebrews 10:12, 13
508 Isaiah 66:1
509 Psalm 2:6, New International Version
510 Hosea 3:1-5
511 Revelation 19:16
512 Matthew 2:2
513 John 1:49
514 Matthew 4:23
515 Mark 14:61, 62*
516 Mark 11:10; Zechariah 9:9
517 See Zechariah 13:1, 2; read also Zechariah chapter 14
518 2 Timothy 2:8
519 See Revelation chapters 1, 7, and 21
520 Revelation 22:18, 19
521 Deuteronomy 23:5
522 See Numbers 23;19 and 1 Samuel 15:29
523 Hebrews 6:13-18
524 Malachi 3:6, 7
525 See Romans 2:9-16
526 Micah 4:8-12
527 Zechariah 12:9
528 See Matthew 13:24-30; 25:31-46
529 Psalm 87*

[530] See Micah 4; Zechariah 8:1-4; Joel 3:20-21; Jeremiah 31:31-33; Daniel 2:44, 45; Revelation 20:4
[531] Zechariah 9:9; 10:6
[532] John Hagee; Earth's Final Moments (Charisma Media/Charisma House Book Group, 2011), pp. 67, 68.
[533] Romans 9:11, 12*
[534] Matthew 20:16
[535] See 1 Samuel 16:7
[536] Romans 11:33-36
[537] See Revelation 21
[538] Zechariah 2:10-13*
[539] See Matthew 6:31-33
[540] See John 8:31-34
[541] Galatians 4:28-29, God's Word Version
[542] John 3:5-8
[543] John 1:47*
[544] Isaiah 1:27, 28
[545] Isaiah 1:18-20
[546] Matthew 16:24-28
[547] Luke 18:35-42
[548] Mark 2:17
[549] Psalm 51:17
[550] Psalm 147:2-6
[551] Psalm 147:4
[552] https://www.gotquestions.org/Jesus-son-of-David.html; Got Questions Ministries; © 2002-2019
[553] Psalm 2:1-12*
[554] Acts 3:20, 21*

555 Matthew 23:38, 39
556 Revelation 1:7
* bracketed material supplied to clarify context

Chapter 13

557 John 1:17; There are several texts equating the Ten Commandments to the Covenant given through Moses at Sinai. Deuteronomy 4:13 states, "And he declared unto you his covenant, which he commanded you to perform, even ten commandments; and he wrote them upon two tables of stone." King James Version; See also Exodus 31:18 and Exodus 34:28.

558 Deuteronomy 5:1-3*
559 Deuteronomy 29:15*
560 Psalm 147:19, 20
561 Romans 2:12
562 Romans 2:13-16
563 See Romans 11
564 Hebrews 10:16; see also Jeremiah 31:33. God states He is going to do this for Israel, not because they deserve it, but to protect His "holy name which you (the Hebrew people) dishonored while you were scattered among the nations." See Ezekiel 36:16-38*.
565 Ezekiel 37:23-25*
566 Read Galatians 3:15-23
567 Galatians 3:19
568 Galatians 3:24-29
569 See Numbers 20:1-12; Deuteronomy 34; The book of Jude suggests that God resurrected Moses, "But even Michael, one of the mightiest of the angels, did not dare accuse Satan of blas-

phemy, but simply said, 'the Lord rebuke you.' (This took place when Michael was arguing with Satan about Moses' body)" (Jude 9); Moses later appeared with Christ during His transfiguration (Matthew 17:2, 3).

[570] See Matthew 5:17

[571] John 1:17

[572] Malachi 3:1

[573] Hebrews 12:24; In Paul's letter to Timothy he substantiated this same truth by saying, "For there is only one God and one Mediator who can reconcile God and people. He is the man Christ Jesus" (1 Timothy 2:5).

[574] Galatians 3:19, 20*

[575] See Genesis 15

[576] Acts 15:28, 29

[577] Antinomianism is defined as "the false teaching that since faith alone is necessary for salvation, one is free from the moral obligations of the law. The word antinomianism is not used in the Bible, but the idea is spoken of. Paul appears to have been accused of being an antinomian (see Romans 3:8; 6:1; 6:15). While it is true that obedience to the law will never earn salvation for anyone (Ephesians 2:8-9), it is equally true that those who are saved are expected to live a life full of good works (see, for example, Matthew 7:16-20; Ephesians 7:10; Colossians 1:10; James 2:14-26). Since we have been freed from the dominion of sin through faith in Jesus, we have also been freed to practice the righteousness demanded by God (Romans 6:12-22)" (Holman Bible Dictionary).

[578] Galatians 6:2;

[579] Romans 8:2, King James Version

[580] Hebrews 4:12, 13

581 Ephesians 5:10

582 Isaiah 2:1-3; Christ, then sitting as supreme Lawgiver and Judge, will establish His judicial hierarchy from among His redeemed faithful on earth. "Do you not know that we [believers] are to sit in judgement upon angels – to say nothing of things belonging to this life" (1 Corinthians 6:3*, Weymouth New Testament). We see this played out in type under King Jehoshaphat of Judah when "he appointed judges throughout the nation in all the fortified cities, and he gave them these instructions, 'Always think carefully before pronouncing judgment. Remember that you do not judge to please people but to please the Lord. He will be with you when you render the verdict in each case that comes before you. Fear the Lord and judge with care, for the Lord our God does not tolerate perverted justice, partiality, or the taking of bribes'" (2 Chronicles 19:5-7). Paul's instruction to the Corinthians was simple: if we are going to be called upon to judge with Christ in eternity, shouldn't we start practicing the same principles of fairness and equity when dealing with each other in the here and now?

583 Isaiah 33:22

584 Luke 6:31

585 Matthew 5:33-37

586 2 Timothy 3:1-5*

587 Psalm 12; see also Revelation 20:11-15

588 Romans 3:9

589 Romans 3:20-22*

590 1 John 2:1-6; see also Revelation 12:10-12

591 James 4:11, 12

592 Romans 14:2-4; We could include a myriad of other issues here, such as style of dress, music, cultural differences, etc. Paul is simply using a few examples to teach a broader principle.

[593] Romans 14:20-23
[594] James 4:17
[595] 1 Thessalonians 4:11
[596] See Matthew 18:15; 2 Timothy 4:2; Proverbs 9:7-9
[597] Titus 3:9, Contemporary English Version
[598] See Ephesians 4:11-13
[599] See Leviticus 26
[600] 1 Corinthians 10:6-11
[601] Here is the warning given to those who received the law from Mount Sinai: "If after this you still refuse to listen and still remain hostile toward me, then I will give full vent to my hostility. I will punish you seven times over for your sins. You will eat the flesh of your own sons and daughters. I will destroy your pagan shrines ... I will leave your corpses piled up beside your lifeless idols, and I will despise you. I will make your cities desolate and destroy your places of worship ... Yes, I myself will devastate your land. Your enemies who come to occupy it will be utterly shocked at the destruction they see. I will scatter you among the nations ... Then at last the land will make up for its missed Sabbath years as it lies desolate during your years of exile in the land of your enemies ... As for those of you who survive, I will demoralize you in the land of your enemies far away. You will live there in such constant fear that the sound of a leaf driven by the wind will send you fleeing ... You will have no power to stand before your enemies. You will die among the foreign nations and be devoured in the land of your enemies. Those still left alive will rot away in enemy lands because of their sins and the sins of their ancestors. But at last, my people will confess their sins and the sins of their ancestors for betraying me and being hostile toward me. Finally, when I have given full expression to my hostility and have brought

them to the land of their enemies then, at last, their disobedient hearts will be humbled, and they will pay for their sins. Then I will remember my covenant with Jacob and with Isaac, and with Abraham, and I will remember the land ... I will not utterly reject or despise them while they are in exile in the land of their enemies. I will not cancel my covenant with them by wiping them out ... I will remember my ancient covenant with their ancestors, whom I brought out of Egypt while all the nations watched. I, the Lord, am their God" (Leviticus 26:27-45). Could this text be referring to the Jews' horrific experience of the European holocaust and the subsequent restoration to their ancient homeland of Israel? It certainly seems plausible.

602 Hebrews 12:18-29*
603 Matthew 12:31, 32
604 Hebrews 3:15*
605 Jude 6
606 Matthew 8:29
607 "For this is what the Lord Almighty says: 'In just a little while I will again shake the heavens and the earth. I will shake the oceans and the dry land, too. I will shake all nations, and the treasures of all the nations will come to this Temple. I will fill this place with glory,' says the Lord Almighty. 'The silver is mine, and the gold is mine,' says the Lord Almighty. 'The future glory of this Temple will be greater than its past glory,' says the Lord Almighty. 'And in this place, I will bring peace ... I am about to shake the heavens and the earth. I will overthrow royal thrones, destroying the power of foreign kingdoms...but when this happens,' says the Lord Almighty, 'I will honor you [Israel]'" Haggai 2:6-22* The book of Hebrews obviously situates this imagery during a time yet future when the Lord will shake the nations at the end of time and gives honor to Israel.

It also outlines Israel and its Temple co-existing at the time of Messiah's return. See again Hebrews 12:26, 27.

[608] Revelation 22:11-13

* bracketed material supplied to clarify context

Chapter 14

[609] Psalm 133:1
[610] Mark 3:24, 25
[611] Matthew 8:11, 12
[612] Revelation 22:15
[613] Many misunderstand what it means to be chosen or elected by God. They confuse those terms with salvation, but they actually refer to a call to service. For example, in Isaiah 42:1 we read, "Look at my servant, whom I strengthen. He is my chosen one, and I am pleased with him. I have put my Spirit upon him. He will reveal justice to the nations ... He will bring full justice to all who have been wronged. He will not stop until truth and righteousness prevail throughout the earth." New Testament biblical scholars agree that the verse refers to the Messiah–Jesus Christ. Though the Lord calls Him "my chosen one," He did not require regeneration or salvation, because He never sinned. Peter said, "He committed no sin, and no deceit was found in his mouth" (1 Peter 2:22, New International Version). Jesus Himself said to His accusers, "Can any of you prove me guilty of sin?" (John 8:46). Though sinless, and not in need of salvation, the Bible still terms Him as God's elect, or chosen one. God selected Him for a specific purpose–to make a blood atonement necessary for the redemption of the human race. Israel was also called God's "chosen one," called "so all the world from the east to west will know there is no other God"

(Isaiah 45:4, 5). Scripture terms Gentile believers as "examples of the incredible wealth of his favor," chosen to live lives different than their past ones as a witness of the power of God's Spirit to regenerate all humanity (See Ephesians 2:1-10).

But not all who are chosen, or elected, will necessarily do God's will. Speaking to His disciples, "Jesus said, 'I chose the twelve of you, but one is a devil.' He was speaking of Judas, son of Simon Iscariot, one of the Twelve, who would betray him" (John 6:70). In His parable of the wedding feast, Jesus said, "For many are invited, but few are chosen" (Matthew 22:14, Christian Standard Bible) Perhaps we could read the passage as, "Many are called by God for service, but few choose to obey the calling." Consider the rich young ruler. When reading his story in Luke 18:18-29, we are tempted to think that he turned away from eternal life and was lost. But Scripture doesn't say he went away lost, but that he became "sad." He missed the opportunity to be not just a spiritual follower of Christ, but to walk with Him in person. Think of all the life experiences he passed up! It appears that in his spirit he had an interest in Christ's kingdom, but his flesh was weak, because he loved his earthly possessions more than the things of God. As a result, he failed to experience what God wanted for him in exchange for a status quo life of earthliness.

The point I am trying to make in this chapter is that if we really desire to know it, the Lord promises to reveal what His will is for our lives, or why He chose us. It will then be up to us to decide whether or not we want to cooperate with the purpose of His calling.

[614] See Acts 26:12-23*

[615] See Matthew 27:1-10 and Acts 1:16-20

[616] Hebrews 12:14-17*

[617] Matthew 20:21-28*
[618] Isaiah 43:10-13
[619] Deuteronomy 28:13-44*
[620] Isaiah 6:13; also see Isaiah 11
[621] Amos 9:8, 9
[622] Isaiah 43:21
[623] Judaism. Ed. Arthur Hertzberg (New York: George Braziller, Inc. Publishing, 1962), pp. 29, 30.
[624] Obadiah 15
[625] Isaiah 41:8-14
[626] Isaiah 43:21
[627] Ronald E. Diprose, Israel and the Church, pp. 10, 11, 17.
[628] See Jeremiah 31:31 and Hebrews 10:16, 17
[629] Matthew 26:27-29*
[630] See Jeremiah 31-33; Ezekiel 37:26-28 and Romans 11
[631] Galatians 4:22-26
[632] Jeremiah 31:22
[633] Isaiah 45:17
[634] Ezekiel 39:7, 8, 28, 29
[635] Micah 7:15, 16
[636] Zechariah 12:10, 11
[637] Dr. David R. Reagan, Israel in Bible Prophecy: Past, Present, and Future (Lamb and Lion Ministries, 2017), p. 7.
[638] Romans 9:25
[639] Ephesians 1:10
[640] Jeremiah 50:4, 5
[641] Zechariah 10:6
[642] Zechariah 12:2, 3

[643] See Isaiah 9:6, 7
[644] Obadiah 16-21*
[645] 2 Thessalonians 2:10, 11
[646] See Matthew 7:15
[647] Ephesians 2:15
[648] Zechariah 2:10-13
[649] See Acts 2:30
[650] Isaiah 14:1
[651] Isaiah 25:6-8
* bracketed material supplied to clarify context

Conclusion

[652] 1 John 4:8
[653] Analogy based on Ezekiel 16 and Hosea 1-3.
[654] See Luke 15:11-32
[655] See Genesis 3:7
[656] See Zechariah 12:10
[657] See Zechariah 2:8, King James Version
[658] John 3:16
[659] Jesus Loves the Little Children; Words by C. Herbert Woolston; Music by George F. Root
[660] See Numbers 22:21-34
[661] See Hebrews 7:25; 9:24
[662] Revelation 6:17; Isaiah 33:10-16
[663] 2 Corinthians 5:10
[664] 1 John 4:9-12
[665] Luke 17:33; Weymouth
[666] See Revelation 21

[667] See Ezekiel 47:13-23 and Ezekiel 48
[668] Psalm 24:1
[669] See Jeremiah 30:7
[670] Zechariah 14:4
[671] See Acts 1:9-11
[672] See Revelation 20 and 21
[673] Isaiah 11:6-13
[674] Isaiah 49:14-17; 22-23*
[675] Isaiah 56:3-8
[676] Galatians 6:16*; Some versions such as the English Standard Version translate "people" here as "Israel." It is a most unique portion of Scripture that identifies both believing Jews and Gentiles as one body – "the new Israel of God."
[677] Genesis 21:12; see also Romans 9:7 and Hebrews 11:18
[678] Ecclesiastes 6:10*
[679] Mark 7:24-30
[680] Acts 13:47
[681] Romans 11:13-15*

* bracketed material supplied to clarify context

TO PURCHASE ADDITIONAL COPIES OF
WHY ISRAEL?
CONTACT

HAYDEN FAMILY MINISTRIES.

SPECIAL QUANTITY DISCOUNT
PRICING AVAILABLE.

https://keavinhayden.org/